Peace, Joy, and Comfort

Daily Inspiration for Living a Meaningful Life with Chronic Pain and Chronic Illness

Copyright © 2025 Chronic Pain Anonymous World Services, Inc.

First Edition

Peace, Joy, and Comfort

Daily Inspiration for a Meaningful Life While Living with Chronic Pain and Chronic Illness

Copyright © 2025 by Chronic Pain Anonymous World Services

All rights reserved.

Cover Art was created and provided by a CPA member.

ISBN: 978-1-7353295-1-2

Library of Congress Control Number: : 2025902085

Chronic Pain Anonymous World Services, Inc.
13802 N. Scottsdale Rd.
Ste. 151-10
Scottsdale, AZ 85254-3403

E-mail: inquiry@chronicpainanonymous.org
Website: www.chronicpainanonymous.org
Phone number: 888-561-2220

CPA World Service Conference Approval

First Edition

CPA Serenity Prayer

*God, grant me the serenity
to accept the things I cannot change,
the courage to change the things I can,
and the wisdom to know the difference.
Thy will, not mine, be done.*

Contents

CPA Serenity Prayer v

Foreword ix

Introduction x

January 1

February 35

March 67

April 101

May 133

June 167

July 199

August 233

September 267

October 299

November 333

December 365

Appendix A: The CPA Preamble 398

Appendix B: The Twelve Steps of CPA 399

Appendix C: The Twelve Traditions of CPA 400

Appendix D: Twelve Concepts of Service 402

Appendix E: The CPA Declaration 405

Appendix F: One Day At A Time 407

Appendix G: One Night At A Time 409

Appendix H: Suggested Meeting Format 412

Index 415

Notes 427

Foreword

Chronic Pain Anonymous (CPA) is a Twelve Step program started in Baltimore, Maryland, by Dale L. and Barry M. in 2004. The fellowship now hosts meetings around the world, helping those struggling with spiritual and emotional debilitation from living with chronic pain and chronic illness.

In CPA, we share our experience, strength, and hope with each other so that we may help one another recover from the disabling effects of chronic pain and chronic illness. Our lives have been characterized by countless doctors, diets, and alternative therapies, and by desperately trying anything to return to the lives that we had before we became ill or injured. This can be overwhelming and lead many into isolation, addiction, anger, fear, and depression.

CPA offers friendship, hope, sanity, and peace. By practicing the Twelve Steps and Twelve Traditions as individuals and in groups, we develop a set of principles for living, inside and outside CPA. We are amazed at how our lives improve by learning from and supporting each other.

There are no dues or fees for membership. We invite you to explore our website, try a few meetings, and discover how CPA may enrich your life too.

Wishing you daily peace, joy, and comfort,
Chronic Pain Anonymous

Introduction

How This Book Came to Print

The members of CPA have dreamed of a daily reader since its early days. It was first noted in 2008, a mere four years into CPA's existence. But, as a brand-new fellowship, other projects were prioritized. The dream did not die, but it did sit on the shelf for a while. It wasn't until 2018 that the Literature Committee decided it was time to make this long-talked-about daily reader a reality. Or at least to begin the process, which meant collecting submissions from CPA members who wished to contribute. From 2018 through 2021, that's exactly what happened. Email and video groups were formed to write entries on various prompts. Along with individual member submissions, the Literature Committee received more than 400 entries! Once collected, these passages were beautifully crafted into 366 vignettes. Through the combined efforts of professional editors, members of the Literature Committee, and the year-long fellowship feedback process of editing, this book came to print, while still keeping the varied voices of our members clear.

Ways to Use This Book

The customary use for daily meditation readers is to read one vignette per day, as labeled. For example, reading January 1 on January 1, and so on for the entire year. However, you do not need to start at the beginning. Feel free to start this journey on any day of the year. If you miss a day, you can skip it and read the present day or continue reading them in order.

Going in order is not necessary. If a page does not appeal to you, that's fine. Just find another one, or use the index to find a topic that is on your mind. Please don't feel restricted by the dates. Any reading can be used on any day. You can simply open the book to a random page. Read and focus on your favorite reading every day for a week. Go ahead; read February 29 more than once every four years—it's okay. The ideas are endless. How creative can you be?

Everything needed to conduct a CPA meeting is in this book, including: CPA Preamble, Twelve Steps, Twelve Traditions, Twelve Concepts of Service, CPA Declarations, One Day At A Time (bookmark), One Night At A Time (bookmark), Suggested Meeting Format, and an in-depth index. Common meeting formats include selecting a reading coinciding with today's date and then inviting each member to share on a topic related to the reading. Another option is to select a topic from the index, read a few of the corresponding pages to introduce the selected topic, and then open the meeting for shares. More details about these approaches can be found in the Suggested Meeting Format found in Appendix H.

Please Remember While Reading

Though there have been edits and changes made to the original submissions, please keep in mind that each entry was, at the outset, written by an individual and is ultimately the expression of that individual's personal opinion and not the opinion of the Chronic Pain Anonymous organization as a whole. Likewise, CPA is not allied with any sect, denomination, political group or party, organization, or institution; does not wish to engage in any controversy; and neither endorses nor opposes any causes.

Any references to a Higher Power by a specific name, gender, number, or pronoun are that of the writer's understanding. If you like, wherever you find it appropriate and helpful for your recovery, please substitute the words for a Higher Power with those which you are most comfortable with. You are free to adapt and alter any language that you find benefits your journey with this book.

Living with chronic pain and chronic illness is not an easy path in life, but we find hope together. This daily meditation book is an avenue to share our members' voices. The hope is that CPA members find peace, joy, and comfort within these pages. Even though we may feel lonely in our pain, we find that listening to one another's experience, strength, and hope eases our isolation. These readings help us stay connected to other members at any time, even between meetings or outreach calls.

We recognize ourselves in one another; we believe that if someone else has experienced hope, then maybe we can, too. We know that we are more likely to find personal growth when we apply these recovery principles together. Because of the nature of living with chronic pain and chronic illness, we compassionately understand that there will be many ups and downs ahead. The Twelve Steps gift us a way of life that allows us to have our bad days and not condemn ourselves for our mistakes. We clean up our messes and move on to do better next time.

These pages remind us to be gentle with ourselves at all times. After all, we are doing a great job at living through challenging circumstances. We remember that our recovery cannot always be perfect and that, over time, we will see our progress. A seed can only grow when it is left to flourish in the soil—we don't do it any favors by digging it up to see if it has taken root. So goes our recovery. We tend to it by doing the work of the Twelve Steps and not judging ourselves too harshly. We remember that years are built by taking life *One Day at a Time*.

January

January 1

In Chronic Pain Anonymous, it is suggested that we don't share specifics about our pain or illnesses. As I have gotten to know members one-on-one, of course, those details come up. But, in a meeting, we have the protection of anonymity, which provides a welcoming, nurturing ground for compassion and understanding.

When I was a newcomer, I was afraid I didn't really belong. Pain wasn't my primary issue; fatigue and other symptoms were making my life unmanageable. I shared vaguely because I wanted to belong, not because I understood that we were supposed to share generally. It took a while for me to hear people sharing about symptoms other than pain. But, by then, it didn't matter. I was relating to their shares: to their fear, isolation, anger, envy, and depression. I wasn't alone anymore.

I can go to a meeting and get just as much from the share of a newcomer as from a person who's been in CPA for a decade. This is possible because our sacred space is honored, starting with the Serenity Prayer and closing with the same. There isn't anywhere else I can go to get those moments to share my thoughts and feelings without interruption. And there is nowhere else where I get to listen to others think and feel similarly about their bodies.

Meetings are what I treasure most about CPA. It's here that I feel seen, heard, and understood. I know I belong—with pain or with symptoms, with this chronic illness or that type of chronic pain—it simply doesn't matter. We are all in this together.

In this moment, I will experience the peace, joy, and comfort recovery offers me, if only for a moment.

January 2

Chronic pain and chronic illness force me to return to Step One often. It is a kind of home base I tag again and again before moving on with some serenity.

Because I've always been a good manager, I suffer from the delusion that if prudent management is good, hyper-vigilant care is better. By seemingly sound logic, obsessive management is best. Unconsciously, I equate the best management with the complete management of outcomes. I am unwittingly suffering from an obsession to control and direct my pain and illness. My obsessions play a role in my emotional and spiritual debilitation, which CPA has helped me recover from.

When my delusion of control became clear, in a deep, whole-body understanding, I turned to the Twelve Steps of CPA. I began to see that I had to let go of a lot of old ideas and my intense need to control if I wanted to survive. In that moment of truth, I was humbled enough to ask for help. I became teachable. I was ready to try having another relationship with life.

In this moment, I will choose to engage in this simple but profound process of CPA Twelve Step recovery.

January 3

Lately, waking up in this body every day is a struggle. One day, while coming into reality and thinking about all I needed to do, I realized the day's events are not necessarily up to me. They are up to my Higher Power, whom I check in with hourly, for guidance.

Today does not look like I wanted it to. I'm tired. I don't like holidays. I wanted to shower, unpack boxes, and prepare to start my new year in an orderly way. Fortunately, God's time does not follow any calendar. At some point today, my body will fall into sync with my Higher Power's plan; I'll spend time with friends in CPA meetings and end the day having fallen through laughter into peaceful rest. I'm hopeful that tomorrow, my pain will be gone; I'll be strong and relieved of impending fears and disappointment when that does not happen.

Now, I have a safety net in CPA that draws me out of the obsession with what I cannot do and the improbability of a physical solution. I know CPA will be there today and tomorrow, no matter how rough the start of my day is.

Part of my daily ritual is reaching out to at least one other CPA member to start my day. I find that, by the end of my day, I've interacted with several CPA members in various contexts. I go to bed at night feeling like my life matters, which, for me, is a feeling of fulfillment, usually sprinkled with some laughter.

In this moment, I will find hope. It is a phone call or text message away.

January 4

I thought I knew about powerlessness and surrender. Each surrender led to tremendous relief and I became a better person living a better life. When chronic pain and illness entered my life, I had to go much deeper and really explore the meaning of powerlessness and unmanageability, as talked about in Step One. I was suffering, isolated, and alone amidst the storms and chaos of chronic pain and illness.

What I didn't comprehend about Step One until I came to CPA was the extreme importance of awareness, not just of bodily symptoms, but of the need for self-compassion as well.

Whenever I ignore this compassion for myself, I inevitably end up in an extreme emotional state in which I can harm myself and sometimes others. In this state, I'm not likely to think about sitting down and meditating; I obsessively berate myself (sometimes all night long).

The difference for me now, in CPA, is that I am willing to describe my suffering to a room full of fellow sufferers, and immediately, I am filled with the camaraderie of others nodding their heads in comprehension and love.

This fills my heart in a way that shared understanding never has before. It can bring tears of joy, which I'm not yet comfortable showing, but for which I am so grateful as I continue to learn to be vulnerable.

In this moment, I will choose to treat myself with the compassion and care I would expend to a friend.

January 5

To actually *Let Go and Let God* takes extreme courage. For me, this slogan represents the principle of relying on my Higher Power, found in Twelve Step programs. When I carry this slogan into my Step work, again and again, I rediscover the power of the Serenity Prayer.

> *God, grant me the serenity*
> *to accept the things I cannot change,*
> *the courage to change the things I can,*
> *and the wisdom to know the difference.*
> *Thy will, not mine, be done.*

My need to control and direct my pain and symptoms causes my life, behaviors, and relationships to quickly become unmanageable. Can I accept my powerlessness over my chronic conditions? Can I seek the assistance and wisdom of something greater than my mind and best efforts? Can I take the risk of really taking a look at my actions, feelings, thinking patterns, motives, and gifts in a nonjudgmental way? Can I set aside what I think I know and be brave enough to change and to be changed? Can I admit to myself and others the exact nature of my humanity? All of this requires letting go of fear and placing trust in my Higher Power. The Serenity Prayer makes all this possible for me.

It takes great courage to stop fighting life, my body and my mind, and those who wish to help me. My bravest CPA change of attitude is believing that, somehow, some way, I am in the hand of a loving Higher Power.

In this moment, I will be given the courage to turn my will and my life over and really mean, "Thy will, not mine, be done."

January 6

I arise in the early morning stillness. My body has become conditioned to these early hours. At this time of morning, I read, contemplate, gather my thoughts, and ask Higher Power to guide my day.

I haven't been able to do much of anything for the past several months. I've been shaken by new medical conditions that will require attention for the rest of my life. I'm not adapting well; I haven't really asked HP to help me endure this life. But now, I am in yet another moment of despair, and I am finally ready to ask HP to guide me.

My prayer is not formal, not religious…just a thought that has now become a prayer through my intentions. I ask, "Is there help out there?" After a few quiet moments, I enter "life with chronic medical conditions" into an online search engine. Up pops Chronic Pain Anonymous, which I would eventually understand as the answer to my prayer.

The connection that I find in CPA is a true gift. Understanding, comfort, and support are openly shared with me. As I've begun to share myself with others, I am also starting to change, learn, grow, adapt, and accept my new conditions. Despair and isolation are continually replaced with peace, joy, and comfort. I am so grateful to have found CPA.

In this moment, I will acknowledge that, despite my fear and depression, my Higher Power stepped in and gave me hope through finding CPA.

January 7

I have accepted that I am physically and/or cognitively functional for only a few hours a day on a good day. But I find I still want to explain, even within CPA, that I can't do things because my brain and body can no longer be forced to function, that my body now will just override and quit. Acceptance, humility and Step One are what I need to repeatedly turn to when setting boundaries.

At one time, I feared being labeled as lazy, snobbish, or uncaring, but now I have a different understanding. I am powerless. This helps me be less critical of myself and others, in and outside of CPA. When I honor my limitations and boundaries, it doesn't mean I'm being rude or uncaring; it means I am powerless and am practicing self-acceptance, self-care, and self-love (the Three S's of CPA).

I still find it so difficult to tell a fellow member who reaches out for help, "I'm sorry, but I just can't talk right now." I used to sacrifice my well-being to others all the time, but thanks to Step One, I now see that my stubborn denial of self-care makes my life unmanageable.

I have learned that practicing self-acceptance, self-care, and self-love is a CPA victory.

In this moment, I will celebrate my self-care boundaries. I am grateful for my new understanding of powerlessness and unmanageability.

January 8

What does admitting powerlessness mean to me?

Admitting I am powerless brings me to accept the reality of my circumstances. Acceptance releases me from feeling I do not do enough or am not enough.

Admitting powerlessness also means I accept reality, even when I find it unacceptable. My dreams of working until retirement and being financially independent are gone. I'm not able to live alone easily; I've needed a cane to walk since young adulthood. I am unavailable as a healthy, physically equal, and capable partner and companion. I can no longer dance, sail, scuba dive, or bike outdoors. I always need a backup plan and can no longer be consistent in my commitments.

Thanks to CPA, I am learning to accept all the feelings surrounding these limitations, broken dreams, and challenges. I am powerless over them. I can now feel them and then let them go, as opposed to staying stuck in grief and suffering. I've learned that I can grieve without endlessly suffering emotionally.

There are lots of positives in letting go of being adversarial with my pain, illness and losses. Surrendering creates a void that begs to be filled with positive emotions, spiritual nourishment, or simple love of myself and others.

In this moment, I will admit my powerlessness, release negative thoughts, and make way for more ingenious, creative ways to live my current reality to its fullest.

January 9

When I attended my first CPA meeting, something happened.

I knew chronic pain and illness isolated me, but until that meeting, I was unaware of how shut off I'd become. I seldom left the house or saw people. My focus was on how awful I felt almost all the time. Isolation had become a comfort to me. But during that meeting and the fellowship after, I realized this fact: my pain and symptoms were easier to deal with when others understood. I relaxed. I can't describe the sense of belonging and rightness I felt. I had come home.

I am someone who loves and needs her alone time. I keep my cupboards stocked. I have as many books as my shelves can handle. I have internet service and plenty of streaming apps. I recharge by being alone. But any asset can be taken too far. I had no idea how much I needed to connect with people like myself. Now that I have friends in CPA, meetings, and service work, I balance alone time with human connection.

My CPA program is based on working and living the Steps, nurturing my relationship with my Higher Power, and finding and strengthening my CPA recovery. But I cannot minimize the value of belonging. Connection with others separates me from my pain and other symptoms so that I am myself first.

In this moment, I will remind myself that although I have chronic pain and illness, I no longer feel alone.

January 10

Starting my day over at any time is a lovely freedom I can enjoy. When my day isn't going according to my design, I can breathe, relax, and release my tension and frustration. I can stop and reconnect with my Loving Source. Joy begins to creep into my awareness when I stop trying to run the show. Sometimes, abandoning my plans is the healthiest thing I can do with my day.

If the pain or illness I am experiencing is more than I expected, I can pause, acknowledge the present situation, and readjust my expectations and plans. This gives me the chance to take care of myself by choosing to rest or cut back on my activities. When this happens, I also have the opportunity to change my perception to one of grace rather than judgment for "taking the day off."

If I'm depressed, fearful, angry, resentful, or experiencing any challenging emotion or situation, I do not have to be stuck all day. I can allow myself to feel the feelings; then I stop, take a breath, and clear my mind. I might feel difficult things, but I don't have to be miserable all day. I determine what I can do to make a change when possible and useful. I might make a gratitude list, grab some literature, look at the resources on the CPA website, or contact another CPA member to help me.

In this moment, I will pause, take a breath, and start my day over.

January 11

Before CPA, I would classify days as all good or all bad. I know now this isn't true. I now consider a good day one in which I wake up, surrender, and accept that not much will be accomplished except self-care, as I make amends to myself for all the years I pushed way too hard.

When I remember past days as all good, it sets up unrealistic expectations for the future. When I see them as all bad, I miss out on seeing all the things that can contribute to happiness. When I wake up with very low energy or more symptomatic than usual, can I keep an open mind? Sometimes, a good nap or some other unforeseen help or event can turn things around.

My sponsor has taught me: 1) If I can't go back to bed, I may as well use the time to do something pleasant, such as connecting with fellow CPA members. 2) Today and this time are precious, even though they're imperfect. 3) I really can't control or predict how I will feel in the future, so it's not healthy to project and catastrophize. 4) Focus on what is possible. When I can't sleep, I can journal, read program literature, connect with friends, etc. It feels good to let go of expectations and remember that physical and emotional feelings are transitory. Labeling things as good or bad no longer serves my recovery or my practice of acceptance and surrender.

In this moment, I will accept that this feeling is just for now, not forever.

January 12

I equate Step One with humility, and my humility was born of desperation. I could not cure my illness or stop the pain from coming, but I also couldn't go on living like I was. I was only looking at the world through mud-covered glasses, feeling hated by fate, hating myself, my life, and my body. I have come to learn that this is not humility. It's humiliation, self-hatred, and a total lack of faith. In CPA, humility means I accept and love myself exactly as I am and realize I cannot heal myself with my attempts to control situations. By trying to control my conditions and pain, I was only creating more unmanageability and despair.

The good news is that it took just a drop of humility and self-acceptance to get me to that first meeting, opening the door to Step One in my life. I knew I wanted to live like the people who shared in that meeting. I wanted to live with humor, hope, and the acceptance that this is who I am today. No more muddy glasses!

Doing Step One with a Step buddy helped me become aware of the unmanageability in my life. I discovered the part I played by not asking for help when it was really needed or refusing help when it was offered. Allowing others to feel needed is a gift I can give by allowing them to help me.

In this moment, I will humbly love myself exactly as I am.

January 13

I have an obsession to control and direct. I have learned in CPA that I only have control over what I choose to do next. So I ask myself, "What is the next indicated action?" If I'm feeling poorly or I don't have any energy, I can rest. Often, I get stuck in keep-doing mode and don't pay attention to what I'm feeling and need. This slogan helps focus my attention so I can take loving care of myself.

When I am not feeling well, and there are items I need to complete, but I am overwhelmed, I think to myself, "What's the next indicated action? Taking out the garbage. Okay, this I can manage. I don't have to complete the entire list right now. Just one thing. Just one thing at a time." If I need willingness, I talk to my Higher Power and pray for guidance, strength, and clarity. I can reach out for support when my to-do list becomes my HP.

When my energy is low, my cognition is unfocused, and my emotions are intense, all I have to do is the next indicated action. I find there is always something I can do. I can listen to music or find something to feel grateful for. I can read something that will nourish my spirit, or I can pray for someone who is suffering. I can just pause, relax, and breathe.

Doing the next indicated action brings sanity back into my life. It brings a feeling of relaxation, of serenity and reminds me that I am not hopeless or helpless. Here, right where I am, there are choices.

In this moment, I will do the next indicated action as guided by my Higher Power, not my to-do list.

January 14

I love the slogan *Progress, Not Perfection* because it is full of grace I can apply to myself or others.

I have been practicing the Chronic Pain Anonymous program for about eleven years. I work the Steps, attend meetings, do service work, and sponsor people. CPA is a very important part of my life. I think that even when I have bad days, am weak, have increased pain, or my symptoms repeat day after day with no improvement, I would know what to do by now because I am experienced in this program.

The truth is, no matter how long I have been in this program, there are still many times when I forget to use what I've learned. I let depression or the fear of never feeling better into my day and allow them to rule my attitude. At some point, however, I almost always remember that I have some tools I can use to help myself. When I remember *Progress, Not Perfection*, I accept that I am human.

I can use this slogan to treat myself and others with kindness. We are all a work in progress. Applying our program takes practice, making mistakes, and learning from those mistakes. It helps to keep in mind while none of us will ever be perfect, all of us can make progress.

In this moment, I will acknowledge that I am making imperfect progress, and that is perfect.

January 15

In my first year in CPA, I learned that *Rest is an Action,* a simple but life-changing slogan. It had been difficult to accept that I could no longer do as much as I once did. Earning potential and the ability to keep up with my responsibilities in my home and with my family were things I had to let go of to let in a new normal.

Even after hearing this new definition of rest, trying not to do too much was still a challenge. I was still confusing rest with laziness. Resting seemed like a waste of time. I was taught that my home, yard, job, car, etc., had to be in tip-top shape. If they weren't, I had failed and was a bad person. Yet, if I did not rest and kept doing what I thought needed to be done, my condition would frequently decline.

In CPA, I've begun to see and act on the fact that resting is doing something. This is a miraculous shift in my perception. Resting has moved in my mind from something lazy and irresponsible to something valuable and useful. It is the opposite of a waste of time. Resting keeps me feeling better and often results in less pain. It is taking care of myself, which makes my life more enjoyable. Rest is a very constructive use of my time.

In this moment, I will become more comfortable with rest as a necessary part of my life.

January 16

I used to think it was human nature to see the troubles in my life and automatically discount anything that was going well. My reasoning was that by focusing on the things in my life that were already causing me harm I could find solutions and ways to make those concerns and fears go away. I was afraid if I forgot about my problems, it would be like turning my back on an enemy that would later attack. I didn't realize just how badly that was *not* working until I developed an *Attitude of Gratitude*.

Gratitude proved to be an antidote for depression, worry, and fear. Bringing gratitude into a troublesome situation felt like a balm or topical medicine for my hurt feelings and fractured thoughts. Being purposefully grateful lifted my mood enough that I could think differently, and often, solutions were more forthcoming.

CPA taught me that gratitude is an amazing tool. I use it to pass the time while waiting on someone or something. It's helpful during a test, such as an MRI, when I must keep my eyes closed and my mind busy! I start with the letter "A" and go through the alphabet. Sometimes when I am relaxing to begin a meditation, I breathe in gratitude. Even in my head, making a list helps me to feel the spiritual elixir of gratitude.

In reality, there is much more in a day that goes right than wrong. I have much more to be grateful for than not.

In this moment, I will relax into gratitude.

January 17

I spent years dreading nighttime because I worried so much about sleep. I grew so accustomed to waking up frequently to manage my condition that I now automatically wake up at least every two hours. Doctors impress upon me the need for restful sleep but have no solutions for the unpredictability of my condition.

In CPA, I heard a lot of people talk about difficulty with sleep. It was a relief to know I wasn't alone. I heard my story, took a personal inventory with my sponsor, and examined where the unmanageability lay. I started practicing a new way of thinking around being tired and the resulting emotions. I learned to let my Higher Power into my obsession about my sleep hygiene.

First and foremost, on days when I've had very little sleep, I seek support from other CPA members. They remind me that I may feel extra hopeless or overwhelmed because I'm tired, and those are the days when I make myself crazy by trying to plan the rest of my life or do too much. Second, I check in with my body a hundred times a day, if needed, to see if I'm tensing muscles and bracing against exhaustion. Fighting physical sensations drains the precious energy I do have. Third, my sponsor often reminds me that my Higher Power gives me all the energy that is required of me that day. If I'm unable to do something, it wasn't required of me. I usually find that I'm stronger than I think, and if I need to cry, I can do so, knowing that the feelings will pass and sleep will come when it can.

In this moment, I will practice changing my attitudes regarding sleep.

January 18

I am so grateful for CPA. I've met such beautiful people and made lifelong friendships. I have learned to have more peace and love within myself. I discovered that my Higher Power was with me all along, even when I felt abandoned and alone.

I'm using the tools and looking forward to studying the Twelve Steps and Twelve Traditions. I've learned to cope and deal with whatever comes into my path. Before CPA, something would get in my way, and I wouldn't proceed forward. I would get stuck. Am I still struggling? Yes, of course. In physical pain? Yup…lots! Emotional pain? Yes, but it's so much better! I struggle less. I now have a support system of people who truly understand and are there when I need them. And I am there to make sure they're doing okay, too!

I've got more obstacles ahead of me, but there are fewer crisis-laden what-ifs—the kind that used to leave me crying uncontrollably and, as a result, suffering more pain. I'm can stop now and tell myself, "Those what-ifs only lead to more suffering." I take a deep breath and keep moving forward.

I am living life with peace of mind and the ability to adjust my reactions, all because of finding CPA and realizing my Higher Power has been with me all along. There is no shame; my eyes simply weren't letting me see in the ways I needed yet.

In this moment, I will honor that my life has changed!

January 19

Just for Today is my go-to mantra when I realize my mind has slipped into another fear-of-the-future spin cycle.

I've been sick for many years and am now aging. Often, as I go about my business I think, "How will this get done once I am a little more ill?" My head begins to spin. This is part of my insanity; I still suffer from the delusion that I can completely control my condition and my life.

Just for Today allows me to feel good about what I can take care of now and stop trying to predict my future. I don't know how I will be able to deal with all that the future holds. Accepting what comes with grace helps keep me firmly in the present. Today is all I am guaranteed.

What I can do for tomorrow is live well today. What I will need most in the future is to be better at the skills I need most today. I practice accepting what is in front of me, focus all my God-directed energy upon it, and do my best. So, today, I keep practicing living fully in the now.

To do this, I often follow *Just for Today* with the prayer, "God, direct my thinking." This sometimes means I take a small step or two on a problem, then let it go for a few days—whatever my health requires and my Higher Power suggests. Once I've done what I can for today, I can, in good conscience, let go.

In this moment, I will remain fully present and let go of thoughts of tomorrow.

January 20

I appreciate the CPA acronym *STOP (Surrender, Time-out, Observe, Prioritize)*.

When my pain is relentless or when my obsession takes hold, a wall is erected between myself and other human beings. The mental and emotional deterioration that I experience at those times creates a cloudy, paranoid barrier that my mind cannot pass. I also lose any connection to my Higher Power.

On occasion, my loving rescue pets can break through the haze. They will give a clear indication that I am not in my loving-kind mind. I get such clear feedback from their intuitive selves that I have learned to turn back from extreme emotional states when they act a certain way. I need this feedback from my tender-hearted loved ones. It helps me remember to put this slogan into action and points me toward recovery.

Today, I can distance myself from brutal and cruel interactions with myself and others. My animals and my body tell me the truth about how I am doing.

This truth helps me *STOP*, reconnect with my Higher Power ,and start over.

In this moment, I will STOP and connect with my Higher Power.

January 21

Before CPA, it would have been hard for me to believe how *Acting As If* would really work in my spiritual life. I would have fixated on the dishonesty involved and how that is truly not me. How could prayer possibly help me if I no longer believed it was helpful? Isn't that like lying, pretending I believe when I don't? I am honest!

There was a time when I did not want to pray because many of my religious prayers are of gratitude, and I was not in a place to feel gratitude. In fact, I was very angry at Higher Power for all the injustices of my life. Then, I read a humorous short story. A sponsee told her sponsor that she didn't want to do something because she didn't feel it and thought it would be hypocritical. The sponsor responded, saying, "That's correct. Heaven forbid—we wouldn't want you to be hypocritical. You can be a glutton, you can be a thief, you can be smelly, you can be disheveled and slothful, you can be a liar, you can be angry and rude, but you definitely cannot be a hypocrite."

That got me to say my prayers. I realized that *Acting As If* is not lying; it is simply giving something different a try. It may contradict things I have said or even currently believe, but being open to ways of improving my life is nothing to be ashamed of. It is natural for us to change throughout life. Here's the good news: *Acting As If* worked for me! I've even started to thank Higher Power when things go wrong and when I'm in a lot of pain. I don't usually mean it, but it does help remind me that my Higher Power is in charge and knows what's best for me—better than I do.

I often just want to be comfortable, but comfort does not help me reach my goals. At times, I have to endure discomfort to get to what I really need.

In this moment, I will Act As If in areas of my life where I am unwilling or afraid.

January 22

In doing my Step Four inventory, I identified the character defect of comparing myself to others and judging myself as lacking.

A saying that helps is, "Don't judge your insides by someone else's outsides." There are times I've dressed nicely, put on a smile, and presented to the world as a healthy person. The truth was, on the inside, I was running on fumes—miserable and disconnected. I became a master at acting healthy, thanks to my invisible illness.

I've learned, in CPA, that my pain and illness have varying levels of intensity and frequency. My body doesn't stay the same from one day or one week to another. On a good day with decreased pain and symptoms, it may look like I'm not that ill. When I'm having a bad day, I tend not to share it with others so they don't know how much discomfort is present. My safe place is in a CPA meeting, where I can share my feelings and struggles. At meetings, others share their inner worlds, so I know others go through the same ups and downs as me.

If I compare myself today with last week, I can get caught in a trap, trying to figure out why I am not as well or why I am better than last week. What did I do wrong or right? Those lines of thinking merely strengthen my obsession. Comparing means living in the past or the future. Sanity, for me, is found in the present moment and the CPA program.

In this moment, I will release judgments about myself and others.

January 23

Every morning, I remind myself that I am ultimately powerless over my condition. As the gears in my head start slowly turning, the stark and simple truth of that powerlessness, once more recalled, drops me into the beginning of the acceptance I will need for the coming day.

This means that I'm not fighting or resisting things as they are. Yes, I can try all kinds of medical treatments, alternative therapies, psychologies, and religions to improve my quality of life. However, I'm not going to escape the human condition in which both joy and suffering exist. My delusional disappointment is that, somehow, I was not assigned the role of God. So, I remind myself by saying, "No, I'm not God. I can't control everything the way I so badly think I ought to be able to. No."

Instead, I pray and meditate, fellowship with those who understand, and engage in activities that help me grow emotionally and spiritually. I act when directed by an intuitive thought, a serendipitous meeting, or an unexpected event. I reflect on conversations with someone who knows me and my defects well. I am not leading but following. I am acting. Powerlessness means I give up insisting, directing, and demanding, not that I give up living or trying.

In this moment, I will take the actions I am guided and inspired to take.

January 24

Surrendering to the fact that I've got this thing called chronic pain and illness helped me understand that if I want any kind of serenity, I have to move towards acceptance. I may not like the situation; I don't have to like it; I just have to accept it to pivot in a more positive direction.

Acceptance of things as they are right now does not exclude the possibility that I may be directed to try new treatments. Acceptance is essential for an open, willing, and teachable mind. I don't have the energy to waste on internal rants about how unfair this or that is. I don't believe that energy helps me or anyone else, and frankly, it's my experience that it's that energy that harms me and those closest to me.

Some days, I find myself beginning to get angry over something —a wrong, a slight, or just the whole damned difficulty of it all—so I shift my perspective and laugh a little. I am not royalty. The world does not defer to me. Instead of saying, "Oh, this can't be"—which is indeed delusional since it is happening—I try to remember to say, "Oh, I definitely do not prefer this, but it is what it is."

By resisting the current flow of things, I acted like a royal pain, harming myself and others. Now, I can take it as easily as I need, do the things I can, skip those I cannot, and become okay with today as it is.

In this moment, I will live life on life's terms, not entitled expectations.

January 25

Loss and grief never seem to get easier for me. The cycle time has gotten shorter, but the pain of loss is always intense. When I face yet another adjustment to how I must live my life, I become deeply angry. The sadness—from the loss of another part of my body or furthered inability to function in this world—fuels my anger.

I've learned that I have to take time and grieve. Sometimes, the functionality or mobility I think was lost comes back. For me, that's the insanity of living with multiple chronic conditions. Symptoms wax and wane. I get both happy and nasty surprises.

I have a condition that produces a loud ringing in my ear. There are weeks and months that it is so loud I can't think clearly. It keeps me up at night. Meditation is impossible because all I can focus on is the roaring in my ear. And then, one day, it is gone. There is no rhyme or reason. At one time, I searched for answers and chased doctors.

As I worked my CPA program on this specific condition with my sponsor, I eventually surrendered it to my Higher Power and accepted that this is just for now. In that process, I grieved the loss of peace and quiet and rejoiced when the ringing left. As with all things in my program, I am never done. When it comes back, I will go through the process of surrender, turning over all my feelings again. I am grateful to have found a solution to living with my chronic, unpredictable condition.

In this moment, I will assure myself that recovery is a journey, not a destination. I'm grateful for the tools that help me each day.

January 26

I am powerless over my obsession with chronic pain and chronic illness—the conditions and symptoms that arise without consent and through no fault of my own—and the debilitating spiritual and emotional effects of both. My life is indeed unmanageable.

In early 2019, I found myself in constant pain, unlike anything I had previously experienced. I was unable to get out of bed, make myself a meal, take a shower, wash my hair, or handle the simplest tasks. I found myself unable to interact with my husband, the person I most love, without becoming angry. I found myself unable to rise out of the pit of constant self-centeredness that turned all conversations back to me and my misery. I found myself unable to wake without wishing I hadn't and wondering how I would get through another day.

I had never felt such despair. I was baffled. I hated myself with a fervor I did not know was possible. This is how I crawled into Chronic Pain Anonymous. This is when my real emotional and spiritual healing began.

I wrote an entire notebook on my reactions to admitting powerlessness. After reading more about powerlessness in our literature, I learned that my reactions to the situation caused the majority of my unmanageability and suffering, not my conditions themselves. This was a great relief. I wasn't a bad person for being sick; I just reacted poorly. I didn't have any helpful tools to deal with my changing life.

In CPA, I am shown other ways of responding that heal the spirit and emotions, soothe the weary body, and teach me that I am powerless, not helpless.

In this moment, I will help myself by working the Twelve Steps of CPA.

January 27

When I first came into CPA, any little bodily sensation surely meant catastrophe. I was obsessed! I calculated every action regarding how it would affect my pain in the future. I would agonize about every choice, assured I was to blame for any flare-up. My belief was that if I just managed my life well, I would be freed from suffering. CPA has taught me that it was this relentless need to control my pain and illness that was making my life unmanageable. Who'd have thought?!

I love that our preamble says, "changing attitudes can aid recovery." It reminds me that there is something greater than my mind that I can turn to when I forget that I am powerless. I can refocus my thinking by turning to that Power. I can write a gratitude list or place something I wish to turn over in my God box. Most important for me is to remember in Step Three that I made a decision to turn my will and life over to the care of my loving Still Small Voice.

Today, when my thinking turns to control and obsession, I pause, take a breath, and remember my program. I tell myself, "Alright…here I go again, thinking I am responsible for my flare-ups. I am doing my best, and I am powerless over my chronic pain and illness. Still Small Voice, give me the next right thought or action." When I do this, I surrender my obsession and trust that I will be guided toward a more peaceful, joyful, and comfortable life.

In this moment, I will remember that I suffer from obsession and turn to my Higher Power.

January 28

Until recently, I had a very difficult time with the concept of acceptance. When I received my diagnosis, I was still working, exercising, traveling, socializing, and getting on with my life. I was in control and made sure everyone knew it. Additionally, I had no relationship with or reliance on God. Then, a traumatic event triggered a year-and-a-half-long flare. Everything was out of control! So I thought, "I better grab on to something, or I'm not going to survive this."

Today, acceptance and God are the most used tools in my CPA program. When my pain is high, I go through a checklist of things I can do to reduce the pain—things that are within my control. Once I've utilized these things, I say, "Acceptance is the answer." Often, this simple act relaxes me. It takes the pressure off and permits me to be okay with what is happening with my body.

When I'm fatigued and don't have the energy to get out of bed, I accept that I need to take care of myself and rest for as long as I need, and that's okay. When I'm depressed because I haven't had a good day in a long time, I remember that I've done my best. I accept the situation and pray for strength. When people look at me and say, "You look fine! Why can't you work, go to a party, stay up late, etc.?" I accept that I know my body and my capabilities. It's none of my business what others think or say about me. I pray that God will soften their hearts toward me. This not only changes how I feel about them, but it also changes how I feel about myself.

In this moment, I will let go of what others think of me and keep doing the best I can.

January 29

When I came to CPA, the first thing that I noticed was that I had found people who could accept their lives. They weren't living in a constant state of resentment over their circumstances. This motivated me to attend meetings.

I began to catch myself laughing with people who were quickly becoming my deeply compassionate friends. My despair began to lighten as I looked forward to attending meetings daily. This changing attitude, although not present at all times, increased my awareness of the aspects of my life for which I am actually grateful.

I started facing the fact that I had been holding a lot of resentment. Chronic pain had stolen my career, my friendships, and my hobby of ballroom dance. Developing thoughts of gratitude, feeling friendship—and a bit of hope—allowed me to be more willing to explore how I was relating to my situation.

After about a year and a half in CPA, my resentment has lifted. I can honestly say that I believe it is possible to create a life that I love, *One Day at a Time*, with the ongoing support of this fellowship. I am even beginning to find ways to be of service in this program and other areas of my life, such as in the building in which I live.

I am grateful I took a chance on CPA.

In this moment, I will express my gratitude by being of service to others. I will take a chance on CPA service.

January 30

I remember learning that nothing is more important than sleep, but it's so fundamental that it can be easy to forget. As a person living with chronic illness and chronic pain, I needed to expand the definition of this basic need to include rest. Mostly, it's because the sleep I do get is often disrupted, insufficient, and non-restorative, but also because my conditions need various kinds of rest every day. Sometimes, I fight this need, thinking I can just tough it out. There are things I want to do, and I don't want to have to stop!

When a need isn't overtly obvious, I can interpret it as a psychological failing or character flaw, which carries a lot of baggage. One thing that helps is getting validation (from myself, others, CPA literature, etc.) that my conditions are real, significant, impactful, and absolutely not a personal failing. I remind myself I didn't choose this, but I do have some choice in how I respond to it.

A Step One inspired process that helps me is to make a list of all my symptoms, diagnoses, conditions, etc. It helps me to see that I am truly powerless over chronic pain and illness. It bolsters my willingness to surrender when I want to keep fighting my reality.

To this end, I find it very helpful every time I'm in a meeting and hear yet another person affirm, "Rest is doing something. *Rest is an Action.*"

In this moment, I will be creative in finding ways and willingness to rest.

January 31

An old proverb says, "If you want to go fast, go alone. If you want to go far, go together." I lived alone with my chronic illness, pain, and exhaustion for nearly four decades. Then, in CPA, I discovered a new way of living.

I never developed a relationship with a compassionate, supportive, and loving Higher Power. As I discovered the consequences of this, I found that I'd never been truly compassionate, supportive, or loving with myself—especially when it came to coping with my chronic conditions. I spoke viciously to myself. I persecuted myself for mistakes, for falling short of expectations. I shamed myself for my illnesses. CPA members helped me change the things I could, but also shared how a relationship with a Higher Power changed them. It seemed I had nothing to lose; I wasn't getting very far alone.

I didn't know where or how to begin. One of my Step buddies suggested I create an advertisement for my ideal Higher Power. I listed all the attributes I wish God had and many I wish I had. I then simply started talking to the Higher Power of my list. I felt silly and didn't expect much.

Before long, I began to realize my ad was being answered! I was feeling lighter. I was treating myself more compassionately and not being such a pain to others. Character defects I had been battling for decades seemed to simply fade out in the light of this newly arrived loving-kindness.

Now, as I continue to "travel far," as the proverb says, I can take my Higher Power and CPA village with me.

In this moment, I will re-enliven my commitment to the spiritual solution of CPA.

February

February 1

My sponsor asked me to make a list of tangible powers greater than myself for Step Two. He said, "God can be kind of an abstract concept and hard to grasp. What are some things that you can directly interact with that help restore you to sanity?"

Here are some of those things:

- Meetings: I almost always feel more sane at the end of a meeting than I did at the beginning.
- Phone calls: Sometimes, I get the perfect answer to my question. Sometimes, I get to help someone else and not think about my issues for a while.
- Literature: It's amazing how, sometimes, the section I read has exactly what I need to hear.
- Working the Steps: When I do Step work, not only do I improve over time, but I also feel an immediate benefit. I'm in better shape spiritually and emotionally, and the rest of my day goes more smoothly.
- The Fellowship: Collectively, the CPA fellowship has more sanity to offer than my fearful thoughts. When I associate with the fellowship, I receive some of that sanity.
- Sponsorship: It often happens that when I'm talking to a sponsee, my symptoms seem to recede. I can't tell whether my pain is less severe or if I'm just less aware of it. And when a sponsee asks a question, I answer and think, "Wow, I can use that too."

For me, it's true that God sometimes feels abstract and far away. At those times, I can turn to one of these tangible powers greater than myself.

In this moment, I will look for ways to connect with a Higher Power of my own understanding, knowing that I can use these tools when I am struggling.

February 2

When no cure for my pain or illness was forthcoming, I found myself in a long, desolate, dark night of the soul. Initially, I felt abandoned by God, and then I became convinced there was no God. I could feel nothing. I was alone. I was sick, I was hurt, and I was empty.

I saw faith in the eyes of the people at that first CPA meeting I attended. I was blown away by the down-to-earth spirituality and wisdom shared by people who obviously didn't feel physically well. Some were in bed wearing pajamas, with stuffed animals and real live pets to keep them company. There might be tiredness around their eyes, some hoarseness or drag in their voices, but they shared about life today as it is, and it was not too bad! I can say, without a doubt, I came away from my computer screen over an hour later, and for the first time in over a decade, I felt my soul again!

As I work the CPA program, I have come to embrace the fact that control is an illusion. If I make plans but then try to force a particular result, I'm closing myself off from possibilities which could be better than my preconceived outcome. The Power Greater than myself that I am coming to understand again may have a plan for me that is out of this world! Somewhere along my short journey in CPA, I realized that all those years, I did not believe there was a God or Higher Power; God always believed in me. God always loved me just as I am. I may not have had faith in God, but God has faith in me.

In this moment, I will practice faith and release the illusion of control to my Higher Power.

February 3

I have come to see that the Steps and fellowship of CPA are necessary for me to heal from the emotionally and spiritually debilitating effects of chronic illness and chronic pain. Collectively, people in the program have a more useful perspective than I do—they have something I want and have not been able to achieve on my own. Even if I have little or no specific faith at this time, I can choose to trust the group and the fact of its members' recovery.

I realize I am powerless in Step One, and I become willing to be open-minded about believing this spiritual process could work for me in Step Two. Then I can decide to give myself over to this method of spiritual living in Step Three. I don't need to be sure if it will work. I just need to decide that I'm willing to try it.

This is an action program; no genuine and lasting change will come unless I let myself trust a Higher Power of my own understanding. I appreciate that I'm only asked to trust my understanding of a Higher Power. This allows me to still experiment a little with surrender to the greater mysteries I don't comprehend but have sensed in my life. I now know I no longer have to struggle on my own.

I grasp that just a part of my fundamental problem is a lack of power. I seek that deep and elemental force that undergirds and animates all. In this way, I can breathe deeply and relax. I can begin.

In this moment, I will open myself up, even just a little, to a Higher Power that can handle today's struggles.

February 4

I am a miracle. I am not who I was before I worked the Steps. Now, I have the opportunity to pass on the miracle which I truly believe saved my life. It also demonstrated that there were great and small things for me to still do regardless of the condition of my body.

Our book *Recipe for Recovery* reminds me the only way to really hold on to this experience is to pass it on to others. I can only do this when I'm ready. The transformation I experienced didn't happen by chance; it took effort. The recipe works when I follow it. When there is discomfort in my life, I turn back to the recipe or speak to another CPA member who has had success and ask for help to see what I am missing. I am not at fault; mistakes are human. In fact, they are inevitable. But the recipe—the Steps and the program—is never far away, and I turn to it to guide me again.

When I am working my program, others can hear it in my shares. Then one day, it just happened: someone reached out to ask if I would journey through the Steps with them. The first time, I was concerned. Did I really know enough to take on the responsibility of being a sponsor? Would I screw it up and make things worse? My sponsor reassured me that I am not doing this alone but with my Higher Power. It could be that the person reaching out to me was the work of that Power in my life, directing things. I need not fear.

In this moment, I will rely on the Step work I've done and carry the message of hope working the Steps has given me.

February 5

My journey with Chronic Pain Anonymous helps me face my fears.

I was scared and anxious to attend my first online meeting. I'd only attended face-to-face meetings with a group of people I knew while at an inpatient pain program. So, I attended my first online meeting alone, from my home, with those fears of being judged, not belonging, and being the odd man out. But, I was welcomed and immediately felt at home.

Then, I went to a hybrid meeting. I took a chance and attended alone. It did not go well. As I shared, a man yelled, "Get over yourself." Ouch! I allowed that to hurt my feelings and occupy my thoughts for days. I asked people what I'd done wrong, whether crosstalk was allowed, and how I should have handled that man's mean words and behavior toward me. I attended once more to pay attention to the sharing guidelines and that man's behavior. The guidelines included no crosstalk; the man proved to just be someone who needed recovery.

I faced my fear by attending again. I realized that I have to surrender; I am not in control. I expected everyone to treat me with kindness and respect. What the man had said was about him and had nothing to do with me.

Today, I go out of my way to welcome new people at meetings in hopes they will keep coming back. I thank that man for teaching me how not to treat someone new to CPA. I am filled with joy at every meeting I log on to by seeing the names and faces of others who are also growing in the fellowship.

In this moment, I will continue to face my fears.

February 6

I will never work my program perfectly. Yes, I have an excellent set of recovery tools and use them regularly. I can make an attitude change. I can find gratitude in a difficult situation. I can reach out to my Higher Power and receive guidance when I am struggling. However, believing I can apply my tools every time I need them turns out to be part of my insanity and makes my life unmanageable.

New conditions show up, symptoms come and go, and my pain waxes and wanes in intensity and frequency. I do my best to work my program through the good and bad times. Some days, I reach out to a friend when I'm lost and confused; on others, I think I have to figure things out all by myself. Then suddenly, I'll remember I can call someone!

Perfection is an unattainable goal. My need to be perfect is sometimes about wanting approval from others and often leads to blame and shame. This does not contribute to self-care, self-compassion, or well-being. I'm a human being with a range of emotions, old habits, and a body and brain that are not always reliable. It takes time to develop new habits, shift attitudes, and let go of old belief systems. This is a process of progress, not perfection.

Progress for me is an ongoing process, with the intention of bettering my life. Surrendering expectations of perfection for myself is progress. I can find meaning in the process. The slogan *Progress, Not Perfection* helps me make sane and skillful choices for my well-being.

In this moment, I will celebrate my progress and know that I am enough.

February 7

Acceptance is not something I can experience once, and then just be able to accept everything about my life. This is a tool I need to use often in my recovery journey as my body changes and more loss of functionality occurs.

Denial is often my starting place. When I lost the sense of taste and smell, I ignored it. I thought, "This is temporary; it doesn't mean anything." It took about a year for me to realize this wasn't going away. Moving past denial, I went to the internet for answers and eventually spent money and time seeking a medical fix. "My body is broken, and the doctors will know what to do," I thought.

Living with a chronic health problem means there are often no solutions. I had to learn to live with a diminished and often absent ability to taste food. Chocolate had always been a treat, especially when I was feeling poorly. Now, most of the time, all I have left is a memory of this delicious experience. I had to accept that this was my new reality, disappointing as it was.

Acceptance is crucial because, without it, I would be spending all my energy mourning this loss and looking for a cure that does not exist. I do not have to like this new version of my body. Although, accepting this version *Just for Today*, helps me stop obsessing about ways to change it.

In this moment, I will shift my focus to gratitude.

February 8

For years, I had to take a type of medication that was risky for me but necessary. I was careful and took it as prescribed. I've recently had to discontinue this medication because it began to hurt more than help. The process of discerning this was very difficult. I had become the proverbial frog in the heated pan—the one where the heat can be turned up in such fine increments that the frog never realizes it's in trouble.

Without a CPA sponsor, the Tenth Step, journal entries, and a great deal of Higher Power's grace, I would never have jumped out of that pan. I felt very scared. I had no idea how I would function without this medication. From previous experience, I realized I was at the edge of my comfort zone, which often led to good things I could not yet see.

Doing without this medication has meant accepting many more limitations. However, I began to experience new freedoms. A mental clarity I'd lost somewhere along the way returned. My program became more meaningful. My conscious contact with my Higher Power deepened. My fellowship relationships dramatically improved. I became much more grounded.

Does this mean I will never use this type of medication again? I don't know. Chronic illness teaches me that adaptations are constantly required. But now I can relax. I have found that staying open and accountable on an ongoing basis with a trusted and experienced person in CPA, like a sponsor, is key when addressing my medication concerns.

In this moment, I will notice if I'm outside my comfort zone and commit to reaching out to a person I trust in CPA.

February 9

Before chronic pain and illness, I was a workaholic. I spent ten years struggling, constantly berating myself for not doing more. I went through cycles of forcing myself to get a new job, to work for a while, and then end up in the hospital, followed by months of inactivity and depression. My chronic pain and illness dominated my life and made it impossible for me to work full-time.

Service in CPA gave me wisdom and helped me grow. It brought me out of this cycle. I was not seeking work when I came to CPA, but my Higher Power had other plans! At the time, CPA happened to need someone in my field of study, and I felt that small, still voice, my Higher Power, telling me this position was perfect.

While doing service, I have felt myself blossom and thrive in ways I didn't think were possible with chronic pain and illness. The people I collaborate with completely understand my situation and limits because they are members of CPA as well. When something doesn't go as planned, everyone is understanding and supportive of the situation. I don't have to worry about flares impacting my service work because I know I have support and help when needed.

Knowing this gave me the confidence to slowly experiment with how much I can work. Using the pacing technique, I've now established a schedule that honors my limits, the needs of service, and other jobs I perform in life. It brings me such joy to see CPA flourish. I was able to help make that happen, and I did it in a healthy, positive way.

In this moment, I will feel grateful for the many life lessons service has brought me.

February 10

I thought I was in CPA because I have a chronic health condition. As I listened to others share about their recovery and read the literature, I understood that my illness and pain are not the problem. It is my relationship to them that interferes with my serenity and happiness.

Some people can drink a few glasses of wine or play slot machines at a casino and never develop an addiction. I know people who have more serious medical problems than I do, but they don't need the recovery program of CPA. They don't obsess over their health. I do. That is why I need to be in CPA.

Someone once told me that if I tell the same story more than three times about my health, I am obsessing. If that's the case, then I definitely was. This made me realize others might be quite tired of hearing that story.

It is my obsession, my constant search for ways to make my health problems go away, that consumes my thoughts and makes me unhappy. It is my never-ending battles with a body that doesn't work the way I want it to that give me so much grief. It is my belief that if only I could get the right answers, I could finally live my life.

As I worked the first few Steps in CPA, I began to surrender my desire to be fixed and my belief that I am broken. This doesn't mean I've stopped taking care of my well-being. It means I'm not fixated on what triggers my symptoms, what I need to be comfortable, complaining to others, how sick I am, etc. My entire life is not fully focused on myself and my body.

In this moment, I will be aware of my obsessions and ask for Higher Power's help if needed.

February 11

I have a bimonthly procedure that is remarkably painful but incredibly helpful, and I dread it every two weeks. The mechanism my head is placed in is so loud that I am required to wear earplugs or earbuds. The first time, I wore the earplugs I was offered. Never having used them before, I got an instant earache that had to be medically treated. This only added insult to injury. What was I to do? The procedure hurts too much but yields such benefits.

CPA taught me that whatever procedure I am presented with, I can ask HP, "How creative can I get in my self-care regarding said procedure? How can I make an intimidating appointment into a time of play? How can I make something that is naturally uncomfortable more pleasant?" HP never lets me down.

The next time I had this procedure, I wore my earbuds and listened to British stand-up comedy. Now, I laugh out loud during the procedure. I discovered that my laughter actually reduces my pain level, and I come out of these experiences feeling lighthearted and giggling. I now look forward to these sessions, and so do the technicians. They have told me they love when I come because they love to laugh at me laughing. My Higher Deeper Self's creativity changed my attitude and brightened another's day.

In this moment, I will look for more ways to be lighthearted and laugh.

February 12

Chronic pain and chronic illness forced me to rest for the first time in my life. I was a superwoman, denying myself any form of self-acceptance or self-care, let alone self-love. Now, I had no choice but to lie in bed and rest. I was bed-bound, barely able to make it to the restroom on my own. As I entered into my awful new reality, I had to force myself to rest. Force rest? The results of this forcing only increased the fatigue and anxiety in my already exhausted body and depressed and terrified mind.

Then I found CPA and heard about resting in the care of a loving Higher Power. Wow! What a concept. It wasn't up to me to rest. It didn't have to be a chore. I could simply allow for rest, trusting this Power to care not only for me but for everything in my life.

Today, when I engage in the action of rest, I do just that. I allow for rest. I relax and soften my body and mind; I breathe deeply and imagine myself wrapped in love, warmth, and support. I have many different images for the concept of loving care; they all support me by truly relaxing not just my body but my mind, emotions, and spirit as well.

Resting in loving care does not always equal a reduction of symptoms and fatigue, but it always creates a more peaceful, joyful, and comfortable feeling in the depths of my being. To me, this is CPA recovery in action.

In this moment, I will look for ways to allow for rest.

February 13

I find I require various ways to shift my attitude to help me discover God's will for me.

When the need for a yes or no regarding a request for my time and energy arises, I find that sometimes the only way to know if it's possible is to try. Like a pair of jeans I try on and discover aren't a fit, I can return them without apology or lengthy explanation. This option lends a lighter attitude.

A daily gratitude practice has been a hugely helpful method to change my attitude. I used to make gratitude lists when desperate; they rarely made me feel better. In CPA, I've learned that gratitude takes cultivation. Daily, noting what's right shifts my focus from only seeing what's wrong. Over time, my outlook becomes more balanced, lighter, and hopeful. I no longer expect to feel better on-demand or hold that maddening requirement to feel better immediately. Instead, I understand it as an ongoing process, a practice.

The biggest attitude shift for me came in developing a daily ritual of admitting that I have chronic pain and chronic illness. I don't have to like it, but I do have to accept it if I hope to live well. Morning reflection on the plain facts of my life wakes me out of the slip back into expectations more suited to my former, non-compromised state of health. Then, with fresh acceptance, I ask God for the courage I need for my current life, its joys, pleasures, fears, and sorrows. I repeat to myself throughout the day, "God, may I go with the flow, be in the now, and do the next indicated thing."

In this moment, I will take action to adjust my attitude if necessary.

February 14

I think I am humble...until I ask for help due to my physical, mental, or even spiritual needs and get rejected. Sometimes, I get no response, or it's clear that I am not going to be someone else's priority that day. I know other people have their own lives to live. Even though they may sincerely wish to help me, they may not be able to.

These responses can be hard for me. It leaves me feeling dismissed and alone. Can I trust that my Higher Power can handle the timing of anything, including what I think I need? In CPA, I'm learning that I cannot force outcomes. Take the example of herding kittens: put several kittens in a room and try to get them to do what you want. It isn't possible. I am learning to stop trying to herd kittens and to instead relax, trust, and truly let go of outcomes.

I learn from listening to others who make an effort to practice these behaviors in their lives. I no longer have to hold myself or others hostage to my expectations. When I am able to practice a little bit of trust in my HP, I discover peace of mind and freedom from the stress my old thinking causes.

Nonetheless, there is always more room for growth in this department. I can always ask for help in any area of my life and then let go of how that need is met. This has worked for me so far, but it is a continual work in progress.

In this moment, I will let go and trust that Higher Power will help me get my needs met.

February 15

When I came to CPA, I'd looked in many other places for support: government and disability organizations, nonprofits, and churches. I wanted help because it seemed so scary and impossible to handle on my own.

In CPA, I learned that I could ask—but I could not force—people to see or hear my needs. I didn't cause my condition, and I would change it if I could. Before CPA, the idea that I would change it if I could was a mission statement. I was searching for purpose, even if it was only to convince others I was worthy of services. Over and over, people denied my requests for help. I felt like a victim, someone no one cared about, and someone people thought wasn't in that much pain or wasn't that sick. In CPA, I found people who seemed more calm and accepting of the unacceptable.

CPA also taught me about the great power of prayer and meditation. I had been relying almost solely on myself. There seemed to be a lot I needed to do to make people understand my needs. But daily prayer and meditation helped me realize my Higher Power was far greater than myself, others, and organizations. The more I prayed and meditated, the more I shed my victim role and could face life on life's terms.

Little by little, my fears dissipated. Today, I don't feel like a victim. Yes, it might be nice to be free of chronic pain and chronic illness, but I am okay and whole in spirit, even as I live with it. CPA helped me see myself as a full person as I move forward with my life, one day at a time.

In this moment, I will turn my fears over in my prayer and meditation practice.

February 16

In the past, I felt short bursts of potential hope because of a promised result from a new doctor, treatment, or medication, but it was always fleeting. The paths I went down ultimately ended in failed results and disappointment.

Then, one day, while desperately searching for yet another possible solution, I found CPA. I believe my Higher Power led me to this program. At my first meeting, a small seed of hope was planted. Although CPA was not what I expected, I felt as though my eyes and my heart had been opened. CPA offered a new and different way to live despite having chronic pain and chronic illness.

I heard shares not about curing disease but filled with heartfelt solutions to our associated emotional and spiritual pain. I knew I'd found my people. As I began to experience a new kind of hope, I found that my body responded. I was experiencing life in a new way, with a new attitude. I felt lighter and more connected to the world.

Life is more joyful because of this changed perspective. Even when I am in bed all day, I can live my life as if the glass is half full. I do what I am able and have genuine hope for my future. With a new freedom from the obsession surrounding my pain and illness, I can truly experience life again.

In this moment, I will acknowledge sources of hope in my life.

February 17

With chronic pain and/or chronic illness, it's natural to feel envious and compare ourselves to others who do not have this challenge. I often compare myself to my pre–chronic pain self and rue the things I'm no longer able to do.

Prior to chronic pain, I was a fairly active person. I had a full-time job and was active in my community. I am also a father, husband, son and brother. I can still do quite a lot, but these changes are still upsetting. Doing things I'm familiar with, while living in an unfamiliar body, can be quite challenging. The temptation to compare myself to others often arises. I sometimes succumb to it, which aggravates my sense of frustration and misery.

I think comparing is part of the grieving process we experience when we try to come to terms with our situation and the changes it involves. This tendency is perhaps heightened by the media. We are surrounded by images of people whose bodies are seemingly perfect and have not let them down. There is a prominent figure in my country who is two weeks younger than me. When I see him on TV or read about him, I often think, "This guy is my age and managing the country's finances. I sometimes barely manage to get dressed for the day!"

I have started asking my Higher Power for help in managing this inclination. I pay attention when it arises but in an impartial, nonjudgmental way. It's actually quite amusing how my predisposition for comparison can manifest itself. So, now, when I notice that I've begun comparing myself to others again, I take a moment and reach for a little self-compassion instead.

In this moment, I will accept myself for who I am and know I do not need to be defined by what I do.

February 18

Hope is a word that has eluded me for several years. I kept trying doctor after doctor, treatment after treatment, and surgery after surgery alleged to relieve my chronic pain. They didn't. Pain became my constant focus, the center of all my thoughts: what can I do to relieve it? How bad is it going to be today? What if I can't sleep tonight because of my pain? How am I going to get any chores done today? How am I going to participate in my relationship with my husband? I lived in moments strung together by fear. I felt like things were never going to get better.

I started coming to CPA and was shocked to find others who understood how I think, feel, and experience life.

I almost didn't come back after my first meeting because I got embarrassed during my share. I focused so much on what I felt about my circumstances that I missed the hope that was there. During fellowship time after the meeting, someone gave me their number. I spent the next week talking one-on-one with another member who is my same age and struggles with my same pain. It was a Godsend. I kept coming back. I now go to meetings every day and am able to hear the hope.

Today, I find hope in accepting myself as I am, no longer seeing my limitations as negative attributes, being kind to myself, and knowing it's okay to be where I am. I hope to learn how to find self-love, self-acceptance…and honestly, just how to find myself again. I lost myself since the chronic pain started, but now I have hope I will not only find but like myself again. And maybe one day, even love myself.

In this moment, I will focus on ways to feel hopeful.

February 19

When the onset of chronic illness stopped me dead in my tracks, I found great relief in pacing to try to manage my energy envelope. It was such a useful tool until it became my obsession. For example, I would wake in the morning and think, "Okay, I have X hours out of bed for the day. Do I spend some of that energy on a shower or not, because showering really takes up a lot of energy, and it's only 8:00 a.m.? Okay, let me account for all the energy needed just to clothe and feed myself. Darn it. Thinking about my energy just wasted energy. Argh!" Pacing controlled me and no longer helped me. I fell under the delusion that if only I paced well, I could defeat reality.

When I arrived at CPA and read the opening words of *Recipe for Recovery*, which states, "The meaning of these Steps is based in faith, humility, and the ability to turn over the problems of our life to a greater power, without trying to control and direct the outcomes," I realized I was trying to control and direct my daily life via pacing. If I wanted to apply the CPA program in all my affairs, I had to begin by giving my energy to my Higher Power.

As I practice *Let Go and Let God*, I find that Higher Power is much more powerful than a metaphor. When I pause and ask for the next thought or action, I find unknown reservoirs of strength, stamina, courage, and creativity that I never knew I had. I no longer overanalyze my energy with extreme pacing. This new normal is peaceful, joyful, and comfortable because my actions or inactions are no longer up to me or my belief that life is limited by pacing correctly.

In this moment, I will ask my Higher Power for guidance on the best way to manage my energy.

February 20

I was living a life of happiness and activity: golf, travel, books, crocheting, and being socially active filled my life. Then, it changed. For two years, I was bedridden, feeling hopeless, angry, and depressed. It felt like my life was over. Over the next five years, I tried all types of pain medications and every type of therapy and surfed the internet relentlessly with minimal relief.

I came to a point where I had to accept there was nothing that could be done to eliminate the pain. I had to learn to manage it. I felt defeated and alone. What was I to do? Fortunately, in my search, I ran across CPA. I found members who embraced me with love, compassion, and encouragement. They spoke my language. They understood me; I felt like I was home.

Acceptance of my situation and a deepening relationship with my God give me hope. I am redefining my life with activities that bring me joy and purpose. Online coloring, music, movies, visits with CPA members and family, walking when able, nature, and seeing babies and puppies—all fill my proverbial cup. I genuinely feel more like who I was created to be.

In this moment, I will notice that I am a blessed person, exactly as I am today.

February 21

When approaching Step Nine, I was convinced the most important amends would be to my children. I had some fear that if I admitted my wrongs, somehow my amends would not work to repair the relationships. I wrote letters to my two children, in detail, about my wrongs and how sorry I was. My sponsor reminded me that I needed to make amends to myself first. The concept of forgiveness, including self-forgiveness, was a light bulb moment for me.

As I started to learn how to forgive myself, my children also opened their hearts, and a new foundation for our relationship was built. Both my children were very forgiving. I changed my behaviors to be kind and gentle to myself. Self-forgiveness gave me a new way to look at myself and, in turn, others. That allowed me to give kindness and compassion to others and to make amends. Some of my amends were a simple apology; that's all that was needed. Other amends required some changes in my behavior; these are still being changed with time.

Working the Steps helps with my ongoing amends. As I learn to be kinder to myself, with the help of my Higher Power, I'm guided to a more peaceful life with the people I love most. Praying for guidance from my Higher Power allowed for all of this to happen. My amazing sponsor also helped guide me to make peace with myself and continues to support and give me strength to carry out my amends.

In this moment, I will focus on being kind and gentle toward myself.

February 22

All my life, I've had conflict with my body. From early childhood, I was engaged in a ruthless campaign of self-improvement. I was never good enough and could never do enough. Driven by self-will, I never succeeded in changing myself. Instead, after periods of frenetic activity, I collapsed into exhaustion and depression. Looking back, this was the only chance my body got to rest. But for me, rest was a naughty word; once I regained some energy, the relentless cycle would start over again.

A huge impediment to my healing was my refusal to rest. I kept trying to force my body to perform the way it used to, the way it was no longer able to. I was unable to treat myself with compassion.

Through CPA, I am beginning to attend differently to my pain. I realize that all my exercise and management strategies over the years have actually been a form of bargaining. I've been saying, "I'll do all these things, I'll be really, really good, and the pain will go away." The pain isn't going away.

I no longer push myself when my body tells me it's time to stop. I am learning that my body is fine as it is. I am not separate from it; when I treat it cruelly, I treat myself cruelly. My developing relationship with my Higher Power is the foundation of this new relationship with my body. Through prayer and meditation, I am discovering how to be gentle with myself. I remember *Easy Does It*. My body is not a thing to be improved; it is a gift to be appreciated. By resting in the loving approval of my Higher Power, I have found, at last, that change is possible.

In this moment, I will treat my body with loving-kindness.

February 23

I have been through many medical procedures since joining CPA, and I'm currently trying to decide about another one. In the past, I've had a lot of anxiety around these decisions. I remember being seventeen, going into my first surgery, and my mom helped me connect with my Higher Power. We held hands and said a prayer together. I was specifically scared about the anesthesia, so she had the anesthesiologist talk with me to help us build trust before I went in.

Fast-forward a couple of decades to me joining CPA. I was getting a common procedure done, but my old fear was bubbling up. I was worried about how this could exacerbate symptoms and about how long it would take to get back to baseline. I scheduled the procedure for after my favorite Third Step prayer meeting, where I got to turn over the experience. This was just like holding my mom's hands and praying. I remembered that, ultimately, Higher Power is my surgeon. That thought is extremely comforting to me.

The procedure went smoothly. I came home to some delicious takeout—a treat for getting through the experience. I cleared my schedule for a week so I didn't feel pressure to accomplish anything while I recovered. This gave me the time and space to go slow.

Now, I am debating this new and major procedure; I am reaching out for help. I am asking my CPA friends for help and understanding. I am turning over my fear every day. I'm an adult now, so when I choose a healthcare practitioner, I can meet with them, ask questions, and build a trusting relationship.

In this moment, I will remember that I am never alone. I have CPA, I have guidance, and I have HP.

February 24

I have learned that I am powerless, but I am not helpless. I have no power over whether it rains. I have to surrender to the reality of rain. But I am not helpless. I can choose to take an umbrella when I go out, wear a raincoat, or just not go out when it's raining.

The same concept holds true for my body. I am powerless over the thoughts that arise, over my digestive system, over my lungs, over my bones. I have to surrender to the reality of what happens with my body. But I am not helpless. There are things I can do to help myself. I can choose what and when to eat. I can choose to put heat on a part of my body that hurts. I can choose to recognize thoughts that don't serve me well, and I can use my recovery tools to shift my attitude.

In CPA, I learned that the outcome of taking these actions is still not in my hands. I am still surrendering when I eat healthful foods. I am making the best choices I can, as guided by my Higher Power. And then, powerless to direct the outcomes and results, I turn them over to that Power.

There are always ways I can help myself. The key is in the Serenity Prayer: knowing the difference between what I can and can't change. I can't change my body. I can ask for the courage to take actions that will help me cope with the realities over which I am powerless.

In this moment, I will ask for the courage to change what I can and the wisdom to know the difference.

February 25

CPA literature tells us that changed attitudes and actions can aid recovery. Yes, and…?

Before CPA, I was drowning in the misery of all the changes my chronic pain and illness brought into my life. On my own, I couldn't change my intense focus on every sensation, negative thought, and debilitating feeling. It took help from something greater than myself for my attitude to change.

Seeing smiling faces and hearing laughter in CPA meetings opened me to the new idea that I could be happy and disabled at the same time. The Twelve Steps taught me to surrender my stories, which led to the spiritual awakening many experience as part of Step Twelve. For me, this awakening came in the form of Higher Power changing my thought processes. I no longer feel the need to label life as good or bad. Additionally, I now have the courage to choose to reframe my thinking when needed.

The freedom this awakening has given me is immeasurable. Some days, I need to honor my feelings of self-pity, grief, and sadness, letting that energy flow through me and exit. Other days, it is helpful to reframe such thoughts rather quickly. When I ask Higher Power to give me the wisdom to choose which action is required, I honor the totality of my attitudes and feelings without dismissal or obsession.

In this moment, I will choose to view life as an experiment, and not a test.

February 26

I really appreciate that CPA asks us not to investigate or discuss each other's treatments. In my other support group of people living with the same disease, many conversations can quickly devolve into who is suffering more or who is administering what treatment better, etc. Part of my experience in recovering from my obsession to control my chronic conditions is learning to handle what I call "the conversation." This is when almost every interaction seems to turn into some mini health update, usually followed up by unsolicited armchair advice.

I'm on medicines that, on their own, will eventually kill me if my disease doesn't first. But to live, I have to use them. I don't come to CPA to hear another person's opinion on this; I've had that conversation with myself and my care providers many times already.

I still find it hard to let each day be its own and accept my health as it is at each moment. When I try to fix or control everything, I add another layer of suffering. So, I continue to work on surrendering and letting go. The shame I experience surrounding my use of medications is a big part of what I am working the Steps around. However, what I have experienced in CPA is that there is an interest in my life that is more than medication compliance or updates on my health status.

In this moment, I will know that I am made of more than my health conditions and how I manage them.

February 27

I could grasp the notion from Step Two that I needed to be restored to sanity. I was demoralized, depressed, and afraid because, on some level, I knew my own resources were no longer up to the task of coping. But I had lots of baggage when it came to God and a deep, irrational fear that I could only trust myself. I could, however, see that many in the fellowship of CPA found a way out. They had what I wanted but could not seem to obtain myself.

It was explained to me that I might not understand this power initially, but over time, I would have real and vital experiences that would reveal it. In the meantime, I could simply trust the evidence of those in recovery who talked of no longer relying only on themselves to cope with the destructive forces of chronic pain and chronic illness.

"It's something like falling in love. You have to experience it to know it. It's like that," my sponsor would say. He suggested I just get started. I could address my petitions for help, "To Whom It May Concern." He said that if things didn't work out, the program could refund my misery.

I thank God for such forthright, kind, and sensible people like my sponsor and others. Finding my Higher Power has become the great experiment of my life. And it's made all the difference.

In this moment, I will trust that experimenting with my beliefs in a power greater than myself is enough for me to experience spiritual growth.

February 28

I was open to a Power greater than myself in Step Two, although the word "God" in Step Three made me wonder if I was in the right place. My belief in a Higher Power developed gradually as I devoted myself to working the Steps with my sponsor's help.

I'd tried my best to address my progressive chronic pain and chronic illness with innumerable attempts to cure or control my physical state. It was only after coming to Chronic Pain Anonymous that I began to see the insanity of my responses to my pain and physical limitations. In CPA meetings, I learned that if I put the Higher Power of my understanding first and then my program, everything else would fall into place. I discovered my priorities had been reversed. I had put my career and other people ahead of my connection with Higher Power. This was indeed detrimental to all my relationships, as well as my recovery, sanity, and health.

I am grateful for the opportunity to apply the Twelve Steps to other aspects of my life where I need help. The Steps work under any conditions. My faith and reliance upon my Higher Power grows as I listen, share, read, and participate in CPA meetings. While I usually prefer hearing the sanity and serenity that old-timers have gained, hearing newcomers share about the insanity helps me realize I am in the right place. I certainly have more trust in my Higher Power than I could have imagined before CPA. Listening gives me the most precious gift: hope.

In this moment, I will trust that I am in the right place and open my heart to listen for the hope that others share.

February 29

Until I came to CPA, I didn't think anyone would understand me and the choices I need to make to get through the day. The first time I shared that I often don't get out of bed and dressed until late afternoon, instead of seeing looks of disapproval, I saw head nods. There was no judgment, merely shared understanding. When I talked to my sponsor about the grief I felt because of the professional dreams I've had to give up, she looked at me with compassion and told me about how she dealt with that in her life, too.

We help each other in CPA by reminding each other that we have permission to be idle, to rest, and to not be productive every hour of every day. We give to each other by listening and not trying to fix or solve problems. Even when I am flat in my bed, eyes closed, I can give to others by being warm and caring toward someone who needs a loving witness as they share their struggles that day. I can pass along the support and acceptance I received from others.

No one in CPA is an expert. We are always learning together on our recovery paths. I'm grateful for everyone who said something at a meeting that positively altered how I responded to a situation later that day. I'm grateful to all the people who answered the phone when I was feeling poorly and showed compassion as I wept or ranted. I'm grateful for my sponsor, home meeting, and the love and support of the CPA fellowship.

In this moment, I will know I am of value even when I cannot get out of bed. I can still be loving and supportive within my limits.

March

March 1

Through decades of chronic illness, I kept working my first Twelve Step program to change my attitude, respond creatively, and grow closer to my God. But still, I felt tremendously alone despite the many ways I tried to break my sense of alienation. One day, I found myself sitting in the parking lot alone after a meeting and weeping. Through my tears came this prayer: "God, I need some kind of support for this pain, for this illness."

I thought of purchasing another self-help book in hopes it would keep me going. While searching, one book mentioned Chronic Pain Anonymous. In a hot minute, I was on the CPA site reading sample stories. One really hit me. I thought about how I'd like to talk to that guy.

So, I found a meeting that night, and the host was that guy. Afterward, he spoke with me late into the evening. It felt like a miracle to me, one that's been hard to beat. I like to recall it because it reminds me that, repeatedly, what I've needed in life has always arrived, eventually.

Often, my basic needs feel threatened by difficult occurrences, but I persevere. Either things sort themselves out or they don't, and in any event, I can find acceptance with God's help. I can't speak to the future. However, when I acknowledge the miracles I've experienced, small or large, I am reminded: Don't quit.

In this moment, I will remember that I am not alone.

March 2

Instincts can be tricky. It's not always easy to tell when my will pushes through or when my Higher Power is trying to communicate. In my experience, HP's will comes from a place of calm and peace, while mine typically stems from worry and panic. Noticing this difference is one way I've learned to identify whose will I am practicing: mine or HP's.

While working Step Three with my sponsor, I connected with and came to appreciate my HP, but I sometimes still feel distanced. During these times, I remind myself that I am trying my best and to *Let Go and Let God*. Letting go gives me a break. Instead of wasting my energy stressing and obsessing over situations—potentially making them worse—I can turn them over to my HP.

I keep items around my house to remind me to let go and trust in HP, such as a Serenity Prayer key-chain that jingles when I walk my service dog, my glass God-box decorated with fairy lights, and various jewelry pieces featuring the Serenity Prayer or other recovery related quotes. There are even some activities I've learned to use, which help me turn things over. I can write about the issue and put it in my God-box, revisit Step Three and my answers to the questions asked when working that Step, talk to my sponsor, or meditate and escape into a peaceful garden I have created in my mind.

In this moment, I will trust my Higher Power to bring me peace, and I will always be grateful for it.

March 3

"Thy will, not mine, be done." In CPA, we add this line to the Serenity Prayer. It reminds me that my serenity is based on accepting reality rather than on asserting my will on it.

When I woke up this morning, I thought it would be a normal day. That was my will. The moment I stepped out of bed, I knew the day would not go as planned. My body did not feel stable, my head spun, and a fogginess set into my mind.

Before CPA, I'd ignore the messages from my body; I'd disagree with reality and pretend I was okay. I've learned the hard way that fighting with reality, fighting with the will of my Higher Power, does not lead to serenity. I might have checked off the items on my list, but I would make myself miserable as a result.

Each morning, the first thing I do is try to recognize God's will for my day. I accept what is true and surrender to reality. Serenity, for me, comes from aligning with what is happening at the moment rather than imposing what I think should be happening. With this shift, I can sort out what adjustments may be needed.

The day has been given over to my Higher Power. I don't know what the whole 24 hours will look like. I can always start my day over again. Living in this way brings me serenity.

In this moment, I will surrender my will and ask my Higher Power what to do next.

March 4

This is what sanity means to me: to have soundness of mind and judgment, be rational, behave reasonably, be realistic, and make sensible, healthy, and clear-headed choices.

When I first came to CPA, I didn't believe I would ever have sanity again. But this program helped to restore my sanity.

My insanity will never be totally gone. That's why I need to attend meetings, talk to my sponsor, and work my program every day. I now know that when sanity eludes me, I can find it again.

Here are a few practices I use to stay sane:

- When I am tired, I go to bed. I rest when tired, even if it is noon.
- When I find a medication change causes problems, I react reasonably. I call the doctor. I don't try to figure it out myself.
- Before I go to a new restaurant, I look up the menu online and select what I can eat. If I need to make special requests, I can arrive with them already planned. If I'm going to someone's home, I may call and ask what they are serving and make a request for myself. If that's not realistic, I eat beforehand, so I'm not hungry.
- When I travel, I start packing weeks in advance. I may arrive a day before an event or stay a day longer. I pace myself. I keep my schedule light before and after the trip.

Sanity can sometimes come from using some common sense and making healthful choices. I didn't seem to be able to do this before CPA. I often made decisions that led to pain and suffering.

In this moment, I will remember that I am learning a new way of living.

March 5

I am very new to CPA. I love the idea of the Twelve Steps and know I have much to gain from them, all while being a little reluctant to jump in.

Just knowing I have a connection to this group is so helpful. I can reach out to someone or go to a meeting. It's such a relief! I no longer feel alone. I am in physical pain almost all the time, but since coming to CPA, I find I am no longer fighting against it. I am learning to practice acceptance and have faith that I can live a joyous life regardless of my pain. On the more difficult days when I have to take it easy, CPA teaches me how to slow down.

One coping mechanism I've started using is helping others. I find it interesting that when I help others, I avoid my pain and suffering. It seems getting outside of my head and focusing on someone else releases the grip on my pain. I am grateful to have CPA, where I can share the path of recovery.

In this moment, I will see where I might be useful to someone else.

March 6

One of the things that has really helped me in Chronic Pain Anonymous is developing a new perspective on rest. In my healthier days, rest was something I viewed as a waste of time. If I was resting, I was not doing anything.

That's changed. I used to only focus on what I could get done, but now I also focus on taking care of myself. It was a surprisingly difficult switch to make.

All my life, everything was about what I could accomplish. At work, it was taking care of my responsibilities and meeting deadlines. At home, it was cleaning the house, buying groceries, and cooking. Everything was about getting things done and crossing them off my to-do list.

When chronic pain and illness came into my life, I soon discovered this mindset no longer served me. If I pushed to get everything done, I ended up worsening the symptoms of my illness—I was in more pain, which meant I could get even less done. At first, I struggled with guilt. There was this constant inner battle: I knew my body needed rest, but I also thought I had to get everything done. I was frustrated and wanted to avoid the reality of my body's new rest requirements.

When I finally accepted rest as a good thing, not an interference, it brought me peace. I now realize that rest does accomplish something. It helps give my body what it needs so I can live a peaceful life.

In this moment, I will accept rest as part of my life without guilt.

March 7

Before CPA, I had no issue asking for emotional support because I had no emotions that needed exploration. Emotions...what are those again? I was just another guy, detached and avoiding feelings of any kind.

It wasn't until my depression and anxiety became unmanageable and drove me into Twelve Step rooms that I became desperate enough to ask others for emotional help. I discovered that expressing my fears, resentments, confusion, and faint hopes to those who understood was enormously beneficial, especially when combined with changed actions.

But, I am still unable to request favors of a physical nature. Something as ordinary as asking for a ride feels impossible. When I was able-bodied, I'd ask for that kind of help readily, but only because I would and could easily reciprocate. Once I was too ill and disabled to return favors, I stopped asking.

I was afraid of being seen as a loser, freeloader, or someone who makes a mess and expects others to clean it up. This is something I'm working on in my recovery. There is a lack of humility, a fear of rejection, and a deep belief that a man acts independently and decides his fate.

The honesty I find in the program has been as important as any specific guidance I've ever been offered. As for asking for help, I am trusting the process. In CPA, the hardest things for me, requiring the most genuine of changes, only shifted when I saw no other choice but to grow through them. Humility gets me to move out of the way, giving my Higher Power the space needed to enter. My experience is that this works.

In this moment, I will remember it is okay to ask for help, even if I cannot reciprocate.

March 8

When I was first introduced to the Twelve Steps, my perception of a Higher Power was attached to a specific theology. But, there came a time when that concept of my Higher Power within that spiritual practice stopped serving me. It became a hindrance to who I was becoming.

As I worked the Steps in CPA and practiced them in my daily life, it became clear that I needed to go back to Step Two and find a new understanding of a Higher Power.

There was some relief in this decision, but it was a spiritual bottom of sorts. When I left that spiritual community, I disappointed my family; I lost friendships. It was especially difficult to do what was needed for my growth and recovery when it meant disappointing others.

My authentic self emerged as a result of working the Steps in CPA. I cannot be authentic if I'm pretending to believe in something. Step Two helped me to see that I owe it to myself to recognize that I have a Higher Power that loves and supports me in every way. It is key to my recovery.

In this moment, I will give myself the permission, space, and time I need to come to believe in my own Higher Power.

March 9

Acceptance is a daily practice for me. Living with chronic illness has meant learning how to wake up each day without knowing what the day will bring. I simply cannot predict how my illness will take shape today. How would I ever find a place of acceptance if I never knew what I would have to accept on any given day?

I was battling my illness, and I was terrified of surrender. It wasn't until I found CPA that I was able to do the deep work I needed to excavate the emotional resistance I was experiencing about accepting my illness.

The first and most powerful result I received from my Step work in CPA was allowing myself to accept my illness—*Just for Today*. When I first heard that was an option, it was like a weight lifted. I was convinced that if I accepted my illness, I was giving up. But when I started cutting things into smaller pieces, acceptance became easier, and it finally clicked. In fact, I usually chop up my day into morning, afternoon, and evening. So, really, I'm only accepting my physical condition for a few hours at a time. It's amazing how much I can handle in bite-sized chunks.

I needed CPA to help me see that accepting this day, just as it is, *One Day at a Time,* was a helpful way to find inner harmony and a sense of peace.

In this moment, I will only face the next manageable period of time. I don't need to overwhelm myself by taking on too much of my day at once.

March 10

The stark, difficult realities of my symptoms are very real: when I hurt, I hurt. When I've not slept for a very long time, it seems I don't have access to the basic brain functions that lead to well-being. I do not deny my illness.

That said, much of my freedom from the emotionally and spiritually debilitating effects of chronic illness and pain comes from becoming aware of the ways that I respond to my symptoms. With growing awareness and continued participation in this program, I see that what I am thinking about my condition(s) causes a great deal of my distress.

I work to become aware of what I am thinking when I'm feeling rotten about life. I ask Higher Power for the grace to accept my life just as it is right now and then for the courage to change what may need to change. More and more, I come to see that what needs to change is my attitude toward my life and my acceptance of it as it is.

I reflect on what thoughts would reveal a healthier and more accurate view of things. I find my stressed thought patterns are often quite distorted. I'm becoming aware that when I choose to continue with help from my Higher Power and practice adjusting my attitude, stress, and disease are often removed.

I am learning that this one seemingly small application of *Awareness, Acceptance, Action* can have a large reward. For me, it's been one of the great gifts of CPA.

In this moment, I will pause and notice my thoughts. If they're mired in negativity, I will take action on behalf of my well-being by asking my Higher Power to help adjust my attitude.

March 11

When I first came to CPA, I wasn't able to set healthy boundaries. I continued to say, "Yes," when "No" was more accurate. Even today, I appreciate those in the fellowship who help me see when I am overextending.

Boundaries can be an act of kindness. They're my way of ensuring I don't spew my feelings all over another person. In the past, this has happened because I couldn't say "No" in time. Boundaries are also a service, tool, and form of love. To me, setting a boundary isn't about strength; it's about loving another person enough to say "No" when needed.

My experience is that life doesn't always allow time for boundaries, but in most cases, I can find room to provide a little relief by saying "No." Even though "No" is a complete sentence, I've found saying something like, "I don't think I can help with or do that today, I'm sorry," is easier for me.

CPA has helped me tremendously in trusting that things will work out and all will get done in time; my Higher Power will never abandon me but always guide me to the next right step. When my connection to my HP is static on my end, I can reach out to the fellowship with an open mind. For me to do this, though, having faith has been key. It relies upon having faith that the other person will understand even if it takes time, faith that what needs to get done will get done, and faith that I can handle any repercussions with my HP leading the way.

Seeing boundaries as an act of love has helped me tremendously. I both implode and explode less, experience more peace and serenity, and can feel the program working in my life.

In this moment, I will trust my HP to guide me about when to go, do, stop, or rest.

March 12

When I first came to CPA, I was in a state of total panic and fear. I felt desperate, unable to think clearly, and trapped, like a wild animal, in my body. I was obsessed with my symptoms and constantly distracted by pain. All I could think of were worst-case scenarios. It took intense effort to listen to shares and really tune in, but as I did, my mind and nervous system started calming down, and my breathing began to regulate.

Little by little, seeds of wisdom from CPA members penetrated my soul as I began applying them to my life. Doing simple things, like reading the CPA "One Day At A Time," helped me stay in the moment, let go of possible future outcomes, and realize God is with me right now. Our Serenity Prayer is another favorite. Many times, I resisted the pain, fought with the pain, and sought doctor after doctor to fix it, but the Serenity Prayer says to "accept the things I cannot change." As I've practiced surrendering control, I find that my pain can actually lessen while my spiritual and emotional states are more manageable.

CPA gives me permission to be gentle with myself and others. When I remember this, I have peace in my body and the world. My attitude is improving. I accept that people don't have to understand my condition or fix it in any way. Many cannot understand unless they have experienced it themselves. I'm grateful for fellow CPA members who not only understand the despair of living with chronic pain but who, I believe, through their constant offerings of genuine love and compassion, actually have the power to heal.

In this moment, I will be gentle with myself and others and use the Serenity Prayer to guide me to the next indicated action.

March 13

As a CPA member, I've discovered that when a new symptom or diagnosis comes, I need to work my program. Even as I explore options, I can practice turning outcomes over to a Higher Power.

Recently, I developed a new condition and found myself weighing how best to work my program. I didn't want to obsess, yet I did want to find answers, identify appropriate healthcare professionals to see, and assess treatments that might be offered. In my opinion, a new diagnosis needs prompt attention and a focus on possibilities for getting well. Could I do all the necessary research and still work my program? Would I be able to avoid making myself miserable trying to control everything and becoming overwhelmed with fear? I met with my sponsor to think through a plan.

It was time to turn myself and the process over to my Higher Power, pray for the best outcome, and not tell my HP what that would to look like. I prayed for my HP's guidance as I did my internet searches, went to doctor appointments, and weighed all the options. I went to meetings and reasoned the situation out with a trusted friend. Was this new diagnosis interfering with my family life? Was I complaining a lot about the symptoms? What feelings did I need to address: fear, grief, or anger? I worked my Steps again to get a new perspective.

Recovery is a journey, not a destination. A new diagnosis highlights the journey once again. Even though I work my recovery program daily, It is helpful for me to start from Step One when given a new diagnosis.

In this moment, I will work the Steps, no matter where I need to start. I will be compassionate with myself anytime I need to go back to Step One.

March 14

I often wonder, "Why do I persist? What drives me?" As a kid, if someone said something couldn't be done, a part of me always wanted to be the first to try it. It was almost like I had no choice in the matter; that part of me just took over.

Perseverance has served me well in my journey through chronic pain and chronic illness, but when I don't put my Higher Power at the forefront of every decision, this very skill can become a liability. CPA has taught me to slow down and not waste precious energy. To the best of my abilities, I try to turn over any situation that is causing me problems and conserve my energy for better use.

Through working the CPA program, listening, praying, and reaching out to others, I can look back and see when perseverance served me and when it's worked against me. I am listening now for guidance on when and how to use my skills to help myself and others. I am so grateful God has given me this asset because there have been so many times I wanted to simply give up. Today, I believe perseverance comes from my Higher Power taking the lead.

I believe my Higher Power has given me exactly what is needed to deal with my chronic pain and chronic illness. I try to remember to breathe and enjoy the process instead of just fighting my way through everything. In CPA, I am learning a new way to work with perseverance.

In this moment, I will turn to my Higher Power and ask for assistance if I'm struggling to slow down.

March 15

For me, faith and humility are necessary to even begin to turn over the problems of my life to a formless greater power that cannot be seen or touched. That takes a lot of faith. Trying not to control, direct, or influence outcomes takes humility.

Each member of CPA is free to find their meaning of a Higher Power. Our literature is made from the collective consciousness of our recovering, practicing group members; we are all human. Together, we do what none of us could ever do alone. For me, that is but one example of a Higher Power.

It's easy for me to hear that faith and humility are required to turn my problems over and to work the Steps in my daily life. I accept that I use these spiritual principles to work these Steps to keep me from living a life with no soul. I lived that life for far too long due to the negative emotional and spiritual effects of chronic pain and chronic illness. Working the Steps in CPA has been a gentle and deeply meaningful process. When my body was sick and in pain, my soul was empty, I felt emotionally bankrupt, and I was desperate for meaning. Having faith and humility helped me to take the First Step. Then, I found more faith, humility, willingness, and meaning in the Steps, literature, and fellowship of CPA.

In this moment, I will find meaning by actively using the CPA Steps and tools.

March 16

As I continue to go to CPA meetings, talk with CPA members one-on-one, and have heart-to-hearts with my sponsor as we read and discuss literature, I have come to embrace the fact that control is an illusion. When I make plans to try and engineer a certain outcome, I could be missing out. The Greater Power, who I am coming to understand, may have outcomes for me that are out of this world!

Somewhere along the way, I realized that God has always believed in me and loved me just as I am, even when I may not have had faith in God.

Knowing this, I now have not only willingness and ability but also enthusiasm for turning over my problems and everything else in my life to a Greater Power of my understanding without trying to control, direct, or influence the outcome. This is how I practice Step Three in my life.

In this moment, I will practice Step Three and turn my concerns over to the care of my Higher Power.

March 17

I very much appreciate the kindness and compassion I have found in CPA meetings. I had no idea that was what had been missing from my life since I became chronically ill. I have truly found my tribe here.

In the early years of my illness, I was bedridden, and housebound, and I never thought I would smile again. I had lost so much to despair. I now have online CPA friends who are inspirational, caring, and often so much fun!

After a conversation with a friend, I regretted a miscommunication. She told me that I never need to apologize to her for what I share when it is honest. She asked me to always just be who I am, without censorship; she comprehends the spirit of what I say to her. I never want to disrespect anyone, so I try to be careful, but I've always valued emotional honesty. I give others wiggle room with what they share with me, even if it is not cordial, correct, or careful. Within my CPA community, I can give myself this room as well—to totally be who I am. I know they will give me the benefit of the doubt if something comes out wrong or not exactly the way I wanted—it's quite amazing. I could not be more grateful for the fellowship of CPA.

In this moment, I will be authentic in my relationships and give others the grace to truly be themselves.

March 18

In Step Seven, I see my powerlessness and ongoing need for help.

In my original Twelve Step program's earliest literature, Step Seven was simply a prayer. I still find that I need to give a human, vocal utterance to my request.

My personal, most oft-spoken Seventh Step prayer goes like this:

"God, take this fear I carry—which seems to be at the root of most of my character defects—and remove it. Give me the strength to bring something good out of the many ills of my self-will. Help me see that You—God, Eternal Presence, Abiding Love, Ultimate Mystery—are the Source of the grace needed to drop all that stands in the way of my becoming as loving as possible. Remind me that in remaining under Your guidance, I may rest."

In this moment, I will use prayer to humbly ask to become as loving as I can be to myself and others.

March 19

I still have lots of difficulty surrendering when I feel I need something in the moment. I know this is something that I need to work on.

I find the acronym *STOP (Surrender, Time-out, Observe, Prioritize)* incredibly helpful. I've been learning in CPA that when I find my mind or body in a state of urgency, I must quit what I am doing and take a moment to myself. Nothing useful, helpful, or productive will come from trying to force a solution.

I'm also working on being more of an observer. Trying to separate all the emotion from an event or decision and prioritizing what is most important can often help me see the next indicated action. But not until I am ready—after the "*Time-out.*"

Another thing I've learned is that almost everything can wait twenty-four hours, especially decisions or things I'm not sure I should say. I try to take a day and sleep on all decisions and responses of magnitude.

Recently, I had a challenging day and did not wait even a few hours before sending a questionable text. The results weren't terrible. I think the relationship will survive, but it's a reminder that taking my time to *STOP* has its benefits.

In this moment, I will remember that I can pause and reach for CPA tools before taking action.

March 20

When I started my CPA journey, I had already been in another Twelve Step program. I thought I had Step One down. I had been in chronic pain for almost ten years, had a diagnosis that I understood, and I told myself, "Well, obviously, I can accept my powerlessness and the unmanageable parts of my life. I've been dealing with this for too long to believe I have power over it."

I recently had to change doctors. At our first visit, my new doctor said she didn't believe my diagnosis was correct and we would need to start diagnostic testing over. Then, I saw the true extent of my obsession. Day and night, all I could think about were my symptoms and how I could speed up this process. I began to believe that if I only thought hard enough about my pain or read enough about the human body, I could figure this thing out on my own.

After a few weeks of this, I became trapped in my brain, and it hit me: I am powerless over this entire process. I cannot force the right diagnosis or treatment to appear. All I can do is continue to the best of my abilities and give the results up to my Higher Power.

Some days, it's easier than others, but when I truly admit my powerlessness when things become unmanageable and turn my will over to my Higher Power, I start to see how much more there is to life than my body and symptoms.

In this moment, I will apply the first three Steps to anything disrupting my serenity.

March 21

It took me years to understand that resting when I feel poorly does not mean I'm idle or irresponsible.

Permitting myself to rest, without guilt or shame, was one of the amends I made to myself when I worked Step Nine. It was such a novel concept. How dare I go to bed in the middle of the day and watch TV! Even though I was ill and could barely function, I thought I had to push and make myself do too much to prove I was not a slacker.

I began to think of my mid-day rests as taking a sick child to bed. As a parent, I would never send my child to school or out to play when she was ill. Why would I do anything different for myself? In CPA, I've learned how to be a kind, loving parent toward myself, too.

I learned when I rested, I actually got more accomplished. When I got up afterwards and worked on a task, my thoughts were clearer, I had more energy, and my body and mind were better rested.

What helped me was to see resting as putting gas in the body's tank. For way too long, I made it operate on fumes, which only made it all worse. I made errors and tasks took longer. I wore myself down and aggravated my symptoms. I was not respecting my own body. I was forcing solutions instead of *Letting Go and Letting God*.

Having faith helped. I trusted that all would get done in Higher Power's time, not mine. The other day, when my body was screaming at me, instead of emptying the dishwasher or finishing the laundry, I went to bed and watched a movie. It was a lovely, compassionate gift to myself, that I need never feel guilty to receive.

In this moment, I will rest when I need to.

March 22

Acceptance has been vital in my recovery and living a really good life despite having chronic illness and chronic pain. This does not mean I give up and that things will never be different. Acceptance, for me, is recognizing reality as it is and still being able to experience peace.

I recognize that my life has changed, and I can do less than I used to, but that is okay. I continue to do what I can to improve my condition. Acceptance helps ease my frustration, despair, and resistance toward calmness, optimism, and hope. Acceptance has given me the courage to make changes that improve my life, and opportunities have come that would not have if it were not for pain, illness, and acceptance.

When I truly accepted the place of chronic pain and chronic illness in my life, I grieved. I went through depression, fear, and anxiety, but eventually, I came through them. These challenging feelings come back, but the longer I practice living in acceptance, the less they affect me. Acceptance brings me peace and the opportunity to continue to live a fulfilling life instead of living a life of bitterness and despair.

In this moment, I will grieve when needed and accept myself exactly as I am.

March 23

When I first started working a Twelve Step program, I had no belief in a Higher Power. If there was one, I thought He or She had abandoned me. My life had fallen apart. My partner had left me. I was too sick to work or take care of my children. I had no money. I was scared, sad, and hopeless. I wasn't sure if it was worth it to keep on living. I had hit bottom. How could I be restored to sanity?

My sponsor guided me through Step Two. He kindly listened as I wrestled with old beliefs of a punishing God. He described his perception of a caring, loving Higher Power and said, "This is a personal and direct relationship."

He asked me to begin by staying open to the possibility that I could be restored to sanity. He asked whether I would be willing to explore the idea of a Power besides my own will and determination. My sponsor had a strong relationship with his Higher Power and said I could borrow his belief. I approached Step Two in baby steps. I needed to trust that someone else believed in a Higher Power and that it could happen for me.

Over time, I came to believe, through my own experiences, that Step Two works. In retrospect, I can see there was a Higher Power working in my life all along, but I didn't recognize it. I was so sure that I was too broken to be restored to sanity and that no Power existed that could help me. I'm so grateful I was wrong.

In this moment, I will allow for the possibility of a Higher Power, and I know I can borrow a friend's belief in such a power if I am struggling.

March 24

Some days, and especially in the mornings, my symptoms can be so intense that it's difficult for me to concentrate, let alone accomplish much. I often feel distressed during these times.

Recently, one morning, I was weak and tired. Life felt dark, and the work that needed to be done seemed endless. I did not have the strength to do any of it. I did not feel I even had the strength to trust God.

I decided to offer God what I had: my nothingness and inability to do. Then, I just needed to trust that God, in His mercy, would meet me right where I was. This brought me peace. I was able to let go of feeling guilty for not getting much accomplished. I accepted that I don't need to try to be something more than I was able to be in the moment. This brought not only relief but sanity and the truth that I am loved by my Higher Power, exactly as I am.

In this moment, I will not expect too much of myself and will turn to my Higher Power to meet me exactly where I am.

March 25

I woke up under a heavy blanket of dark thoughts today. I am trying to learn how to surrender in these moments. This feels counterintuitive on all levels—spiritually, emotionally, mentally, and, yes, even physically.

When I remember not to fight and to take time to stop, pause, and connect with my Higher Power, I can actually feel a hint of meaning and purpose in the uncertainty and fear of being chronically ill. In the quiet space of my heart, underneath the turbulent thoughts, I've always known there was a powerful opportunity here for spiritual growth. I knew this reality but didn't want it to be true, so I spent all day, every day, scrambling desperately to find a solution.

But today, I feel slightly different. I am more in touch with my emotions and slowly accepting my reality. Observing my fear allows me to be more open and receive moments as they come instead of reaching so hard for some kind of hope that my life will be different. I don't want to run away from this reality anymore. It's too painful to live like that. I want to learn how, in the heat of these moments, to pray and find peace, ease, and total acceptance.

In this moment, I will surrender so that I can actually see, feel, and know the beauty that is always within me.

March 26

A lot of my amends have turned out to be best made as living amends. There are a few that I have kept on paper as amends that I will make if my Higher Power brings me into contact with that person again. Reaching out to some of the people I owe amends to, after not seeing them for at least a decade, could cause more harm than good. However, I can make living amends by changing my behavior, and staying willing to make those amends, should the time come.

My rule of thumb with amends is to put myself in the other person's shoes for a moment and imagine someone had done this to me. Would I want to hear their amends, or would I want them to leave me alone? Sometimes this can help me clarify whether I'm making amends because it's right or because I'm trying to clear my conscience, regardless of how it affects others. As long as I turn it over and stay willing, my Higher Power has always shown me what to do next.

In this moment, I will focus on improving my behavior to work on my living amends until a situation arises to foster other Step Nine amends.

March 27

I practice Step Ten by taking a small daily inventory most nights, along with my gratitude journal. If I am able, I write down the things that disturb me as they pop up, and then at night, it's a little easier to recall the events of the day. For example, if someone did or didn't do something that I had an expected, I write it down and then look at it in the evening.

Since working the Fourth and Fifth Step, I have become aware that one of my greatest defects of character is being too hard on myself. That's why it's essential for me to focus on what I have done well each day.

My inventory is very simple, out of necessity. Brain fog and pain issues tend to cloud my thinking more in the evening. I write at least three things I did well, sometimes more. I also write anything I feel I could have done better. For me, it is as important to practice my daily inventory as it is to practice the Eleventh Step.

In this moment, I will practice Step Ten and think of at least three things I did well.

March 28

It's hard to remember to allow God into all areas of my life, big and small; I require spiritual practices like Step Eleven.

Mine currently includes praying every morning that I be given "knowledge of God's will and the power to carry it out" in all areas of my life. I read selections from spiritual writings that seem right for the concerns of the coming day. Daily meditations have become essential to increasing my ability to detach from distorted thoughts that add stress to my already stressed body.

All day, I ask God to direct my thinking, specifically to help me stop worrying about what I can't control. Often, I'm directed to take very small actions, letting the larger problems be managed or resolved *One Day at a Time* or accepted slowly. I ask for courage or strength to do difficult things, such as making a phone call I've been dreading. I pray for discernment in perplexing issues and then listen for direction. If I feel guided to act yet unsure, I ask myself, "Is this direction increasing peace and clarity?"

I've also begun practicing gratitude. Throughout the day, I am on the lookout for items for my gratitude list. Late afternoon, I jot down all those I can recall. Not only does this lift my mood when I'm most fatigued, but it gives my mind something positive to focus on. Once I have my list, I review it, looking for a special blessing embedded there, one thing that nourished me spiritually. This allows me to enter my evening feeling blessed.

In this moment, I will ask my Higher Power for the courage, discernment, acceptance, gratitude, and emotional strength needed to nourish me spiritually.

March 29

Letting go and admitting powerlessness were foreign concepts to me. I was so miserable when I arrived at CPA that I was willing to try anything, even though being powerless seemed ridiculous to me. How could letting go be the path to serenity and happiness? It was hard to believe. It was the complete opposite of how I lived my life; I was a great manager. However, my sponsor suggested I try it out. She said I could always go back to my old way of living.

Well, I never did go back. As I worked Step One I felt relief, for the first time in years. I had hope; I was no longer lost and alone. It is a Step I return to daily, guiding how I live in all areas of my life.

Admitting my powerlessness seemed like the worst way to live, but so far, no longer living in the delusion that I have control over people, places, and my illness has been the best way to live.

In this moment, I will admit I am powerless and become willing to be teachable.

March 30

When I began working the Steps in CPA, I realized in Step Two that my concept of a Power greater than myself needed to grow. The Twelve Steps gave me the freedom to explore my relationship with this Higher Power. It's a freedom I treasure.

Sometimes, my Higher Power is the program itself, and sometimes it's the fellowship.

The Traditions help me feel safe in CPA. We have a primary purpose. We have unity within our fellowship. There is no expert or guru making sure that I'm doing things perfectly. I'm safe here. I believe in the power of these Steps, but first, I needed to become willing to believe that following these Steps might work for me. That is all that was required of me to work this program.

Today, I would say that my Higher Power is the power of the unity that binds us together. I'm seeking a spiritual solution to emotional and physical problems and am willing to do the work. If I show up to meetings or work with my sponsor on a specific Step, I'm doing the work. Living with chronic illness and pain is not an easy way of life, but it becomes manageable with the help of CPA and my concept of a Higher Power. CPA members inspire me to keep growing. They help me stay willing to believe there is a spiritual solution.

I worked Step Two with hope, an open mind, and an open heart. As a result, I came to know my Higher Power, myself, and others in ways that changed my life forever.

In this moment, I will recognize how a Power greater than myself, through the Traditions, provides a safe space for me inside the fellowship of CPA.

March 31

I struggled with how to practice Step Three in CPA. In my first Twelve Step program, I collected coping mechanisms. I attended tons of meetings, dissociated using the internet or TV, set aside feelings to do service, made endless lists, and basically just moved until I wore myself out.

These activities kept me from self-destructing. I'm grateful I found them! But, when my health issues arose, it became clear they were not sustainable. I couldn't physically show up in the way that I had. Bombarding my discomfort with solutions that weren't working left me exhausted, symptomatic, and depressed. Feeling betrayed by circumstance, I became sicker, lonelier, and more ashamed. Plus, I didn't know how to ask for help. I thought I could wield powerlessness in a way that would leave me invulnerable to pain and uncertainty.

Today, after a brief time in CPA, my Third Step toolbox includes economy of motion and energy, meditation, writing, gratitude lists to Higher Power, angry letters to Higher Power, and connecting with program friends I've never met in person. When it's time to turn over a medical issue, I reach out to my doctors instead of the internet. And when these efforts don't fix me right away, I put my hand on my heart and let myself cry. I trust that feelings pass.

Today, there's more space for me to examine how my fear motivates me. I now turn toward this fear with compassion, visualizing the fear behind the impulse to act as the voice of a worried family member who truly loves me. I am so grateful I found CPA.

In this moment, I will look in my Step Three toolbox for methods to help me practice letting go.

April

April 1

Through working the Steps, especially Step Four, I discovered I often felt obliged to be obedient—afraid to rock the boat and stand up for myself—when working with my healthcare providers. At times, the medical settings were intimidating. I didn't want to upset the people I relied on for care by coming across as difficult.

With support from my sponsor, I began to make amends to myself by practicing self-care. The ways I took care of myself when it came to changes in my treatment plan included going slowly, asking questions, doing my own research, and speaking to other patients. I realized I could even say "No" to my medical providers if necessary.

As a result of working my program, I believe I make better choices regarding my health care most of the time. And, yet, just last week, I had a bad reaction to a new medication; I had to surrender and cancel my plans. Unlike in the past, I didn't freak out or get angry.

This experience was a reminder that the unexpected is a part of this journey; it's guaranteed as a part of living with chronic health conditions. I can do the footwork but am always powerless over the outcome.

In this moment, I will make a choice that honors my integrity and self-care.

April 2

Before CPA, my pain frequently came between me and my loved ones. Disguised as self-justified anger or depression, pain hijacked my emotions. The loving part of my soul was clouded by fear and frustration. I was too angry and ashamed to ask for help. I turned away when helping hands were extended.

Early in my recovery, I was taught that the Twelve Steps could help me to change my relationship with God, with myself, and with others. This was a process; I did not believe in God then, and I did not trust anyone. I had fully relied on my abilities. I believed I was the only person qualified to run the show. This changed when I found my sponsor and started making my way through the Steps. I slowly became willing to share my insecurities; her impartiality and acceptance led to trust. My sponsor was the person who put my hand into the hand of a Higher Power.

My relationships are more loving, trusting, and fulfilling now that I'm working the CPA program. Meetings are an opportunity to share with others who understand and empathize. I've learned I can be honest about my condition and ask for help without shame. My spouse is extraordinarily grateful for the newfound serenity and acceptance he sees in me now that I am living with chronic pain rather than suffering from chronic pain. I can see innumerable good people in the world want to help, and it benefits them as much as it helps me. When I don't ask for or accept help from someone else, it deprives both of us of the chance to spiritually connect.

In this moment, I will remember that admitting when I could use some help is a beautiful way to exemplify the saying, "I can't, God can."

April 3

I still hadn't stopped whirling when I did my first CPA Fourth Step. I was still trying to do everything, be everything, and control everything. That might sound like I needed more time with the first three Steps, but those Steps just ask us to believe and make a decision. So, I attacked my Fourth Step with the same vigor as I was attacking life. I came out the other side a bit different.

As I worked on Step Four, I discovered things, not only about my behaviors and my faith but about others' behaviors, too. When it came to others, I mostly learned how to have compassion and assume they're acting with good intentions. I realized they were trying to help me: a person going through something they'd never experienced and didn't understand. Or maybe they had a somewhat similar experience and would offer unsolicited solutions or advice (usually things I'd already tried that didn't work for me). But in all cases, I realized they were loving me in the best way they knew how.

It took another Fourth Step to find some compassion for myself. Today, I am working this Step around why I feel shame when people treat me graciously. I want to be free of that shame. I want to feel that I am deserving.

For me, practicing the Fourth Step begins the road to freedom. I do this frequently and have so many amazing realizations about myself and how I view the world. This Step is a way to free myself of the weights pulling me down. What a great gift.

In this moment, I will remind myself that if I have difficult feelings about a person or situation, working Step Four can provide clarity, compassion, and freedom.

April 4

There are bad days when I can't function at all. And days when I am happily walking along, and I suddenly run into a brick wall that was not there a second ago. I know these days will come, so I have movies saved to watch. When I feel wiped out and weak, I need movies that are light—that have no violence or tension. I treat myself with compassion and gentleness on those days. I cancel my tasks and crawl into bed. I do this with the gratitude that I have all I need to rest and be kind to myself.

This attitude was not possible before CPA. There was a time when I got angry and frustrated, when I lashed out at family, when life seemed terribly unfair and cruel. I would fight reality, and that only made me more miserable. I have discovered over time that bad days do not last forever. They do pass. And there is nothing I can do to make them pass faster. With the acceptance of reality comes serenity.

I'm no longer scared or angry on days when my ability to participate in the world is curtailed. This is the rhythm of my life. I can attune to reality and have harmony, or I can fight it and have dissonance and suffering. It is my choice.

Through working the Twelve Steps, the love and comfort of my CPA friends, and trust in the love of my Higher Power, I've found a new way to be in the world, which brings me joy and makes my life meaningful.

In this moment, I will remember that bad days do not mean this is a bad life. I have CPA, so I have choices.

April 5

In Chronic Pain Anonymous, we employ the principle of anonymity, putting humility and compassion into practice.

If, in a meeting, I say I used to be a rocket scientist and giving that up made my life particularly difficult, I am expressing myself. I am asking to be heard, hoping to be understood, and perhaps being of service to those who could profit from identifying with me. But, am I sharing or comparing? Have I—innocently, with no malice whatsoever—suggested something that is possibly off-putting, even hurtful?

Is it equitable to imply I feel an especially keen sense of loss at the inability to engage in my previous vocation because, in my case, it was so special? Did I consider that others' losses are as significant as mine? Am I unconsciously trying to bolster my self-esteem by making sure everyone knows my former five-star status, real or perceived? Is this helpful for others or for me?

I could say, "I used to get a lot of meaning out of life by setting challenging goals and achieving them," or, "I am still grieving my career loss." I may want to talk about it more specifically outside of a meeting. Perhaps I could speak with someone who identifies with my situation, who has found help in the Steps, and who has been able to adjust and let go of what used to be in their own lives.

In CPA, I focus on the similarities I have with anyone who has chronic health conditions. In these similarities, I find compassion and healing. We are people of all backgrounds and stages of life and illness. I want to avoid setting myself apart or above when I speak in meetings and instead focus on the spiritual solution we find in the Twelve Steps. When I put anonymity into practice, the fellowship is about us, not me.

In this moment, I will remember everyone's experience is valid.

April 6

Many of us in CPA with sleep problems learn, and though we may know a lot about good sleep hygiene, it often just isn't enough. My sponsor taught me that sleep is just another thing in life to accept I do not control. For example, there are days and weeks when I wake up at night and know I am not going to be able to fall back to sleep, so I've stopped trying to force myself to do so. I quickly get out of bed and do something productive, like write in my journal.

I cannot control when I will be able to sleep through the night, but I can control how I respond. It's often the case that when I'm up in the middle of the night, I have a lot on my mind, so I journal to help process it all. This is a beneficial use of my time, and I feel better spending it this way.

Part of accepting my sleep situation is knowing I probably won't be my best self the next day. For this reason, I almost never schedule early morning appointments. When people ask, "What time can you be available in the morning?" I often respond that it depends on my sleep, and I can't really know. Not having morning commitments helps me relax and not worry about what will happen if I cannot sleep. I strive for acceptance that this is exactly the way it is meant to be, and I cannot change it.

One day, I may have greater insight or more tools to help with my sleep. *Just for Today*, this is my best solution, and I find it increases my serenity and deepens self-compassion.

In this moment, I will listen to and respect my limits.

April 7

After spending years trying every treatment under the sun to manage my pain, with none of them working, I was left hopeless, with no will left to live. I surrounded myself with others who, like me at the time, were angry, disappointed, and dissatisfied with life. It was the only place I felt minimally understood. We spent our days complaining, commiserating, and basically embodying the cliché misery loves company. I engaged in self-destructive behaviors, doing anything I could to lessen my pain and avoid dealing with the reality of my life. With every choice I made, my life became more unmanageable.

After spending years living in misery, I was sick and tired of just surviving. I wanted to live. I was so lonely and thought no one would ever understand my physical or emotional pain. But I was wrong. I am truly grateful to CPA to have a fellowship of people experiencing similar issues! I feel connected and very lucky to learn from others' experiences.

The people I surround myself with have a significant influence on my mental and physical well-being. We learn from connecting to others. When I see acceptance around me, it helps me to accept my situation. When I see others focusing on gratitude for what they have and what they can do—the yeses and not the nos—it helps me do the same. I've even regained hope for my future.

In this moment, I will choose to not just survive, but to live.

April 8

The slogan *Just for Today* is a workhorse in my program. Often, I apply it this way: just for the next hour or just for the next minute. I remind myself that the pain I'm in is not forever. So many of my health issues have changed over the years, with some going away, some lessening in severity, and some getting worse. Nothing stays the same. All I need to deal with is this moment; that is what I can do.

This slogan applies when I'm happy as well as when I'm miserable. I want the happy moments to stay, but they don't—at least not any more than the unhappy ones. Using this slogan's perspective, I can be resilient and get through any experience that feels overwhelming, impossible, or unbearable. And I can enjoy the good times with no expectations that they'll last.

More often than not, I realize I'm okay in this moment. It may be hard; I may not want it in my life, but I am okay. I ask, "What might I use for support?" That's when other tools in my program show up, such as praying to my Higher Power, saying the Serenity Prayer, or calling a program friend.

This is not always as easy as it sounds. There are times I want to fight against this moment—it should not look like this, it's not fair, I want it gone, I'm angry that I have to feel this awful or have this treatment. In these moments, I can return to the slogan *Just for Today*, remembering that as dreadful as it is, it will end. This gives me hope when I am suffering. The situation will change. It has happened many times, and it will happen again.

In this moment, I will focus on what I can control.

April 9

Chronic pain, illness, and the accompanying medications often affect my ability to engage in sexual activities. But I now know that we can adapt. It doesn't need to be an all-or-nothing thing. By listening to others in CPA share their trials and tribulations around this topic, I have learned to acknowledge my basic human nature.

But am I not also free to choose to let sex go entirely if that is my wish? Might it not be valid to work a program of acceptance rather than change? And I have let it go entirely at times of great duress or simple loneliness and then asked, "Isn't there a way to experience my basic need for touch?"

Some of us who have no partner may have gone years without loving touch. I recall when I was single, I'd save money and indulge in a good, deep-tissue massage when I could. I'd garner hugs wherever I could find them. I got a dog and pampered it with physical affection, including nap-time spooning! I bought a weighted blanket and a body pillow. Those didn't do much for me, but experimenting is part of the path to finding what does work.

I found that even amid my chronic pain, I can find activities that are physically pleasurable, if only for that moment. By practicing willingness and open-mindedness, I learned that I can still find joy.

In this moment, I will allow for physical affection.

April 10

I have discovered different degrees of rest.

Rest can be doing any activity, even active endeavors, that leads to overall restfulness in time. Whether it is an artistic endeavor, playing gently with my dog, or washing the dishes slowly and methodically, it can be restful. Sitting at the window and noting which birds come through my yard works sometimes, as do the times I can take a slow walk.

Rest can mean taking a breath and tuning in to the moment, saying a little prayer, or releasing the desire to be in charge of everything. A quick, heartfelt Step One, Two, or Three is a source of enormous rest.

Rest can mean going slower and doing half of what I'd planned, a fourth, a tenth, or nothing at all.

Rest can mean choosing to just listen and let others talk at a meeting.

Rest can mean doing my morning and afternoon meditation. Rest can mean lying down and listening to music or an audiobook.

What I term "Emergency Medical Treatment Rest," or EMT Rest, means total rest. I brush my teeth, drink some water, eat a little something, and then go to bed—no phone, email, text, or mail, no chores. I do as close to nothing as possible, not even thinking. I may listen to music or something I am not really paying attention to. I may, hopefully, nap. EMT Rest means the world turns without me this day.

CPA has helped me understand that resting is doing something. It's listening to my body, slowing down, and rebuilding strength. Despite my dislike of it at times, and because I need so much of it, I accept it. I rest in knowing it is the next indicated action.

In this moment, I will honor my need for rest.

April 11

Someone who lives with chronic pain and illness once told me, "It's hard to be on the physical plane and the spiritual plane at the same time." At the time, I was still trying to make it to in-person meetings, but when I would go, I would be in so much pain that I couldn't hear any of the messages. It's hard to let my spirit go to a spiritual plane when physical pain firmly tethers me to my body.

It took some time, but I finally gave myself permission to attend virtual and phone meetings. I could stay home and lie down in my most comfortable position during the meeting, making it more likely that my spirit would absorb the readings and the shares.

Sometimes, when I meditate, I have moments when I become completely unaware of my pain. I go back and forth, back and forth, switching from the physical plane, where I feel all my body's discomfort, to the spiritual plane, where I am unaware of my pain. I also experience these moments of relief, oscillating between the physical and spiritual planes, when I serve others.

My friend's admission is a reminder to be kind and not beat myself up if I don't spend the entire day feeling spiritual because my body is almost constantly pulling me back to the physical plane. Furthermore, I can celebrate the moments when I'm able to be on both planes at the same time.

In this moment, I will support my spiritual journey by honoring my physical needs.

April 12

How do I keep moving forward through times when pain, exhaustion, and overwhelming emotions are so relentless? Five minutes with this pain can seem like too much. Five minutes in a doctor's waiting room can be excruciating. But trusting my Higher Power's sense of timing helps me to be patient and let the process unfold.

The tools I have learned in CPA help me navigate my medical care, while the program helps me learn how to competently apply them. Sometimes, the answer about a surgery or procedure is "not yet." One of my favorite prayers is, "God, bless it or block it. Please let your will for me be clear and show me a red flag or obstacle if I am not meant to continue." I am more accepting of not getting the answer I desire. I used to plow headfirst through life without as much consideration as I devote now.

Today, I have spiritual resources. I remember the outcome could be beyond my wildest dreams. I have overcome seemingly insurmountable challenges with help from my Higher Power and CPA. The inspiring messages I hear in CPA meetings encourage me; if my friends can do it, so can I! And if I have trouble envisioning the possibility of a solution or a miracle, I know I can ask one of them to share their experience, strength, and hope with me.

One of the greatest miracles in my life was finding CPA, and I am truly grateful. Five minutes with CPA is much better than five minutes without it.

In this moment, I will remember I am not alone and have a whole community of resources.

April 13

Sometimes, I'm so far from acceptance that I can't see it at all. It's nowhere on the horizon. Not even a silhouette in the skyline. I don't know; maybe it's somewhere on the other side of the world?

During these times, I lean on the CPA program the hardest. I lean on my sponsor. I lean on the friends I have made, the meetings, and the literature. I know that I will get through the current situation.

I won't always be in acceptance, and I won't always be out of it. I'm just grateful to know what to do, either way: accept what is before me, and if I can't, lean into the program even more. For me, acceptance is cyclical. It waxes and wanes. Each time I'm in acceptance, it seems deeper and truer, and the times I'm out of it have lessened. That's *Progress, Not Perfection* in action.

In this moment, I will acknowledge being on the path of acceptance, wherever I am on this journey.

April 14

Humor is a go-to tool for me, especially after surgery.

At my post-op appointments, I continue to call the chief resident assigned to my case, "The Devil." He gets it. I'm joking. Humor helps, and I enjoy these post-op encounters, even when I am there to deal with serious complications. It is not their fault my body is resisting the treatment. With the Serenity Prayer and a dose of good humor, we are progressing toward finding solutions I had never imagined possible. Though the recovery is taking longer than expected, all I have to do is ask, and unexpected solutions show up. But in the meantime, adding a bit of levity to an otherwise heavy situation helps me to cope.

Humor doesn't just help me to deal with uncomfortable topics. I also use it to improve my mood. After a particular meeting, a group of people regularly stay for fellowship and just tell jokes for twenty minutes or longer. Every time I attend, I leave feeling better emotionally, spiritually, and on lucky days, physically as well.

In this moment, I will allow for humor in my life.

April 15

On a very high-symptom day, I was in fellowship time after a meeting; we were all brain-foggy, trying to remember the definition of recovery in CPA. One member recalled part of it: we have the ability to live joyfully. My reaction, and I even said it out loud, was: "There is no joy in chronic illness!" A difficult day can really cloud my perception.

Joy is a different feeling from happiness. Joy is bone-deep for me; it locks in and has lasting effects. There can be plenty of joy in living with chronic pain and illness. It is all around me if I'm willing to take the time to look for it. And that's the key: taking the time. Often, when I'm bogged down with daily tasks and doctors' appointments, or my symptoms are flaring and my pain is high, it's a challenge to stop that frenetic energy. But when I pause and take the time, I recognize that joy is floating just below the surface, and I can reach down into it if I so choose.

I'm reminded of the joy in my life every day. It lives in the love I have for my fellow CPA pals. It lives in the love I have for my family. It lives in the love I receive when our kitten wants to cuddle. It's in my memories of the way I used to savor my old life. And it's in the fellowship time after a meeting where I can be me, whether I am in my joy or I'm seeking it.

In this moment, I will take time for joy.

April 16

Recently, I realized I did not know what surrender meant or how it worked in my life. I thought of surrender as something that happened in battle: I give up, you win, I lose. I read the dictionary definition of surrender. Still lost, I committed to trying an action I did not fully understand, like when I began to practice praying a couple of decades ago. I didn't believe in prayer then, but I do now! That practice led me to believe in a Power greater than myself. My strategy to learn what surrender meant was to get outside, throw my worries to the sky, and say or shout, "Surrender," two or three times.

I recently did this during a particularly hard trip to the grocery store. A friend drove, and I finished shopping first. Exhausted, I could not find an available chair. I pushed my overweight buggy through the automatic doors. Standing outside, I threw my arms to the sky and shouted, "Surrender!" twice.

I must have looked crazy. I went back inside, as there was still no sign of my friend. Aimed toward the flower department, I found a bench turned backward against the wall. I was able to sit and wait for my friend more comfortably. It worked. I surrendered.

As we walked out, I glanced at the place where I'd stood and shouted, and I thanked my Higher Power for making space available for me to rest. No one knew what I had done but me. Now you do, too. I'm continuing this practice. I open a door and shout, "Surrender!" whenever I can. Through this performative exercise, I'm learning to embody surrender.

In this moment, I will remember that surrender is a practice.

April 17

I received some stunningly good news. It could be said that there was dancing in the streets, yet I responded with trepidation rather than joy. After taking my inventory, I realized my guarded stance against joy, hope, and relief had protected me from crushing disappointment most of my life. This unskillful reaction had particularly protected me regarding my chronic conditions. My need to brace for the next cycle of pain, the next random symptom, or the next diagnosis was my attempt to feel safer and less vulnerable. Ironically, this inability to feel joy at this welcome news made me feel sad and out of sorts, the opposite of safe!

My CPA sponsor suggested I greet all emotions as welcomed guests, with as much self-compassion as I could muster. I heard myself say, "This is a moment of genuine suffering and concern. I'm sure I am not the only person responding this way. What kindness can I offer myself in this moment?" I asked my Higher Power to allow these ambiguous emotional energies to flow through me without resistance because I believe that which I resist persists.

After a few deep breaths, I was able to gently detach from my feelings of difference, isolation, and the belief there was something wrong with me because of this unexpected reaction to good news. I told myself, "You are awesome. I love you, and feelings don't define you." I gently patted my chest, saying, "It's alright, it is all right." Self-acceptance, self-care, self-love, and self-compassion are perhaps the greatest gifts CPA has given me.

In this moment, I will show myself compassion.

April 18

When I came into CPA, I was feeling beaten down by my body and the people in my life who pushed me to do more than I was able—emotionally, physically, and financially. I took on commitments that further limited my time and energy, which might have been used for self-care. I was only adding to the mess.

I first came to a Saturday night meeting, then another a week later. That second week, I felt a tad more courageous. I'd taken on one of the suggested challenges: letting go of at least one of my outside commitments. I kept coming back, each week for a month, reporting each time about that feeling to my group—courage.

I realized I could go to as many meetings as I wanted and keep cultivating that seedling inside of me. I was able to remove an abusive ex-partner from my life after struggling for over a year to do so. I set limits on how much time and energy I would invest in my family and started moving toward a safer and healthier home environment.

Thus, with the help of other CPA members, my sponsor, and Step study group, I was able to surrender. That took courage.

Today, I sit surrounded by boxes I'll slowly unpack in my new apartment, trusting in my Higher Power that I'll have courage to continue to face life's ongoing challenges. I'm learning to stand up for myself and the serenity I need to progress. I no longer make decisions under duress or based on fear. I'm embracing this challenged body with the love and attention it needs.

In this moment, I will remember it takes courage to participate in my recovery.

April 19

Anonymity is the spiritual foundation of our recovery because it puts my personal agenda second to the common good.

In a meeting, saying "I used to be an Olympic swimmer, so giving that up makes my life especially difficult," is like saying, "I have a more difficult time than you." Plus, it encourages and promotes our differences rather than similarities.

When I want to share on this topic, it's useful for me to examine my motives. Am I unconsciously trying to grasp my self-esteem by making sure everyone knows of my former status? Have I considered that others' losses are just as significant? For instance, there are those who fell ill or were injured so young they never had a chance at a career. For all I know, that might hurt more than having lost one.

Certainly, my process of letting go of my former identity, roles, and activities needs to be shared in meetings, even at times with some specificity. But it can remain inclusive, not exclusive. Rather than saying, "As a former member of the NYC Ballet, it's different for me, having to settle for short walks," I can say, "As a former member of the NYC Ballet, I miss dancing keenly." Or simply, "I miss dancing; it was my life." The latter statements do not claim that I am any different. We all have activities we miss and past lives we grieve. In the end, I am free to share as I like. Meetings have breathing room. I can be direct and still be inclusive, not exclusive.

For me, the spiritual practice of anonymity is worth thinking about because I need a fellowship that is about us, not me.

In this moment, I will focus on the similarities I have with others.

April 20

Decades prior to my chronic pain and chronic illness, I hated my body; my chronic conditions only exacerbated my self-loathing. I could never walk past a mirror without something harsh to say about what I saw: ugly, haggard, too thin, too old, too sick, too weak, too frail, etc. I employed every positive affirmation any self-help guru had to offer to alter my poor self-image. I took pride in loving those close to me unconditionally, yet I could not extend that same love to myself.

In one of my first CPA meetings, I heard about CPA's *Three S's*: *Self-acceptance*, *Self-care*, and *Self-love*. I added a fourth "S": Screwed. I didn't know what any of these really meant, let alone how to apply them. How could I love this body that continually let me down and, frankly, went out of its way to torture me? How could I accept being bedbound? How could I practice self-care when I couldn't even shower?

My sponsor assured me that a willingness to work the Twelve Steps of CPA was all I needed. As I came to really accept my powerlessness to control and direct my illness, symptoms, and pain, I found the tone of my self-talk began to shift. After my Fifth Step, my black-and-white thinking moved into kinder, more compassionate, gray tones. I knew the spiritual awakening promised in Step Twelve had occurred when, for the first time in my life, I had nothing to say when I looked in the mirror. The Twelve Steps of CPA and my Higher Power did for me what decades of my best efforts could not: enabled me to outright love my body, exactly as it is, at any given moment.

In this moment, I will practice self-acceptance, self-care, and self-love by speaking kindly to and about myself.

April 21

My partner and I have gotten playfully creative in an attempt to avoid the inevitable amplification of my humanness when I am in pain. They know that when my door is shut, that means, "Enter at your own risk!" Their tentative, gentle knocking comes with this playful knowledge of said risk. We have found this inside joke not only lightens both our moods but also diffuses my painful situation. This way, future amends are rarely needed.

"Thank you for your patience with me" has been another helpful tool and helps me avoid constantly saying, "I'm sorry." Not only does it indicate to those around me that I am not at my best, but it is also a beautiful reminder to treat myself with compassion and patience. When I am at my worst, the pain makes me feel unsafe and angry or tries to tell me lies about my self-worth. But humility tells me I can still love myself exactly as I am and ask my Higher Power to help me not wreak havoc with those around me.

CPA has led me to real *Self-acceptance*, genuine *Self-care*, and authentic *Self-love*. I feel safer with the awareness that, although pain can bring out my most unskillful human aspects, I can still be loving and lovable.

In this moment, I will accept my whole self, skillful and unskillful characteristics alike.

April 22

As a person with chronic pain and illness, I have learned that much of my anger is simply my body expressing pain and fatigue. There is no defect to uncover; no complex analysis is needed. What I need is rest and self-care.

When experiencing legitimate anger, I've come to understand that most of it is rooted in fear that I won't get or will lose, something I think I need. When an insurance company refuses a claim, I get upset. Isn't it because I'm afraid I'm not going to get what I need? Or, when I learn that someone said something unkind about me, I can start scaring the dog with my ranting. Isn't this from the fear that others do not think highly of me?

What about all the extra frustrations and difficulties that come with chronic illness? Don't I have a right to my anger about that? Absolutely! But if I start getting stuck there, I find that returning to Steps One, Two, Three, and sometimes Four helps the process.

Anger can jump up quickly. So, the first thing I do is employ the suggestion: when unbalanced, practice restraint of pen and tongue. In this way, I don't damage others. I observe the anger passing through my body and bite my lip. If I do lash out, I make amends as soon as I cool down. If it is rest I need, I take it. If there's a serious issue, I take an inventory, looking especially for fears. Finding these, I take them to God. Focusing not on the person, entity, or situation that has prompted the upset, I pray for my fears to be removed.

In this moment, I will remember that anger and fear are normal human emotions.

April 23

Doing the next indicated thing often refers to narrowing my focus to what needs attention right now. It is a way to move forward when I'm feeling overwhelmed.

Sometimes, just picking up the simple tasks of life, one after another, as they present themselves is a very profound practice. What's indicated is governed by the next obvious need. However, I think of this process, too, as an indication from a Higher Power.

Sometimes, my actual needs are not obvious or are a consequence of my choices. In such moments, I turn to a specific meditation practice: I ask my Higher Power for direction, pause during my day when agitated or doubtful, ask again for the next indicated action, relax, take it easy, and trust the answers will come, as long as I separate myself from dishonesty, self-will, and self-pity.

It's not always easy to see those character defects at play. I find it helpful to ask, "Is this a Godly thought? Would a loving parent suggest this? Could it lead to greater clarity, peace, or connection with my fellows?"

The ability to sense God's will for me increases with my willingness to listen to any answer that comes, including ones I dislike. I need to listen, reflect, and possibly discuss some things before I can act and let go. Whatever the outcome, the experience helps me develop this sense.

In this moment, I will use my actions as a way to connect with my Higher Power.

April 24

Facing fear and managing worry is a large part of my CPA recovery. I relax knowing I am doing all I can with God's daily direction. Currently, I am having repeated panic bouts about finances; I have some hard, scary decisions to make and imperfect data. Such is life. I am not special in facing this challenge. But no one can expect to be free of fear, so I ask for the courage and the grace to continue with purpose.

I meditate, talk to my CPA people, go to meetings, and address what I can, using small chunks of time and energy. Sometimes, I will <u>not</u> face my fear directly or right away, but I will find a distraction, like going outside or watching a movie. This gives me a break and allows for a shift in perspective. I also take care to not get overtired because fatigue is, to my fear, like a struck match to a pile of gasoline rags. At such times, I don't need more counsel or another plan; I need a nap. Rested, I can think clearly and listen for God's direction. I am continually learning what works for me is surrendering with humility to a personal Higher Power. Though I sometimes doubt, my faith is renewed when I realize that through the most difficult times of my life, I somehow had the strength to face my fears and recover.

In this moment, I will remember I am not alone when facing my fears.

April 25

Working Step One in CPA, I was surprised by my shame around admitting I was ill. I had never really admitted, even to myself, the true state of my mind and body.

Admitting illness, in my mind, was cementing it in my consciousness. I thought it was my responsibility to transcend it. I was in a no-win loop. If I am intrinsically defective, this is all my fault. Then, I had the huge realization that shame is a subtle form of control—a means to grasp power. Somehow, it seemed better to feel at fault than to feel powerless. But, taking Step One fully demanded I relinquish the shame and guilt around experiencing illness and pain.

Fortunately, the rest of the Steps in CPA addressed and released shame and guilt—giving me a way out. Though I lived with the Twelve Steps daily for decades prior, I could never shake the shame before CPA. Now, when I feel shame arise, I meet it with compassion and kindness, knowing that part of me feels terrified and powerless; that shame was the only survival tool it knew.

Thanks to Step work, sponsorship, the literature, and the fellowship of CPA, I now have an expanded concept of a Higher Power—love. I am certain I'm safe, loved, and cared for in a way that includes a joyful invitation, patience, compassion, tenderness, and tactile comfort.

I am more grateful to CPA than I could ever convey.

In this moment, I will greet shame with compassion and kindness.

April 26

I spent a number of months working on my Step Four inventory. It was largely an emotional inventory, which was quite radical for me because, prior to CPA, I falsely categorized my pain as 95 percent physical. My sponsor lovingly guided me through the process of finding and facing my pain. I read about, did written exercises on, and used guided imagery to examine my feelings of powerlessness, fear, anxiety, isolation, anger, rage, ambiguity, blame, jealousy, grief, and exhaustion. This multifaceted approach resulted in a number of "ah-ha!" moments.

I had a few of these moments surrounding blame. In particular, I would tell myself, "I should have known I would react poorly to the anesthesia," and, "This person on the phone is a useless idiot, and my health insurance provider is out to get me," or even, "My boss is putting pressure on me to perform the way I used to, but I'm too scared to tell him about my increasing pain." I discovered that, frequently, my response to an ambiguous situation is to blame! Surgical outcomes are uncertain, financial coverage by insurance is not guaranteed, and the ability to continue working with chronic pain and illness is questionable. I feel comfortable when things make logical sense and uncertain, insecure, and fearful when things are ambiguous. I was trapped in a cycle of anger and blame. These are harmful emotions, yet this cause-and-effect behavior continued until I became aware of it. These days, I admit powerlessness, accept my uneasiness, and then take action,

In this moment, I will be grateful for the awareness and acceptance I am coming to through my Step work.

April 27

The *Three A's* is a frequently used tool in my recovery program. The first "A," *Awareness,* is something I still work on. There are ways in which I live in denial and am not aware of my behaviors and attitudes. When I first heard someone in a CPA meeting say they used their illness to get out of doing something they didn't want to do, I recognized I did the same thing on occasion. Until that moment, I was not aware of this. My first reaction was disgust with myself. I felt ashamed that I'd used my pain and illness as an excuse and was dishonest with myself and others.

The next part of the formula is *Acceptance*. Now that I was aware of what I'd done, I spoke to my sponsor and worked Steps Four through Nine. In this process, I accepted that I was not always truthful. My illness had become a way to avoid going places and doing things that did not appeal to me.

The last stage is *Action*. In this case, the action was to make amends. I am making living amends by no longer using my illness as an excuse. For me, this means only giving my pain and illness as a reason for my lack of participation when it truly is, which is often.

The *Three A's* provide specific steps applicable to any situation or challenge. I have gradually altered the way I interact with others and how I respond to my pain and symptoms. As a result, I live with more serenity and peace.

In this moment, I will be honest with myself and act accordingly.

April 28

Acceptance is not a judgment. When I accept something, I am not implying it is okay, good, or even God's will. Acceptance is simply acknowledging the situation, good or bad, happy or sad, easy or challenging.

In CPA, I am leaving behind an unrealistic obsession about how I want things to be and starting to see reality as it is. I may feel it is good or bad, happy or sad, fun or challenging. Through meditation and prayer, my emotions about my reality can help me understand the next best action to take.

There is an ease with which I can move forward as I shed the frustration of my unrealistic ideals and begin to tackle life as it really is. The fight and struggle are relieved. I believe that if I'm fighting and struggling, I am working too hard, proverbially trying to force a square peg through a round hole. I can stop such behaviors when I can accept the situation.

Acceptance is a strength for me—the same as surrender. It strengthens me because I stop wasting energy on what I cannot control and can begin dealing with what is right in front of me.

I don't often start in a place of acceptance, but through meditation, prayer, daily Step work, and discussing my frustrations and fears with others in CPA who understand and can help me see reality, I get there. My close friends in CPA are a huge aide in my coming to a place of acceptance. They are lovingly honest and help me see what I cannot see on my own.

In this moment, I will see things as they are. If I need help, I will reach out to another member of CPA for support.

April 29

I hate having to take medications. Finding acceptance feels impossible. I struggle with each medication change. Every time, my self-esteem takes a hit. I even try to convince my doctors not to prescribe necessary additional medications. Often, I try to appear stronger than I am to persuade, or even trick, my doctors into cutting back on my medications.

When I was working my Fourth Step, this pattern showed up as resentment toward medications, the doctors who prescribed them, and myself. In the past, I addressed these negative emotions by trying to control the situation. I would simply stop taking the medications. Then the downward spiral would start. My symptoms would increase, and I would feel shame for not being able to overcome the need for medication or for having stopped it in the first place. Fighting the need for my medications never worked.

After I worked Steps Four through Nine around this issue, my relationship with my doctors and medications became far more serene. I now view myself as a member of my medical team, fulfilling my role as the one who describes my symptoms and my efforts and letting my doctors recommend treatments. I can discuss any resulting emotional upheaval with my sponsor. I'm not alone anymore.

When I let go of the isolation and the illusion of control, acceptance becomes attainable.

In this moment, I will receive and accept the help I need.

April 30

Before I began this process of recovery, my days always felt like they were building toward something. So, when my chronic pain or chronic illness would inevitably flare, I felt like these bad days were holding me back. Now, I break the day into sections, moving through each one as it arises.

Even though this has been a helpful tool, things that are difficult to handle still happen.

Recently, there was a day when my symptoms got worse, and the pharmacy mismanaged my medication. Once again, the cyclical narrative of despair, loneliness, and being burdensome arose. I picked up my *Recipe for Recovery* book. Hearing my own story reflected to me reminded me that recovery is day by day, moment by moment.

I find myself increasingly paying attention to the quality of moments in my life. My disease and pain do not allow me to miss any moment. They actually stretch the moments out. So, my choice now is to try to make my time meaningful and a part of my spiritual path.

For me, this is about making the path the goal. With that emphasis, I can start a day over at any moment, even right before bed. I've found I only have true influence on the next moment, not the previous ones. So I turn my mind, at the moment, to freshness, sanity, and authentic positivity...again and again.

In this moment, I will focus on the journey, not the destination.

May

May 1

One of the many weaknesses unveiled in my CPA program was that I prided myself on not asking for help, and, as my needs increased, I would become even more heroic in my inability to ask for help. Through recovery, I can see things from the other side, and it's clear that what I once thought was a sane and rational response, was actually a symptom of my insanity.

As more and more people were pushed away by this behavior, the isolation I was left with became further proof that I should never ask for help or ever get in the habit of asking. I'd become an ouroboros, the proverbial snake chasing and devouring its own tail. I was even quoted once, saying, "For me, asking for help is like pouring hot acid down my throat."

Recovery has shown me that asking for help is part of surrender, but it is also an opportunity to practice grace. This is all easier said than done, but the quality of my relationships has only increased the more I directly ask for help. I am beginning to realize that I may not be the only person in the universe who finds meaning and value in helping other beings.

This is, and will be, a constant struggle for me, but I am learning that recovery is lifelong. So, too, is learning to ask for help. I will struggle again. I will forget or refuse to ask for help and suffer again. It's a pattern that accompanies me. What is different now, is that I meet each of these moments with recovery tools, and that is making a huge difference.

In this moment, I will risk asking directly for the help I need. I will trust that honesty with those I love increases the quality of my relationships.

May 2

In Step Five, I found great healing in making myself known to another. I chose this person carefully. I knew I needed someone who'd already worked this Step. Also, someone with the insight and compassion needed to help me put things into perspective.

We thoughtfully discussed behaviors that no longer served a purpose and made life harder. I began to set down and leave my old ideas, fears, and resentments behind.

It was scary to let go of my old ideas, but I was able to trust the process, having seen what it has done for others in this program. They had something I wanted. By giving up my blame, resentment, and unreasonable fear, I opened myself to new energy, which I can now use for more constructive endeavors.

I learned there is no shame in letting my humanity be seen. This is a fellowship where we confess our faults freely and search to understand them. Still, I was relieved to finish the process of taking and sharing a searching and fearless inventory. I can relax more now and no longer put out extra energy to hide and reject my human traits.

I remember waking the day after taking this Step with a feeling I'd known once but could no longer name. I decided that I must have felt connected—to my God, my fellows, and myself.

In this moment, I will practice accepting my humanity.

May 3

Every share I've heard in a CPA meeting has taught me something. Only four months into the program, I still identify as a newcomer, but I know I'm in the right place. I see what I want in others. They have learned to be happy and serene. I could not see that as being remotely possible before I came. There is room for us to be ourselves as we learn to walk this road of CPA recovery. But what I especially appreciate is the humor!

I realized recently that, for years, I've been overly sensitive with able-bodied people. I was constantly angry, had hurt feelings, or felt my boundaries were violated. Ergo, I was very overprotective of myself. My brother visited recently and told me my edge is gone. He said that since I've been sick, there's been an edge to me. He thought he needed to be careful with how he spoke to me and what he said, but now he's beginning to feel comfortable with me again. This made me think about how a CPA friend told me never to apologize for sharing honestly. That is something I want: for others to be open with me and not feel like they need to censor themselves. And, according to my brother, I must be picking some of it up.

My desire for compassion and understanding is being met in this program and fellowship. So, for the most part, I've stopped seeking those things from people who don't recognize that I need them. As a result, I no longer get hurt or angry when they don't meet my vague expectations.

I'm quite amazed that, in CPA, I'm actually learning new things when it looked, for years, like my life was going to be a series of forgetting things.

In this moment, I will examine the role I play in my relationships.

May 4

When I see a character defect crop up—such as self-pity, non-acceptance, or being a pain because I am in pain—it does not serve me or anyone else to beat myself up over my lapse. I am a human being, not a robot. When I notice that I am not living in the solution, I remember that life, including my emotional and spiritual status, is an ongoing process, not a static state of being. I can't expect to move immediately into feeling better.

Instead, I can note that it is growth for me to notice I'm forgetting the solution. I know, then, to ask my Higher Power to gently remind me to give myself the same compassion I routinely show friends as we struggle with the very real difficulties of living, day in and day out, with chronic health problems.

Sometimes, I begin by asking for help, accepting that I'm not in a state of acceptance or serenity at all. I might ask for help letting myself be sad over another loss without slipping into paralyzing self-pity, or accepting, for a while, feeling anger without nursing that anger into a corrosive resentment my health can ill afford. Often, I need to acknowledge that my fear is still there, like the crow that comes to sit awhile atop the tree outside my window. Then I can go on with courage.

I'm endeavoring to remember that living in the solution in deep and meaningful ways grows out of facing difficult emotions and challenges. The blossom is rooted in darkness. Let me be that perennial flower that comes back, again and again, more lovely in its bloom because of its regular, necessary absence.

In this moment, I will accept my recovery as an ongoing process.

May 5

When I walk over the threshold of any medical room I shrink, instantly, from my tall, adult stature to that of a five-year-old, voiceless child. I do not wish to either blame them or shame myself any longer. CPA has provided me with new ways of seeing and communicating that allow me to act and eventually feel differently.

When I don't ask for help from my Higher Power, the painful memories of times I have been belittled, misdiagnosed, shamed, and dismissed by those to whom I have turned to for help, often surface. However, there are also countless instances when those people, and plenty of others behind the scenes, have cared for me in ways I will never fully realize, and without whom it is doubtful I would be alive. Remembering that changes me, and thus my experience.

Step One invites me to admit that all of us, including medical professionals, are human. They are also powerless to know what they never learned and unable to fix the unfixable. Perhaps they want to help me and even feel frustrated at their own powerlessness. Additionally, each human I encounter has battles they are fighting, about which I know nothing. Now, when I walk into a medical appointment, I ask each staff member and the doctors how they are doing and listen with an open heart. Instead of feeling beholden to an authority figure, I both fear and depend on, this simple practice allows me to feel shoulder-to-shoulder with others.

In this moment, I will be kind to those I encounter.

May 6

I often find myself stuck between should and want. I wake up, and I think, "I should start off my day with prayer, but I want to just lie here before eventually getting up and starting my day." In the afternoon, I think, "I should do my physical therapy exercises or take a short walk, but I want to zone out and keep watching TV." At night, I think, "I should meditate, but I want to go to sleep."

Then, one day, it occurred to me that the center of should and want is feel. How would it feel if I began my day with prayer? Would I feel more connected to my Higher Power? How would it feel if I did my physical therapy or took a walk? Would my body feel stronger? Or does my body feel like resting today? How would it feel if I meditated before bed? Would I feel more at ease with a quieter mind? Would I feel proud of myself?

When I find myself struggling to get motivated to do something I should or beating myself up for doing things that I want, I ask myself, "How would it feel to do that particular activity? How would my body feel? How would my spirit feel? How do I think I would feel about myself after I do it?" When I remember to check in with myself in this way, I find that I am more motivated and less likely to "should" all over myself."

In this moment, I will do what feels right for my mind, body and spirit.

May 7

The other day, I picked a fight with my wife. She was not doing anything wrong. I was in a lot of pain, feeling quite cranky and irritable, and I lashed out at her. Thanks to my Higher Power, I remembered to STOP: *Surrender, Time-out, Observe, Prioritize.*

First, I *Surrendered.* Pain was all-consuming. I was miserable and powerless over how uncomfortable I was at the moment. I realized I needed to step away, to take a *Time-out,* so I told my wife I was not going to continue the fight we were in and walked away. I O*bserved* what I needed and *Prioritized* that need by taking some medication for the pain and going to bed.

When I felt better a day later, I realized how insane I'd been acting. The issue I was fighting about was not real; it was my unhappiness with my pain showing up as unhappiness with my wife. There really wasn't an issue between us. I dropped the matter and made my amends to her.

There are many times when my pain or symptoms are the catalyst for my being unpleasant to others. When I am able to *STOP,* I get clarity and don't create any new wreckage.

I can use *STOP* whenever I find myself spinning out of control, having a challenging health day, struggling with a decision, or having a conflict in a relationship. At those times, if I keep pushing, I become obsessive, lost in confusion, and overwhelmed by my pain and symptoms. I just barrel ahead, forcing solutions rather than pausing to work my program. But if I *STOP—Surrender, Time-out, Observe, and Prioritize*—I can find my way back to feeling balanced and sane again.

In this moment, I will remember to STOP when facing a challenging situation.

May 8

I struggle with grief all the time. Much of the difficulty I have with my illnesses is the unpredictability of never knowing what to expect. I've been known to act like a fortune-teller—to think I know how things will look in the future.

My resistance to my current situation or expectations of the future make me feel worse. When my sponsor and I discussed Step One and accepting the unacceptable, they told me about the concept of rolling grief. When I accept my life as it is, I am accepting that I will have a continual relationship with grief. There will be many ups and downs in life, and I will react emotionally to those circumstances.

Once I understand that grief is here to stay, I don't have to resist it. I look at it like the current of a stream. The current is moving downstream, and it's only hard on me when I try to walk against it, cling to a rock, and stay in the same place. The joy of the journey happens when I let go and allow the emotion to wash over me and actually carry me to my next destination.

When I feel overwhelmed, I remember that I can pray to my Higher Power to remove my resistance. I can attend a meeting, share my struggles, and reach out to someone and let them in. This helps me realize that many outcomes are possible, and I'm not a fortune-teller. I can let go.

In this moment, I will remember that my grief becomes less all-consuming when I stop resisting it and share the load with someone else.

May 9

When I began to forgive myself within this journey of chronic pain and illness, I wrote a letter to myself. The following is an excerpt from that letter:

"…I am not only forgiving you, but forgiving the society that has made us feel abnormal. It's been a difficult road. I've learned we enjoy being alone. Solitude allows for us to be creative in our own space, giving us room to pursue different levels of freedom. This includes practicing meditation in quiet places, reading, studying, thinking, writing, crocheting, sewing, and other crafty projects.

"I forgive our past mistakes that led to negative emotions, thoughts, and behaviors. I see now that self-directed negativity makes us sicker. I'm working on changing the narrative and examining my standards and expectations. I'm giving the past less of our time and focus to allow for more creative freedom in the present moment. I forgive myself for getting stuck in the past. I am learning not to repeat past mistakes, and I'm excited about what's to come.

"I forgive our body. I've been given more chances than most, and I want to spend the rest of our time doing what we enjoy. I am letting our body have the grace it deserves. I have been praying for more self-acceptance and to accept what I cannot change about our chronic illness. I resolve to live with more self-care and kindness."

In the process of forgiving myself, I'm finding more joy in the little things. I'm also taking care of my body, recognizing the ability to be creative from within, and feeling grateful for my new knowledge and understanding. All of this fills my soul with more room to be forgiving and at peace.

In this moment, I will honor forgiveness as a journey and respect wherever I am on the path.

May 10

Just doing the next indicated action is an important tool and a core practice in my recovery. While it's valuable any time, it becomes increasingly useful the more overwhelmed I feel or when my mental faculties aren't working well.

For example, it is difficult for me to manage many different kinds of tasks. There is always more than I can do. But instead of being immobilized by anxiety and feeling overwhelmed, narrowing down my focus to what I can do next helps me to take action. Sometimes, the next action is to take a break, rest, sleep, check out of the mental whirlwind, and tune in to my deeper source of wisdom and discernment—to seek guidance. Or it may be to seek help from a recovery buddy who can stay on the phone with me while I get started on the next indicated thing and then check in afterward for accountability and to celebrate the achievement. Sometimes, I'm only able to take a simple action that is unrelated to a critical task.

Sometimes, I give myself permission to do anything. This provides freedom from the internal pressure to get the most important things done first. Inside this freedom, it's easier for me to check in and receive the guidance my Higher Power has to offer. There's less mental static. I'm not buying into the judgments about what I must do.

As I use this tool over time, my stress and feelings of being overwhelmed decrease. I can remember that I've used it before; it has helped me take action even while feeling overwhelmed, uncertain, and lacking clarity. I don't have to figure out or be responsible for the bigger picture. It is a form of practicing *Let Go and Let God*.

In this moment, I will take everything one step at a time.

May 11

CPA has no opinion on sexual morality, preferences, or behaviors. But the values CPA points to as important for a life well-lived, like honesty, empathy, awareness, and some modicum of selflessness, may be important to consider when looking at my need for touch. Chronic pain and chronic illness express themselves within my body and mind and, thus, affect all aspects of my life. I am a physical, emotional, and spiritual creature, so it's no surprise that my physical maladies, as well as my emotional and spiritual conditions, are not separate from my sexual practices.

I've learned that both my character defects and assets play out in the sexual arena. For example, if I have difficulty communicating with my partner in the bedroom, I typically find emotional disturbances, not physical limitations, to be disabling my sex life. I've lost much of my self-esteem and, almost unconsciously, I've withdrawn to avoid further disappointment. I've stopped trying because sex can feel too much like a chore. I also have some old ideas about what sex ought to look or be like. If I can no longer be the brilliantly skillful sexual partner I once imagined myself to be, why participate?

And what about my partner's emotions surrounding our changed circumstances?

I've found that with sex, as with many issues, it's better to take the time and find ways to sort things out. Investing time looking at an issue pays regular dividends that require less and less effort over time. In the area of touch, I've found having a program for emotional recovery can really help.

In this moment, I will remember I can use my program tools in all areas of my life.

May 12

Chronic pain and illness can turn our lives upside down. Many of us can no longer follow the path we dreamed for ourselves or do the work we prepared for and set out to do. Some of us believed that achievement equaled success in life. Loss of our abilities, jobs, finances, potential, friends, and spouses left us not only grieving but wondering if there was a reason to go on living.

CPA can help us discover new and meaningful ways to live. When my illnesses severely progressed, I needed to depend on caregivers to help me get through the day. I had to rest for hours at a time. My brain became so foggy that it was hard to put together a sentence. Then, I found CPA.

Quickly, I discovered that finding a group of people who understand and are going through a similar journey provides a sense of belonging. Attending meetings provided a purpose for each day. As I listened to others share, I learned to be compassionate to myself and even love myself, creating more purpose and meaning in my life.

The Serenity Prayer was my new mantra and helped me face and grieve losses. I could not control my illnesses or how the doctors, and the people who did not understand or believe how ill I was, treated me. Letting go and letting love into my life became a mission. Daily, I can surrender to this Power of Love, ask for guidance, and seek to do its will. I realized this new purpose for life had more depth and seemed far more important than my old purpose of doing and accomplishing.

In this moment, I will remember I can still find purpose and meaning whilst living with chronic conditions.

May 13

When chronic pain and chronic illness irreparably altered my life, I lost all sense of direction, purpose, and identity. I struggled every morning with thoughts of dread, having awakened, yet again, to another meaningless day. I was bedbound and hopeless. A friend intervened and taught me to crochet. It brought color, texture, and a sense of accomplishment right into bed with me. I began collecting all types of yarn. For my birthday, my husband installed shelves to hold it all.

In CPA, I've learned the value of self-acceptance, self-care, and self-love. Nonetheless, I still believed that because I could no longer work and bring income into the house, I should not be spending money. I began hiding yarn purchases in the car until I could bring them into the house without my husband's knowledge.

As time went on, my dishonesty ate away at my serenity. It made me feel worse and worse. I prayed for the courage to come clean and confess what I had done. My husband's response shocked and amazed me. He viewed my crocheting and all it included as part of my medical treatment—he had witnessed the benefit it had on my spirit. I knew crocheting was meditative—it gave me fulfillment and joy—but I didn't know he could see that, too.

In this moment, I will consider the things that bring me joy as necessary to my well-being. I am worthy of experiencing joy!

May 14

How do I know the difference between my will and Higher Power's will? My will always comes with an urgent, pressured, and panicked tirade of mental dialogue that propels me into exhausting action and exacerbated symptoms. When I listen to that voice and act, it almost always ends with the need for even more frantic action or, worse, having to make amends.

My Higher Self speaks in a quiet, brief voice, with a sensation that is comforting, enlightening, and often humorous.

Praying, *"Thy will, not mine, be done,"* releases me from my obsession to control and direct everything. It reminds me that when I listen to that small, still voice, my life is always easier, lighter, and, dare I say, miraculous in ways I could never have achieved by myself.

I have come to believe that something greater than myself knows what is best for me; my only job is to stay grounded in the present moment and ask and listen for Higher Power's guidance. This works for me every time; I know a new freedom and ease of living amid chronic pain and chronic illness.

In this moment, I will be quiet and pay attention to the small, still voice inside.

May 15

Even on my best days, I know I will reach a point where unless I isolate myself and dial down the stimuli dramatically, I'll collapse emotionally. If I'm with others, I'll lash out at them. It doesn't matter how resolved I am to be pleasant or how much I pray about it. At that time, I don't need another suggestion; I need a nap.

I live with my girlfriend and let her know when I'm approaching that point—without burdening her with the details —by simply indicating it is that time now. It's time I isolate and rest entirely. Later, we can be together pleasantly, even if I am only partially restored. We both know I won't be up for much conversation and certainly not for problem-solving discussions, but we can still enjoy the other's company. When I am rested, we communicate well. That allows for the mutual understanding and accommodation necessary for a healthy relationship, even those with crushing burdens.

Before CPA, I thought I never blamed others for my pain. In truth, this is what I expected: I am the sick one here, so you ought to be working on your character defects so I won't have to be patient with them. I've since learned that it is probably my issue and that, perhaps, I am too tired to judge the situation at hand with clarity.

I am thrilled to have the awareness and opportunity to do self-care, communicate with care, and be less of a pain, friendlier, and more loving.

In this moment, I will take time for myself if necessary and make amends for any poor behavior toward my loved ones as soon as I can.

May 16

Forgiveness is like sunlight—a gift from my Higher Power. I didn't do anything to deserve it; I can't bend it to my will. When considering forgiveness, I think about the parts of the word, specifically "give" and "for." So, it's about finding what I am willing to "give" "for" something, what it's worth. In this case, that something is the freedom to live each day as I am—in this body, with this life. This isn't the life I thought I would have, but it has become precious nonetheless.

In my experience, forgiveness is something that comes through the actions of prayer and meditation. From spending time with and paying attention to my Higher Power, I gain awareness. This isn't always a comfortable process, and I am learning to be compassionate and gentle with myself when I have uncomfortable feelings. I discovered the first person in need of my forgiveness was myself.

I still struggle with knowing I have contributed to the worsening of my chronic pain. Engendered by my need to control, my frantic desperation and fear led to actions that exacerbated my injuries. But I am learning about the gentle and compassionate care of my Higher Power. This relieves me of the need to control. When I give myself over to that care, my desperation to be cured is lifted. While my physical pain remains, my mental and spiritual anguish has eased.

In this moment, I will acknowledge that forgiveness and acceptance bring me freedom. Through connection with my Higher Power, I find that I am exactly where I need to be.

May 17

In taking Step Five, I value being transparent and not feeling that I want or need to hide my faults. It's freeing to recognize and admit my shortcomings to another person and my Higher Power and to have the understanding and acceptance of both during this process. So, it's important to choose my partner in Step Five carefully.

I shared my Fifth Step with my sponsor. I found it so helpful to have someone else's perspective. There were some things I was ashamed of, but when I shared them, I found they were natural and understandable results of things in my life. I was able to quit carrying guilt and give myself compassion as I experienced acceptance from my sponsor and God.

The process of talking through these things gave me the wisdom to know that it was time to drop them out of my life if they no longer served me. It was a healing Step. Taking it left me free of secret problems and with a greater sense of self-worth. I love that Step Five fits right where it belongs in the process of working all of the Twelve Steps.

In this moment, I will take action, if there is something I need to share with a trusted individual.

May 18

Thinking that progress is only linear—forward and upward movement—is unrealistic. It's not how life, health, or the recovery process works, let alone pain or anything else in the changing world. I have to let go of the insanity of trying to make life happen the way I think it should.

I now see progress as moving forward from wherever I am. My health may have taken a dive. My ability to remember my recovery tools and use them may be significantly impaired or shut down for a while. Onward does not always mean upward.

Sometimes, progress looks like accepting that sometimes I go into survival mode, and it is okay to just make it to the next day. But survival mode is not a foundation upon which thriving happens. The more challenged I feel, the more foundational my responses need to become. Harm reduction is a useful strategy during these times, as well as self-acceptance, self-compassion, and prioritizing self-care.

Progress, for me, is taking the risk of trying a different coping strategy and experimenting to discover how it might turn out. I can turn a mistake into an opportunity to learn new ways of responding. Progress is also forgiving myself when I get caught playing out old strategies that come with unpleasant consequences.

Rather than remaining immobilized by uncertainty and fear, I take a risk with whatever scraps of willingness I have left. Being able to see the possibility of progress gives me hope and trust that this may be my best way forward.

In this moment, I will recognize how fear impacts my ability to discern the next indicated action.

May 19

My pain can coexist with my faith. I tried it the other way; that was dark, scary, and depressing. When I let chronic pain and illness take over my life, I lost the ability to recognize faith or anything like it. I expected to be let down over and over, especially when it came to being sick. I once had a very strong faith but found I had none left at all.

After I attended a CPA meeting, where I saw and heard others who lived like I did and talked with them in fellowship afterward, I got some hope. Eventually, faith followed. I think that I needed to connect with others, but I may never know exactly what changed for me by going to CPA. I know that life is good today—despair and darkness are gone. I'm okay with not knowing why anymore; it's not necessary. Today, I have faith that I will be continually guided in this program.

My understanding of Higher Power has expanded. It includes a much grittier, down-to-earth version. It's also a stronger version. Life can be harsh and unfair. But I've come to see terms like "harsh" and "unfair" are based on expectations. My world has become smaller in many ways, but my vision of life has expanded.

So, yes, my faith can coexist with my chronic pain and illness, but more than that, I believe it exists because of my chronic pain and illness. Today, I don't worry that I don't believe in God because I've found that God definitely believes in me.

In this moment, I will allow my pain and illness to coexist with my faith in my Higher Power.

May 20

It took me a long time to come out of my shell in CPA. When I first started coming to meetings, I was quiet, reserved, and shut down. I felt like chronic pain and chronic illness had sucked all of the life out of me. Then, one day, I opened up and was vulnerable for the first time. I think I expected everyone to stop, take notice, and give me special attention. Instead, the meeting went on as normal. I sat and stewed, feeling like I'd just exposed a very raw part of myself, and no one cared.

Fellowship time began, and no one said anything about my big, brave share. I wrote in the chat, "I can't," meaning I couldn't do the vulnerability thing and left. The topic being discussed was dancing; apparently, other members thought I'd left because I was saying, "I can't dance." Later, someone reminded me that we don't crosstalk by talking about what a person has shared in a meeting, and that's why no one had addressed my share. I began to feel better.

While I still have vulnerable moments in meetings, I've learned to share the really raw stuff with my sponsor and close friends, especially when I'm looking for any sort of feedback. I've let the fellowship get to know me in my good, funny, and dark moments. It took time for me to learn to trust the fellowship and the program. Now, I look back at my "I can't dance" outburst with laughter. It brings me great pleasure these days to watch newcomers come in and slowly start to share their experiences and personalities in meetings.

In this moment, I will appreciate seeing others grow in this program.

May 21

Sponsorship is a significant responsibility; a person's spiritual life is being fostered. So, when I sponsor, I like to review our literature carefully.

I'm not a preacher or priest, and even if I were, my role as a CPA sponsor only includes sharing my experience, strength, and hope, as I've discovered them through working the Twelve Steps. I am well-steeped in other Twelve Step programs. I naturally draw upon these, but when sponsoring in CPA, I focus on how our literature presents the Steps.

Reflecting on our books is a great way to see the differences between what my head thinks and what the literature actually says. I once saw myself as so wise that I unintentionally started selling my way of approaching a Higher Power. I've also used other techniques that have no business in Step work. Returning to the CPA literature has helped ground me when sponsoring.

Sponsorship has meant that I work the Steps again, to some degree, from start to finish with each person. When a sponsee responds to a Higher Power they've encountered through working the Steps, I can see and feel their spirit ignite, which reignites mine.

In this moment, I will remember I can maintain unity in sponsorship relationships by aligning my experience, strength, and hope with the CPA literature.

May 22

Since I've had my pain and illness, I've struggled with getting restful sleep. Even on days when I seem to get enough, I wake up exhausted. Doctors and specialists have told me sleep is important, especially when dealing with pain and illness. But the medications they've provided have only made me feel worse. I felt utterly defeated and had given up hope for a solution.

Another suggestion was to take naps during the day. As someone who only found meaning in productivity, the idea of a nap seemed wrong. I could not wrap my mind around it, so I completely dismissed it. The denial only increased my suffering. My body was screaming, begging, and pleading with me to sleep.

I suffered for three years until I found CPA, where I learned that *Rest is an Action*. People in meetings shared their experiences with sleep and rest, and I saw that I was not alone in my experiences with sleep or my attitude toward it. This helped me realize that I could be productive and take care of myself. I discovered that I actually became more productive when I rested and took naps.

CPA may not have solved my sleep problems, but it has helped change my attitude. It's given me a gentler outlook and allowed me to change my toxic belief system. When I gave myself permission to rest, much of my suffering diminished.

Through CPA, I do what is best for me and my health by listening to the voice of recovery rather than the voices of obsession, pain, and illness.

In this moment, I will give myself permission to rest when I need it.

May 23

When I found CPA, I couldn't believe I found a fellowship that understood my pain, isolation, and fear. But, more importantly, I couldn't believe I found a place where I could laugh again.

I've noticed many health benefits from bringing laughter and humor into my life. It has helped my immune system, improved my overall mood, and even helped relieve some of my pain. This kind of medicine is not only free but readily available. Therefore, I not only practice this kind of medicine but I share it with my CPA fellows as much as I can.

We are all on this journey of recovery. We are all trying to get by and live another day. This life is not easy. So, I suggest trying humor. Practice laughing in the mirror. Watch a funny video. Or even try telling a corny joke.

The best thing that can happen is laughter—yours and others. I can't eliminate my pain or someone else's, but I can invite someone to smile, giggle, or laugh. I find that keeping a sense of humor is helpful not only to me but to everyone around me as well. My goal now is to include a corny riddle or joke every time I share a gratitude. Maybe everyone won't find it funny, but if two or three get a giggle or laugh from it, I think I've made the world a better place—a lighter, more enjoyable place right at this moment.

Knock, knock.
Who's there?
Cereal
Cereal who?
Cereal pleasure to meet you!

In this moment, I will remember and apply Declaration Eight: "We will laugh and see the lighter side of situations."

May 24

I have periods in my life when it seems like every time I think I'm on solid ground, another tsunami comes to wash me away. Sometimes, it seems like I just can't catch a break.

This is where my program helps me. Yes, I go down. I feel defeated, and I am angry. Then, I have to fight to get up again. But the cycle time is getting shorter, and the intensity of the experience is lessened when I use CPA slogans, Steps, literature, meetings, and friends.

Step One: I surrender to my reality, even though I don't like it. Step Two: a Power greater than me is there for me, even though it doesn't look that way right now. Step Three: I turn myself over to the care of my Higher Power.

Once I feel sane again, after the storm of feelings, I ask my HP, "What am I supposed to receive out of this experience? What am I supposed to learn?" I pray for guidance. I trust that there is something of value. That doesn't mean it isn't awful, that I would rather not be doing it, but using this practice gives me agency and hope. I am not a victim. I am resilient, and HP will show me the way forward.

When I don't know what way to go next, I have faith. That is how I navigate these experiences. It looks pretty on paper, but it is not in real life. It is not graceful or easy, but with the program tools, I get stronger, and my faith gets deeper.

In this moment, I will allow my feelings room to express themselves, then turn to the first three Steps to help me feel grounded once more.

May 25

"But, but, but…I want, I need, I must…" This was how I lived before CPA.

When I committed to turning my will, life, and body over to the care of my Higher Power in Step Three, I had to constantly remind myself to relax, soften, and breathe. I had to accept HP's will and timing as perfect, even when circumstances and appearances frightened me. I didn't give up my hopes, dreams, and desires; I just surrendered the form and timing of the outcomes.

I knew I wanted to move to a place that felt like paradise… and it took seven years of waiting. Things had to happen in those seven years for my dream to come true. I knew that forcing my will in pursuit of my dream would only get in HP's way, create frustration in me, and exacerbate my symptoms. So, while I waited, I continued to put my best efforts toward research, footwork, and preparations. I treated it like a hobby instead of a job, and when HP pulled the trigger on the move, everything fell into place as if by magic. This complex endeavor was the easiest thing I had ever done. And it was, indeed, perfect!

Chronic pain and chronic illness do not have to rob me of my dreams, but, for me, living with their effects does demand reliance on something greater than my best efforts. When I surrender my wants, needs, and musts, I trade struggle and hardship for divine ease.

In this moment, I will practice Step Three and look for the path that HP has opened for me.

May 26

Rest was once a condemnable action, a negative word used to describe laziness. It has become a necessary tool I use in my day-to-day life. Chronic pain and illness forced me to realize that I am unable to move at the pace I once did. This felt unfair, especially given my young age, and I didn't accept it.

I did start resting at various times during the day, but not until I'd pushed past my limit and hit a wall. Bruised, tearful, and unable to keep pushing, I would concede and rest, but never without the shame of being in bed while the sun was still out. I'd look at myself through the eyes of a judgmental authority figure, the word "lazy" hissing in my ear. I'd look out the window at the bustling city, imagining I was the only ambulatory person lying in bed.

Because of Chronic Pain Anonymous, what I once saw as laziness is now something I do to restore myself. I can return to a state from which I can greet the rest of my day with some peace and serenity rather than frustration and anger. Now I know I am not wrong, bad, and lazy for retreating to a restful space to care for myself—even though it often means lying in my bed with the sun shining and the city charging forth around me.

In this moment, I will take time to rest even if a part of me still resists my need for it.

May 27

When I first became sick, I was the breadwinner of the family. As I began losing my ability to work, my fear of what would happen to us grew. I wasn't sure how our family could survive without my financial support.

One of the first things I realized was that my faith in my spouse's ability to handle financial matters was really low. Money was an area where my controlling nature hadn't eased. My fear was tearing me up inside and causing strain in our home.

One of the practices an old sponsor helped me with was inviting HP into all my financial affairs. When creating a spending plan, I'd write a prayer on the top of each page. Some of my favorites were "HP, guide my dollars" and "HP, help me remember that You are my employer." Prayers have now found their way into my passwords and comments on our financial spreadsheets.

The biggest change in my behavior has been talking about money with my spouse regularly. We hold hands and pray before we discuss financial issues.

My general sense of doom is underscored when there is vagueness around money. I still write down every dollar I spend, and so does my spouse. We discuss how much money will be needed in the future and where we stand right now. By watching my spouse handle financial problems and discussing them openly, my faith in their ability to hold our family together has grown. They have done a great job. We've even been able to move into a more accessible home because of their efforts.

In this moment, I will remember each day that I am guided and loved by my Higher Power that has solutions I cannot even begin to dream of on my own.

May 28

It took me a while to learn that the quality of my sleep is not the determining factor of my happiness. I have no control over whether I can fall asleep, stay asleep, or go back to sleep after waking in the middle of the night. I'm powerless over my sleep. This is a new concept I'm learning with the help of my CPA program and friends.

I discovered that being angry at 2:00 a.m. only makes things worse. Obsessively trying to figure out a solution makes me more tense and less able to sleep. Taking care of myself in those wee hours is the best way to deal with the nights when sleep eludes me. I listen to an audiobook and close my eyes. Although I may fall asleep, that's not my goal. I may go into another room, turn on the TV, or read a magazine. I have a friend in another country where it is daytime during my nighttime, so I call her. All this helps me get to the morning. I've let go of solving the problem, and instead, I accept the moment. This brings peace, even when it doesn't bring sleep.

I've also let go of the belief that if I don't get enough sleep, I can't function. As it turns out, I can! And if I notice that my thinking is compromised, I cancel my activities for that day. When I'm irritable and snapping at others, I choose to be alone until I can regulate myself again. I love the days when I wake up after a night of refreshing sleep, but I no longer dread the days when that's not the case.

In this moment, I will stop judging my sleep and telling myself stories that hold me back from enjoying my day.

May 29

All my life, I've heard, "You're so hard on yourself!" I responded by being hard on myself about being so hard on myself! Once my body required me to slow down, all of my fearful thoughts and resulting behaviors were magnified. I couldn't avoid them anymore. How was I supposed to generate that elusive thing called self-compassion?

Working Step One with my sponsor led me to the realization that I hadn't felt safe in my body for a long time. It occurred to me that self-compassion might be instinctive—not something I could conjure in my mind. As someone who always dissociated from situations to cope, I hadn't spent much time staying with discomfort.

I allowed myself to begin to feel my body and slowly built a meditation practice that focuses on sensation. I spent time relaxing my shoulders during the deepest part of my exhale, allowing my parasympathetic nervous system to take over for a few seconds. And then I cried a lot. I realized I always pushed away feelings of sorrow, demonizing them as self-pity, before I had a chance to gently investigate them. Witnessing these feelings of sorrow while in moments of release, I saw that my fear and anger were perfectly human experiences my Higher Power had afforded me. Shutting my feelings down was effectively shutting out my Higher Power.

CPA changed how I see myself and my life. It made me realize that I can choose what to do next—call my sponsor or a program pal, write, yell into a pillow, cry, or listen to other people exploring self-compassion as a practice.

In this moment, I will allow my emotions and sensations space for expression and release. I can ask my Higher Power for support as I do so.

May 30

"Don't just lie there, do something!" My mind always told me I had to do something to be worthy of love and acceptance. I must do more. I must be better, stronger, and faster than I am. Then, chronic pain and chronic illness stopped me dead in my tracks. I could no longer distract myself from these unskillful beliefs with activities. The emotional and spiritual debilitation that arose paralyzed me, and my self-loathing continued to grow.

At one of my first CPA meetings, I heard, "Do half of what you think you can do," and "I am enough. I have enough. I know enough. I do enough." It took time for these concepts to become a working part of my mind. I had to practice. My mind tells me I should be doing this or that. CPA taught me, when this happens, to pause and ask Higher Power for the next right thought or action. Sometimes, there is a gentle whisper, "Go do the dishes," or "Stay flat."

When I listen to those old habitual thoughts, my life becomes unmanageable. I've learned to listen to something greater than my mind. For instance, if HP tells me that taking a shower is the next indicated action, and I actually get the message but can only wash my face and hands that day, this is cause for celebration. Doing HP's will to the best of my ability allows me to live peacefully, joyfully, and comfortably, no matter what my body and mind are doing.

In this moment, I will quietly pause and ask my Higher Power to direct me to take the next indicated action.

May 31

Around age twenty-seven, chronic illness arrived in my life. Right away, I had to accept that my illness did not have a cure, clear timeline, or life expectancy. I always hoped my life would turn out a certain way, but I had to change my expectations. After a hopeful treatment with nearly fatal side effects, I changed my understanding of acceptance to include a lack of control. It was clear that time was limited.

My spouse and I lived the next several years doing as much as we could to organize our life. We managed to accomplish many of our goals, and our efforts were fulfilling. We both had our professions. I loved working two miles from the Pacific Ocean. Our daily life was good. Then, the illness and pain progressed. I tried to hang on to the life I loved but could not do it anymore. Retirement disability was another opportunity to practice acceptance.

To my surprise, I have lived beyond doctors' expectations. (Another lesson in no control!) My husband got a once-in-a-lifetime job, so we moved. I think I will always grieve my sunny southern California lifestyle, but believe it or not, my days are better now because I finally found my place in a CPA meeting.

Sitting in my meeting, I realized how practicing the Steps has turned around my thoughts. Most days are actually good now. It's still hard for me to receive yet another diagnosis. But I just return to Step One, realizing I am powerless, my life is unmanageable, and acceptance is all there is. I'm still living so gratefully and with much more acceptance, mindfulness, and understanding.

In this moment, I will be grateful for being able to live exactly the life I have.

June

June 1

I live with chronic conditions and develop new medical issues routinely. For my recovery, acceptance has been key.

I used to accept a bad turn by trudging forward and staying positive until life got better or I adjusted to a new normal that I could accept. Nothing was wrong with doing that; it worked at the time

But at this stage of my life and conditions, this process no longer works quite as neatly. I had to admit that my so-called new normal is that I am now constantly changing and likely always will be as I age. So, I no longer have the luxury of waiting until I have a new normal I can fully accept and be okay with living.

Now, I accept that I will always experience some new change in my life's conditions. I deny some and grieve some, but ultimately accept everything as it is and call it okay. Meanwhile, the process goes round and round.

When I start my day and recall the ultimate unmanageability of my life, I am reminded to continue accepting things, small and large, as I go through the day. I am not preoccupied with inner narratives spun to convince I-don't-know-who that something isn't right and isn't okay. I now have the mental space to allow for new thoughts, beliefs, and actions. I can now see what I do have, what I can do, and that I can still have meaning and purpose.

In this moment, I will remember that when I look through the glasses of recovery, I see the world differently.

June 2

I remember the first months and years after chronic pain and illness entered my life. I was devastated and depressed because of how much my life had changed and how much I'd lost. So many activities that brought me joy, fulfillment, and self-worth were now impossible. I felt lost. I struggled to keep up my pre-illness pace because I thought I should. This was my insanity. The whirlwind of confusion, feeling worthless, not knowing what to do, grief, and wondering why this happened to me made me feel out of control.

CPA helped me see how my Higher Power could change all of this. It gave me direction on how to turn my life over to Her when the whirlwinds would inevitably come. With the help of members and the tools of the program, my insanity began to be dismantled.

I was able to address my sadness, grief, and other issues with the help of my Higher Power. I learned to turn things over to Her—to make new decisions and life changes that shifted much of what was making me insane. Those changes and decisions happened in Step Three; working Step Two made all that possible.

Step Two gave me the hope that supported me in Step Three. This has resulted in a life that is fulfilling and good. It is not perfect. There are still problems, struggles, and times of sadness and grief, but Step Two brought me out of my insanity and despair. *One Day at a Time*, this helps me transition into a satisfying, fruitful, and better future.

In this moment, I will remember that turning to the Higher Power of my understanding can restore me to sanity.

June 3

Through working my Steps, especially Step Four, I discovered I often felt obliged to be obedient—afraid to rock the boat and stand up for myself. This was especially true when working with my healthcare providers. At times, the medical settings were intimidating; I didn't want to upset the people I relied on for care by coming across as difficult.

With support from my sponsor, I began to make amends to myself by practicing self-care. The ways I took care of myself when changing my treatment plan included going slowly, asking questions, doing my own research, and speaking to other patients. I realized I could even say "No" to my medical providers if necessary.

As a result of working my program, I believe I can now make better choices regarding my healthcare most of the time. Just last week, I had a bad reaction to a new medication. I had to surrender and cancel my plans. Unlike in the past, that didn't freak me out or make me angry. My emotions and catastrophic thinking did not overtake me. I responded with acceptance and serenity.

This experience was a reminder that the unexpected is a part of life's journey—it's guaranteed as a part of living with chronic health conditions. I can do the footwork but am always powerless over the outcome. What I can do is relax and surrender.

In this moment, I will make choices that honor my integrity and self-care. I will relax and surrender all outcomes.

June 4

I revisit the Twelve Steps every few years and work through them with another. Because I'd done Step Four many times, my sponsor suggested I focus my inventory on fear this time.

I decided to answer one question again and again and again: what am I afraid of? I did this over many weeks in many different situations. As I repeatedly answered the question, I discovered more fears. Some were oldies but goodies; some were new.

It was liberating to have all my fears out in the open. All the demons which haunt me and keep me stuck and unable to move were exposed and, therefore, no longer so frightening. There was a clear map of all the ways I was paralyzed by fear and a list of all I would give to my Higher Power in Steps Six and Seven.

After I spoke all the fears out loud in Step Five, I felt such relief. My sponsor heard my list and defused many of my fears. He helped me see how they were not real; my mind was playing tricks on me. Some were past experiences still haunting me; some were negative projections into the future that were only based in my imagination, not the truth.

One surprising result of this inventory was hearing my Higher Power's guidance clearly for the first time. This led to a major life change. I now have a real, interactive relationship with this Power. It is the miracle of the program. I didn't have any expectations when I started. I wasn't looking to make big changes. Today, when a fear shows up and starts to loom large, I work all Twelve Steps on just that fear. This has become a powerful tool I use to work my program.

In this moment, I will shine a light on my fears by sharing them with another.

June 5

In Step Six, I became entirely ready to have a new relationship with pain, illness, and myself.

I am not defective. Steps Four and Five showed me I am human and that I've developed skillful and unskillful responses to my pain, illness, and life itself. After decades of believing and behaving as though I had to be superhuman to be worthy of love and acceptance, I am now entirely ready to have God remove this delusion.

I recently had an extremely high-symptom, high-pain day that required medication. As a woman in long-term addiction recovery, I am mindful of taking medication as prescribed, yet I had a human brain-fog moment and took two pills instead of one. My pain was addressed; however, I had become slightly intoxicated and felt buzzed. I now know that feeling didn't mean I'd relapsed; it just meant that I am human and made a mistake. This experience served as a reminder that reliance on my Higher Power is needed in every action I take.

Instead of beating myself up, fighting the side effects of my error, and allowing my mind to launch me into *False Events Appearing Real (FEAR)*, I shared my error with another CPA member and took the rest of the day off. Thanks to CPA, I have a new relationship with pain, illness, and myself. With humility, I understand that my responses are simply human, not defective, and my Higher Power is always there to lovingly support, guide, and comfort me regardless of my mistakes.

In Step Six, I became entirely ready and willing to accept my humanity and trust that when I seek guidance from my Still, Small Voice, I will be lovingly directed toward my greatest potential.

In this moment, I will forgive myself for making mistakes.

June 6

I am a new member of CPA but have been dealing with chronic pain for twelve years. I was active all my life, and when that changed, I was reluctant to accept the idea that my Higher Power knew what I can handle. CPA has been a blessing, to say the least.

Early on, my bad days were filled with anger, self-pity, tantrums, and depression. Today, I can accept my bad days for what they are. My current struggle is with wanting understanding from my spouse and other family members. My chronic pain can't be seen on the outside. Not one of them knows how much energy it takes to be somewhat normal, how I'm able to hide the pain to just have a taste of what life was like, or how it can then take days to recover. Coming from a family that values work—where no one has ever dealt with chronic pain—they cannot relate. So, now, on those bad days, I practice self-compassion to recover and heal; I extend the same compassion to my loved ones. I remember this is a challenging journey for them as well.

I try to do at least one kind act for someone whether texting, calling, emailing from bed, or just being an ear to listen. I'm fortunate that my kids have accepted what "Mom" can do now, which is listen, be present, and be there when they get home from school.

I refuse to lose hope on bad days because I know I'm still here for a reason. The catch is it's up to me to recognize that reason every single day.

In this moment, I will remember I am lovable not for what I do but for how I express love.

June 7

It's so interesting how each of us can feel so alone and be in such dark places at times. When I think no one can possibly understand what I feel, I attend a CPA meeting, and someone shares the same feelings I have. It's inspirational, comforting, and allows me to exhale.

I recently tried a new prescription and had bad mental and physical reactions. It took me to a dark place. I felt very confused and disoriented. This meant I couldn't participate in a family celebration; instead, my family had to take care of me. The guilt I felt was excruciating. I was angry at my Higher Power, thinking, "How much more do you want me to go through?" The medication finally cleared my system and my mind. My family and support team held me up through prayer and provided what I lacked. I am so fortunate.

My strength and hope come from my HP, which takes many forms. A beautiful picture can warm my heart. Often, a song will remind me to take things *One Day at a Time*, and the spring returns to my step. My CPA friends exemplify and inspire me to be raw and real. They lend me their strength, which allows me to exhale. When I share my experiences and see others experiencing inspiration and comfort as well, I know I am connecting with my HP.

In this moment, I will pause, take a deep breath in, exhale, and trust in CPA.

June 8

Two very important aspects of living with chronic illness and pain are surrender and acceptance. I find both are necessary to live with peace and serenity. I'm not sure I've considered the terms "surrender" and "acceptance" separately. I've often used them interchangeably.

Do I need to surrender to have acceptance? Do I need acceptance to surrender?

I see surrender as an action I need to take frequently. In Step One, when I accepted that I was powerless over pain/illness and my life had become unmanageable, I surrendered and began to relax a bit. I gave up the frenzied search for a solution that would give me back my former health. This resulted in less stress.

In Step Two, I came to believe and accept that there was something greater than my best efforts. I surrendered control. In Step Three, I surrendered my pain and illness after accepting that this was a chance for a more peaceful life. The combination of Steps One, Two, and Three led me to a place where I could begin to accept my life and surrender my obsession to control everything.

As time passed, it became more natural and less of an effort to surrender and accept the situations in my life. I remember in my first months in CPA, going through grief, anger, fear, panic, and confusion. Those feelings still appear from time to time. However, they are now the exceptions and not the rule. I am very grateful for this journey of surrender and acceptance and the peace it has brought me.

In this moment, I will remind myself that peace and serenity are possible through acceptance and surrender.

June 9

I have, at times, struggled with comparing myself to others in the fellowship. I'd think, "They are sicker than me," "I'm sicker than her," "They are smarter than me," "He lives in a better place," "Their recovery is stronger than mine," "My recovery is more spiritual than theirs," and so on. I could easily see the distortion and insanity in my thinking, but I couldn't stop.

My sponsor suggested that I actively begin to look for similarities rather than differences. While focusing at meetings, I heard the shared dilemmas of living with serious, chronic health issues: loss of friends, medications, mobility problems, isolation, lack of necessary help, pressing financial concerns, and more. Focusing on these similarities helped me identify with others and participate in this program. I was freed from the despair of comparing myself to others.

Then, one evening, during a meeting, I had a personal epiphany. I asked myself, "Who am I to know how troubled a person is over an issue just because I think it's trivial or catastrophic? Do I not have a few issues that I know others would think of as small things but are incredibly difficult for me?" My obsessive, negative reactions to life have been my problem, not the ways that I am different from everyone else. Working my CPA program is how I am finding relief.

In this moment, I will let go of comparing myself to others by focusing on my CPA program.

June 10

The most difficult moment for me when facing the healthcare system is when I need some new, different, or uncommon treatment, especially if it's a surgery. Due to past experiences, a form of PTSD kicks in. My heart beats rapidly, my gut clenches, my knees weaken, and the ghosts of past hospital experiences begin to pass through me. When this happens, I understand that, with PTSD, one does not so much expel these types of demons as one learns to accept them with care and awareness.

Instead of being thrown by these upheavals or blaming myself for not having gotten over them, I recognize them as the symptoms of another ongoing condition I have. It's predictable, just another condition, an outsize fear I live through at times. I must treat these symptoms with self-care and God-care. This helps me not run in desperate circles or force feelings to go away.

The best medicine for me is knowing I can talk to other CPA members. I am never judged as a whiner, overly invested in my ills, or someone who doesn't really want to let go. Fellow members lend me their understanding for as long as it takes. They gently remind me of my Higher Power until I slow, and that little empty hole I seem to carry brims again with love.

In this moment, I will remember I cannot force my pain away, but I can reach out for comfort and support.

June 11

I tend to discount gratitude as a tool for achieving serenity. It can sound so ordinary—everyone's always talking about a gratitude list. It sounds like a nice little task but not something that really accomplishes anything significant. I've been surprised to find my perceptions were not accurate.

Gratitude has become an important tool for me. Thinking about things I'm unhappy about—such as things I can no longer do because of my chronic pain and illness—brings me down. When that happens, I've found that thinking about the good things shifts my spirit and outlook on life.

My illness resulted in me having to leave my job, which made me sad. But the extra time I have now gives me opportunities to spend time reading, praying, and doing other things I love, which I didn't have time for while working full time. Whenever feelings of sadness or negativity are weighing me down, I can always find things to be grateful for. I pay attention to those things and actually list them. When I do, I always feel better. When I'm in pain and writing is nearly impossible, I still make an effort, and the results are inevitably positive. My pain somehow shifts. It's like my gratitude list becomes a kind of prayer.

Now, I encourage my sponsees to give gratitude a try, whether for the first time or using a new practice and see how it shifts them. It is one more tool we have available to enhance our well-being, and it's free!

In this moment, I will write down something I am grateful for and see if anything shifts in me.

June 12

One of the gifts CPA Step work has offered me is the renewal of my creativity. Chronic pain and illness robbed me of my adventurous, creative spirit. I was, and still am, mostly housebound and, more often than not, bedbound. My excitement for life vanished—it was just me and these four walls. I was losing my mind to boredom, depression, and a general sense of uselessness. My sponsor suggested I humbly request that my curiosity and courage be returned as part of my Step Seven work.

Higher Power sent me a surprising response via a rare trip to a thrift store. First, I found a beading kit for $2.99 and couldn't wait to get back into bed and begin investigating. Next, it was a bag of crochet needles and some yarn. And thanks to online tutorials, I am now an unstoppable crocheter. It provides immediate gratification as I see art develop by my own hands. Playing with color and textures literally brightens my day, and I find the repetitive hand motion to be downright meditative. Bed-crafting is one of my Step Eleven practices, as it reconnects me to the present moment and quiets my fearful mind.

These are all things I can do in bed! I even take my crochet supplies with me for hospital stays. I am grateful I discovered that although I usually cannot get out into life, I can bring creativity and play into my bedroom.

In this moment, I will creatively honor my Higher Power-given creativity in my most comfortable location.-

June 13

To me, surrender means letting go: letting go of results, letting go of outcomes, letting go of trying to figure it all out, etc. It's also the opposite of control. It is acceptance of what is and of human nature.

My debilitating obsession to control and direct my pain is part of what brought me to CPA. Sometimes, I struggle with the surrender suggested in the First Step because I want to make the healthiest, most proactive decisions regarding my health care. I find myself obsessing and second-guessing whether I made the right decision and ultimately blame myself for not being good enough or smart enough. Obsessing over these things only causes me more anxiety and pain. My pain feeds off of my anxiety, and my anxiety feeds off of my pain. Surrender means gently making a decision, letting go of the results, and trusting that my loving Higher Power will take care of the details.

When I try to manage the details of my life, I end up struggling against or outright fighting what I have no control over. And for me, that is the definition of insanity. Sometimes, surrender can mean asking for and accepting help so I can be restored to a state of clarity. Asking my Higher Power to guide me toward the next indicated action is the best example of surrender I know.

In this moment, I will surrender what I am trying to control to my Higher Power.

June 14

Looking at my history with chronic illness, I see just how early I was aware of something not being right with my health. I also see how early I started pushing myself to try and keep up with my peers and feel normal. Even after receiving a difficult diagnosis, I continued to try and work. The debilitation got worse, but I continued living on a push-and-crash cycle, behaving like most of my peers.

Before coming to CPA, I judged myself for all this pushing; I blamed myself for how sick I had become. I obsessed about whether or not I made my health worse and got mad at myself for possibly doing lasting damage to my body.

That being said, I am beginning to really believe the *Three C's* regarding my chronic illness: *I didn't cause it, I can't control it, and I can't cure it.*

CPA and the *Three C's* help me to forgive and have compassion for myself for staying in that push-and-crash cycle for so long. I know I did the best I could with the information I had at the time. Living with chronic pain and illness is hard enough,—why make it harder by holding myself responsible for causing it? Besides, I'm not that powerful.

With my Higher Power's guidance and the support of my CPA family, I now try to make more healthful decisions and let go of the outcomes, whatever actions I have taken. Along the way, I practice the *Three S's: self-care, self-acceptance, and self-love.*

In this moment, I will release the belief that I caused my conditions, that I can control them, or that I can cure them.

June 15

How could I feel joy while in pain? It seemed so mysterious at first. When I heard a CPA member crack some jokes shortly after having surgery and when I saw a friend meet a new diagnosis with a shrug and a smile, I was stunned.

Lightheartedness through difficult circumstances is modeled in CPA. I've heard people share how grateful they are for a simple pleasure in their day. As I went to more meetings, joy began to feel attainable again.

When joy is shared, it is multiplied. Sometimes, this can be a welcome shock that blows aside my despair. I also know that sorrow shared is sorrow lessened. I can set aside my pain and my negative emotions by sharing them with people who understand. Letting go of those emotions makes space for joy to flow in and splash back out into my days.

I recently had a joyful moment after surgery. I was sitting outside in the sun and felt a delightfully warm breeze tickle my hair. My best friend saw me smile and smiled back. Then we both chuckled. They asked, "Why are you smiling?" I said, "The spring air feels so nice rippling through my leg hair!" Our chuckles turned to joyful peals of laughter that reverberated when I told a CPA friend about this unexpected delight from my post-surgical hygiene challenge. Being present and accepting each moment as it comes helps me to be joyful, even when in pain.

In this moment, I will remember I can find joyous moments when I am in pain.

June 16

My new spouse and I received a letter notifying us that the interest rate on our mortgage payment was changing. We feared the worst, as published rates were considerably higher than we had been paying.

As a couple in long-term recovery, we had already decided to turn our marriage over to the care of a loving Higher Power, but I just wasn't able to do the same with our finances. After all, I was responsible for the original mortgage decision that allowed the rate to be changed at any time. After seven stressful days, I told my partner that I was willing to take responsibility for my risky decision; I was powerless over the past but now decided to turn my marriage and mortgage over to HP. I surrendered, accepted my powerlessness, came to believe HP could help and made a Third Step decision to turn it over. One week later, we received another letter informing us that, beyond all logic and reason, our new rate was ridiculously low, and our payment actually went down a lot.

My HP is way more powerful than percentage rates, bank balances, and financial institutions. My job is to get on board by surrendering all my affairs to the care of my loving Higher Power. When I do, things always turn out better than I could ever have imagined. My faith revitalizes when I trust that my HP does, indeed, have my back when I let It.

In this moment, I will come to believe my finances are in the loving care of my HP as I practice CPA principles in all my affairs.

June 17

My greatest fears fester in the unknown. Becoming severely debilitated took me on a journey into that dark, terrifying space. I don't know what condition my body will be in each morning if the next treatment or surgery will help or harm me, or how many years my body will be able to go on like this. I face unknowns every day.

When I first came to CPA, I wanted out of the unknown. I wanted answers. I was on a quest, desperately seeking new treatments and doctors with determination. Though my wife, son, and friends are wonderful, everything they suggested annoyed me. I felt completely alone.

Working the CPA Steps with my co-sponsors has given me the strength and courage to see what underlies my fear. My biggest fear is becoming a burden to my family or leaving my son without a mother too soon. Facing my mortality hasn't been an easy path, but I'm doing it. I can walk hand in hand with my fear now, making the most of each day I have with my family.

I used to believe fear and faith couldn't live together, but now I believe the essence of courage is the marriage of faith and fear. I have learned how to develop a close connection with my Higher Power, which helps me in those times of excruciating fear. Prayer and meditation are where I find comfort, and I often get immediate guidance as to how to face my present fear and make a new choice. I can't prevent death or stop any further debilitation from happening. But, with my CPA friends and close contact with my Higher Power, I can create the best today possible.

In this moment, I will live peacefully, joyfully, and comfortably with my fears.

June 18

In my recovery journey, I learned a lot about the importance of not revealing who and what was shared in the meetings—that we leave our professional titles at the door. It was drilled into me that we are simply members among members. I learned the importance of keeping our meetings safe so members can share intimately. As I grew in CPA, I realized there were even more types of anonymity supporting me.

One of the things I love about anonymity in CPA is that when we share our medical concerns, we share generally and leave the specifics to private conversations. I consider that to be very important because it reminds me that I am just a member among members. If I don't know another's specific diagnoses, I can't compare their severity to mine. Before CPA, I constantly compared myself to others. *To Compare Is To Despair* was a slogan I heard early on in CPA. Now, I am on the lookout for my comparative thoughts and remind myself that my chronic conditions and pain are no greater or less than another's. We all belong because we all suffer from the emotional and spiritual debilitation of living with chronic conditions, not because we suffer from "X," "Y," or "Z." Every one of us is simply a member among members.

In this moment, I will embrace anonymity as a spiritual principle that creates humility in recovery for me.

June 19

It's been very hard for me to have compassion toward my body since I had to stop working. So much of my identity was wrapped up in my work and the recognition I received in my community for my contributions. I was really angry at my body for failing me.

In CPA, I am learning to have compassion for whatever is going on with me, whether it's physical or mental distress. Working the Steps is helping me cleanse any remnants of self-loathing and self-doubt so I can love myself no matter what.

Early on in CPA, I joined a self-compassion workshop. I attended for a few months. Then, I began to be overwhelmed with all I was doing. I went to many meetings, did lots of service, worked the Steps, and started as a co-sponsor, meeting with a group to work the Steps together. I also had a lot of doctors' visits because, for the first time in a long while, I was advocating to get good health care for my pain and illnesses. One day, it occurred to me that the most self-compassionate thing I could do was drop out of the self-compassion workshop. I stopped going to as many meetings, knowing that my Higher Power was guiding me to the best outcome possible.

With almost two years in CPA, I have learned so much about self-compassion and am taking much better care of myself. I have pain, but I am not being a pain, as is often said in meetings. This now rings true for me.

In this moment, I will forgive myself for overdoing and remember that I am powerless over chronic pain and chronic illness.

June 20

I am having a moment of genuine suffering. I am angry. I am angry at my body, my doctors, my medications, and my gods. Thoughts like, "This isn't fair," and, "Why me?" play in an unstoppable loop. *That Which I Resist, Persists.* My body tenses, and my anxiety increases.

I breathe deeply and remember: in CPA, I have learned not to fear my anger but to honor it by allowing the angry energy to move through—and thereby out—of my being.

I also remember that others are experiencing the same kind of feeling. This brings me comfort—not that others are suffering but knowing I am not alone. Anyone experiencing these circumstances would probably be angry as well. It's not just me.

The CPA principles of self-acceptance, self-care, and self-love encourage me to ask, "What do I need in this moment of suffering?" "How can I be kind to myself in this very moment?" and "What wisdom is my anger trying to impart?" I can greet my anger as a self-loving emotion. It is a signpost that a self-care boundary has been crossed, indicating that self-love is possible for me. My anger actually demonstrates that the obtuse concept of self-love is actually present in me. With self-compassion and my Higher Power's guidance, I can arrive at a place of serenity, peace, and true self-acceptance.

In this moment, I will choose to gently and compassionately acknowledge my anger.

June 21

My first glimmer of hope in CPA came when I read the *Recipe for Recovery* preface: "Many of us with chronic pain and chronic illness have cognitive and energy deficits, and reading can be challenging and overwhelming. We have written this book to present the Twelve Steps in a way that is manageable for anyone, whatever their condition." Oh, thank heavens, they get me!

When I went to my first online CPA meeting, I saw folks in bed saying they hadn't showered in seven days. Again, "They get me!" runs through my head. I heard people laughing about crying and crying about laughing, and I'd think, "Wow, they really get me!" As I delved into the literature and heard that we suffer from the emotional and spiritual debilitation of living with chronic pain and chronic illness, "Glory be, I'm home!" was all I could think. I finally had hope because I was no longer alone. Others understood the suffering I was experiencing!

Before CPA, no one understood the impact my conditions were having on me; no matter how much they loved me and wanted to, they just couldn't get it. CPA gave me the priceless gift of identification. Its absence had been a huge part of my isolation, depression, and the mounting frustration of having to constantly explain or reassure others about my illnesses. CPA gets me. And I will be eternally grateful.

In this moment, I will celebrate having found Chronic Pain Anonymous.

June 22

There are days when I tell myself I should no longer be allowed to have negative feelings, but I've learned that this is just another way of avoiding acceptance. When fully accepting the positive and negative aspects of myself, I can continue to grow and become my better self.

Working the Steps brought up many different emotions and forced me to lay everything out on the table: the good, the bad, and the ugly. I quickly realized I'd been unhappy with myself for a long time. I had lost my identity. What I thought made me a helpful friend, hands-on parent, and joyful partner, what made me "me," was gone.

I haven't always lived a conventionally healthy lifestyle. For many years, I told myself, "Tomorrow will be the day I change; tomorrow, I will not be negative or hard on myself and others; tomorrow, I'll work on choosing more healthful habits." It had been my decision not to be physically active and to avoid engaging in social activities. Then, I was robbed of the choice to do so.

Now, my whole life revolves around my pain and disability. It's exhausting. The uncertainty of when, if, how, and why a flare comes keeps me from knowing when I'll be able to be present physically and mentally.

In Step One, I came to see that my unwillingness to fully accept the situation was holding me back. Experiencing true powerlessness has allowed me to surrender and pray for the willingness to change and become the best version of myself.

In this moment, I will lovingly honor all my feelings, whether they be the good, the bad, or the ugly.

June 23

I obsess about my level of suffering: am I a warrior, or am I a wimp? I like to think of myself as a warrior. Many days, I have to push through tasks when it would be easier to rest. Frequently, I feel overwhelmed by trying to be actively involved in the lives of my spouse and children.

But how can I know if I'm exaggerating how badly I feel? How can other folks with the same diagnosis or similar symptoms do tasks and activities that I can't? How can I do some tasks and activities that some other ill people can't? How can I know if my perception of level seven pain and fatigue is higher or lower than someone else's level seven? What if someone else uses stronger pain medication than I do? How can some folks still hold a job and others can't?

I am beginning to see this type of comparison as an obsession that doesn't get me anywhere. I need to listen to my body and trust what it tells me. If my body dictates that it needs to stop and rest, I need to pay attention. Allowing myself to trust my perception of my symptoms' severity and choosing self-care accordingly gives me peace.

Comparing myself to others and obsessing about their perception of me brings anxiety, guilt, and shame. Getting caught up in that obsession clouds my thinking. It hinders me from making clear choices and moving ahead with the next steps to fully live and enjoy my life.

In this moment, I will listen and take direction from my body, regardless of what others are doing.

June 24

My understanding of how to share my experience, strength, and hope dramatically changed for the better a few years ago.

Some of my recovery friends were at my house, chatting about this and that after our Step study meeting ended. One of my friends, a relative newcomer, urgently asked us for some feedback about a situation that had come up in her life. She was planning to reunite with someone she had a falling-out with and was unsure how to act at the approaching reunion. The woman to my right responded by asking for more information and details about the falling-out, which my friend gave. I felt emotional about my friend's plight; I tried to use words to support my friend with positive energy and love, but not much else. Last to chime in was the wise and reflective woman sitting to my left. She started off by saying, "I was once in a similar situation. I don't know if this applies to your case, but the way I handled it was by…"

My friend's gentle sharing of her experience, strength, and hope entered the conversation like sunlight through a window shade. Since then, I have kept in mind that my personal experiences are the most treasured assets I have to share with others. I also remember that this sharing is best kept for when the other party is actively seeking suggestions.

Unsolicited advice is something I find far less of in CPA than in the rest of my world, and I am grateful for that.

In this moment, I will remember my personal experiences are the most treasured assets I have to share with others.

June 25

For me, acceptance is seeing the reality of my life and not being at war with its circumstances. I don't get to that point right away. I need to go through anger, grief, forgiveness, guilt, sadness, and the humility of surrender before I become open to change.

I can't have acceptance until I have awareness.

Accepting reality does not mean I like that reality all of the time. I don't have to like it. I felt sad and disappointed; I needed to grieve. But surrendering liberated me from misery. I could experience serenity even before acceptance.

By sharing my recovery journey with my sponsor and fellow CPA members and turning to a Higher Power greater than myself, I can accept my circumstances just as they are. I can then make choices based on self-care and kindness as guided by my HP.

I can choose to rest because I can see the reality that sitting at the computer for two hours is too much and accept it. I can choose to take care of myself by sitting for shorter periods, using the computer in bed, or not using the computer for a day. I surrender to reality, my Higher Power's care and accept what is.

In this moment, I will creatively adapt my self-care needs.

June 26

The principle of anonymity brings about humility in me. Members don't compare pain or symptoms; no one gets a medal for dealing with the most amount of misery. I'm just part of the fellowship and am appreciated for showing up. I don't have to compare myself to anyone else. In CPA, I am an equal—not better or worse than others.

Anonymity makes CPA a safe place. No one will reveal I'm a member or anything I've shared in a meeting. This makes it possible for me to be honest about what I'm struggling with and how my program is helping. Since I'm not worried about being judged, the harsh voice in my head has been able to quiet down and no longer criticizes me for all I can't do. I feel safe knowing I will be heard and cared about just for being me.

I lost so much when I became ill, but in CPA, I am enough just as I am. Even on the days when I'm angry at the world and my body, I can speak of my experience and no one tries to fix me or tell me what I'm feeling is wrong. They listen with kindness. My sanity is returned simply by being heard and understood by others.

In CPA, anonymity ensures our unity. No one gets judged by external criteria. It doesn't matter what we do, or did, for a living, where we live, or how our body does or doesn't function. Our unity and focus on recovery is all that matters.

In this moment, I will be grateful for CPA's foundational spiritual principle, anonymity.

June 27

I find contact with other CPA members to be incredibly enriching, soothing, and inspiring. Whether through a phone call, in-person meeting, online group, or text, connecting with someone to express whatever I need to express has been critical to my recovery in this program.

There are times I may not feel like going to a meeting or taking time to respond to someone's message, but I'm almost always rewarded when I do. Sometimes, I'm able to help someone else just by being present and available, but it's also a gift to myself. Often, I say to them just what I need to hear. Someone else's experience may help me in that moment, or it may become part of my toolbox to use in the future. Being around others who are growing and learning about living a fulfilling life in spite of chronic pain and illness helps me cope, make decisions, and improve my attitude.

When a healthy person gives me advice or input, I'm much less likely to give it credence than the input that comes from my CPA friends who have lived my challenges and heartaches. They understand the difficulties of travel, struggles with self-value, and how seriously I have to think to make decisions about things that are simple to most people, like, "Should I try to bowl on the family outing?" or "Should I just stay home?" They understand the guilt I sometimes feel because, once again, I committed to do something but then had to back out. The comfort I receive from my CPA friends knows no equal, with the exception of the unconditional love of my Higher Power.

In this moment, I will remind myself of the great gift of fellowship. I will relax in its comfort and inspiration.

June 28

The *Three A's: Awareness, Acceptance, and Action* have profoundly changed my relationship with my pain and powerlessness.

Awareness was a challenge for many years; I fought through pain and disregarded my well-being. I was obsessed with controlling my symptoms but still pushed myself to carry out tasks. My body had to reach its limit before I became willing to look at myself. I saw that I was doing things to avoid situations I did not want to face. Today, awareness lovingly shapes how I live with pain and illness.

Acceptance has been key to dealing with circumstances that are beyond my control. Surrender, acceptance, and admitting powerlessness form a peaceful trilogy. Together, these words have come to mean tranquility and trust for me. Acceptance has opened up new opportunities. I'm now more open to seeking help. I've found support through various organizations and individuals who only appeared after I made myself vulnerable by sharing the true nature of my condition.

Action has become a gift instead of a burden. Because I have seen and accepted that my energy is limited, I budget it more sensibly. Sometimes I'm unable to participate in the way I would like. Other times, I'll still push myself to be able to participate, but I no longer feel like that is my only option or that I have to go over my limits. I've also learned to stay in regular contact with others in CPA, be open with my loved ones, and practice these principles in my daily life. All are actions that have supported my health and spiritual growth.

In this moment, I will practice loving Awareness of my capacities and limitations, Accept help where appropriate, and take gentle, respectful Actions where possible.

June 29

There are a couple of areas where my humility has deepened through my experiences in CPA. The first was status. When I began attending meetings, I noticed financial status, educational status, social status, etc. The differences between others and myself initially felt significant to me. As time went on, these perceived differences faded. It did not matter what type of work someone did or how much money they made. Nothing that might separate us really mattered at all. The common "chronic" bond we share made everything else unimportant and brought us together for mutual support.

Another area focused on comparing my pain/illness to others. At first, I thought, "Why me? Why did I have to have these problems?" It felt unfair, "Did I do something that caused this? Was I being punished for something?" Constant dwelling on this only caused me more unhappiness and anxiety. Then came the opposite thoughts, "I am so fortunate compared to some people in the world. Others have much worse problems than I have, so why should I need any understanding or help?" Again, I was focused on differences out of my control.

For me, the solution to all of this was learning to act with humility and accept where God has placed me in life. Humbly accepting where I am has been relaxing and allowed me not to waste energy dwelling on things that are not important.

In this moment, I will consider humility as one of the keys for my serenity.

June 30

My daily spiritual practices include morning and afternoon meditations, attending at least one meeting, and connecting with a fellow CPA member. I am mindful of my thoughts and emotions, and if needed, start my day over several times. If I have an emotion that needs expression, I do my best to acknowledge it, feel it, and let it pass in its time without clinging to it. I am also mindful to not act impulsively when emotions are intense.

This isn't always easy. Maintaining balance takes effort. I need to routinely adjust my thinking and attitude when I find myself holding on to or fighting challenging emotions. I am just beginning to make some real progress. I find naming my feelings out loud reduces their power and immediately shifts my attitude toward self-compassion. And when it comes to living with illness and pain, daily mental and spiritual mindfulness seems to ensure I have healthier relationships and more serenity.

Having daily practices makes adjusting my attitude more accessible. One new development for me is making my gratitude list. Instead of things to be grateful for, I now look for answers to the question, "What's right?" throughout the day. Actively looking for little mercies makes the entire day more pleasant. When I find myself in my old, typically unconscious, default mode of only seeing what's wrong, I pause, take a breath, and start my day once more on the lookout for blessings.

In this moment, I will remember that maintaining mental, emotional, and physical balance takes effort, but I am rewarded with greater serenity and joy.

July

July 1

As I learn to replace my old thoughts, habits, and behaviors with ones that serve me better, I have found that laughter nourishes my soul. When I feed my soul with happy behaviors, the pain fades into the background, and the tight grip it had a moment before loosens.

I choose laughter every day, no matter how bad I feel. It is good medicine for my soul, which has suffered from my physical pain. Through choosing this action and actively laughing every day, I can separate how my body feels from my inner self and feelings and heal from the disabling effects of chronic pain and illness.

One way I can accomplish this is by being present and engaged with all that is around me. Only then am I able to find joy in all the little things. Meditation, mindfulness techniques, and the Steps help me focus on the present instead of the past or future. CPA has helped me realize I have choices about how I think and what I focus on. My favorite tool in my recovery toolbox for getting back my smile and regaining some ease is laughter.

In this moment, I will choose joy. I will find at least one reason to laugh today, and when I do, I will allow myself the pleasure.

July 2

I had a pretty chaotic childhood, and for the most part, my escape came through hard work and self-determination. As life progressed, I could not shut off this go-go-go attitude and practice. It became addictive in its seductive illusion of control. Chronic illness and pain changed that, but not all at once. It took years for me to hit my bottom of total hopelessness. Then, as my CPA recovery started, I began to see my inability to rest—just rest.

If it weren't for my illness and pain, I would not have slowed down. Being present and learning to rest have, in fact, become the heart of my recovery. I meditate a lot—that is my full-time job now, training to be at rest in the world. I also paint in a slow process where the breath connects with each stroke, and everything is examined in eternal time. I wouldn't have this type of rest in my daily life without sickness. I believe that training to rest and paint in eternal time may be of far greater significance than anything I've done before.

I believe that when my body is sick and needing care, it's asking for rest. Because I live with chronic illness and pain, I must train my body to know what being at rest feels like so I can live, so I can listen. It is training and it's hard, but the payoff has been both rewarding and tremendously unique.

In this moment, I will make time to rest. I will allow myself to be still and know that by just being, I am enough.

July 3

When I found out about CPA, I doubted that it was what I was looking for because I was facing illness more than pain. Would these people understand me? Would I feel a sense of unity in CPA, the kind I'd known and relied upon in my other Twelve Step programs?

In phone meetings, I found myself stuck comparing everyone. Whenever I heard someone talk about driving or working, I thought, "They don't understand me; this isn't for me." But I always got a nugget of truth I could identify with, so I kept coming back.

In video meetings, I found my connection. I saw others in bed, on disability, not able to work, and sharing about the struggles of trying to take a shower. I saw others in pain, illness, or both laughing and courageously facing their struggles. I shed my cloak of comparison and picked up that old tool, looking for common ground.

Today, I feel united with all my CPA friends, those who go to work every day, and those who can barely get out of bed. Questioning my body, emotional pain, accepting my normal for today, and wondering how I'll get through the next twenty-four hours are the thoughts that bind me with others.

CPA is my place to lay it all on the line and be totally open. My family will never truly comprehend the absolute joy of successfully showering, but my CPA family celebrates with me each and every time! I found the unity and support I was seeking in CPA because I stuck around and didn't quit before my miracle happened, and I was able to connect with others who understand.

In this moment, I will listen in a CPA meeting for similarities, not differences, and keep coming back. I will trust there is something here for me.

July 4

Last week, our family went camping. We headed for a campground we'd never been to before and missed a turn, ending up on a dirt road. My wife knew of another campground farther along this road, so we decided to keep going and check it out. We traveled that dirt road for twelve miles, only to find the campground not to our liking. So, we turned around and bumped back over the road again. By the time we arrived at our original campground, my body was done being jostled around.

The next morning, my symptoms were worse. The camper bed was not overly comfortable; I didn't feel rested. I felt raw and became emotional over trivial things. I wished I didn't have to deal with anyone. It was also our wedding anniversary.

My wife and kids went for a walk to the nearby lake. After they were gone, I tried to figure out how to salvage the situation. I remembered a CPA tool: *STOP (Surrender, Time-out, Observe, Prioritize)*. I pulled up the CPA Toolbox brochure on my phone and thought about how I could use this slogan. I determined what would soothe my mind and body. I took pain pills, put on my sunglasses, did some slow breathing, observed the trees, heard the sound of the wind, and felt the warmth of the sun. I repeated relaxing words to myself, did some writing, and poked at the campfire. Later, I could walk down to the lake and play a game with our daughter.

Using *STOP* has helped me to clarify my out-of-control symptoms and feelings, become aware of my needs, and choose the next action to take.

In this moment, I will listen to my body. I will use the tools of CPA to give my mind, body, and spirit what they need.

July 5

My first couple of years in CPA were difficult. I was trying to understand the art of acceptance while, at the same time, attempting to find a way to fix my condition. I thought the two ideas were somewhat opposites. I couldn't accept my condition, especially when it flared, so I kept obsessively searching for a cure. I remember very difficult days when I would call my sponsor and ask how she coped. "*Just for Today*," was her reply. "I can do anything *Just for Today*." She told me she added it to the end of her sentences, whether they were thoughts of worry or thoughts of achievement, to remind her that everything, regardless of how it is judged, is *Just for Today*.

I tried it. "I fixed myself breakfast *Just for Today*." There was a freedom. I didn't have to worry anymore about all the days I couldn't make myself breakfast! I didn't have to worry about the days I was unable to manage my condition and found myself in the ER. I'd tell myself, "I am in the ER, *Just for Today*." A trip to the ER could easily turn into a week-long stay, but I would take each day one at a time.

Over time, this phrase helped me learn to stay in the present moment. It helped my brain slow down and sometimes even cease its incessant desire to look to the future for the worst or the past for all that I should have done. I've also realized that I can have acceptance and hope for change. Because I can now accept my condition *Just for Today*, I can also accept there is no cure *Just for Today*. Maybe tomorrow will be different.

In this moment, I will remember to take life One Day at a Time, knowing that my daily condition is fluid and This Too Shall Pass.

July 6

In Step Six, "we were entirely ready to have God remove all these defects of character." The word "entirely" has sometimes caused confusion. My own experience has made it clear that a quick temper, tendency to distrust, and stubborn insistence to control are not qualities that easily depart, despite my wish they'd go. To do that, I needed help.

As I accepted help and began the Steps, I had experiences that showed me I could change for the better. In Steps One, Two, and Three, I began the process of releasing my debilitating ideas. Humbled by emotional pain, I became willing to let go of the grandiosity and stubbornness that was keeping me from the road to freedom.

By listening at meetings to those who openly share the traits they've had to abandon to ease their self-inflicted suffering and reading stories of hope and recovery that tell of releasing emotional hindrances common to living with chronic conditions, I've become more open to change. Steps Four and Five brought into focus my specific and often deeply set, maladaptive personality snares which can hold me back.

When I understood how these traits have caused me more pain than I'm willing to accept, I became willing to have them removed. I chose to believe that my Higher Power could lead me toward this ideal.

The sheer amount of recovery I've seen in others from working the Steps gives me hope. It invited me to begin the lifelong journey of distancing myself from the critical voice in my mind. I can now listen when I'm told that I'm lovable, just as I am. I am willing.

In this moment, I will realize I am lovable just as I am.

July 7

Step Seven is about humility. In this Step, I am deepening my understanding that I am not in charge of anything—not even my defects of character.

At the end of our Serenity Prayer in CPA, we say, "Thy will, not mine, be done." That is the essence of Step Seven. I don't get to tell my Higher Power how and when to remove my defects or in what order. When I do Step Seven, my mess is out of my hands.

What a relief! With this Step, I am turning myself over to my HP and doing the next indicated action. With this shift in my attitude, there is greater ease and peace in my life.

But it isn't like I am sitting around doing nothing—I am actively learning and utilizing the tools of my program. Through these efforts, my HP removes my defects. Some of these actions are talking to my sponsor to help reason things out when problems arise, doing my Step Ten inventory, journaling, and getting help from special workers, such as a therapist.

A specific action I've taken in this Step is using a God box. I write down all of my defects and put them in the box; I can also write them down, go out to the desert, and do a ceremony to give them to my Higher Power. In all these actions, I am practicing humility and asking HP to do for me what I cannot do for myself.

In this moment, I will do the next right thing for my recovery. I will listen for Higher Power's guidance and trust in the process.

July 8

I came to CPA as a novice in Twelve Step programs. I had heard about the Twelve Steps before, but it seemed a bit too much like a cult to me.

I'd been struggling with chronic pain for about six months due to complications arising from an elective procedure. My emotional pain was as bad, if not worse than the physical pain. I saw CPA on a social media post and thought it was worth a shot. I felt I had nothing to lose and hopefully everything to gain.

I gingerly joined a CPA meeting online and was overwhelmed by the sheer friendliness of all those attending, who were clearly struggling with a variety of chronic conditions. I immediately felt at home and made some amazing connections with fellow members. It was a bit strange, but also comforting, that I was hanging out and making friends with people in different countries, of different ages, and from all walks of life—people I probably would never have encountered in any other situation.

In this moment, I will make an effort to connect with someone, remembering CPA's First Declaration, that "fellowship, rather than loneliness and isolation, will be present in our life."

July 9

I was fortunate to find a sponsor very early in CPA and started working the Steps right away, but I was not quite ready. I was balancing many commitments outside CPA; it felt like too much. Also, I felt a bit out of place. It was clear that many members had previous program experience and were quite comfortable talking about concepts like having a Higher Power and powerlessness. As much as I tried to incorporate program principles, it felt inauthentic. I found the statements in the literature promising a better life hard to believe. In short, I didn't have much faith in the program.

I took a hiatus from CPA. I was offered the opportunity to have a medical procedure that might significantly reduce my symptoms. It became all I could think about; I convinced myself it was my ticket to a pain-free life. I obsessed over it, reading about it online at every opportunity. I had the procedure, and it did not go as well as planned. So far, it has not really helped, though I still have hope.

I returned to CPA and my Step work. I have a fresher outlook now. I notice I am applying program principles more easily. I find the Serenity Prayer is an excellent tool. My physical pain continues, but my emotional response to it has significantly improved.

Applying the Twelve Steps to dealing with chronic pain is a work in progress for me, but I am learning to turn it over to my Higher Power. It is not easy, but I am clearly heading in the right direction.

In this moment, I will be comfortable moving at my own pace. I will do what feels right for me without judgment.

July 10

When faced with anything difficult in my life, habit sometimes causes me to become preoccupied with the worst possible outcome. In CPA, I'm working on a new habit instead, asking myself, "What's the best thing that could happen? What if it turns out really great?"

For instance, I needed to move. My health conditions mean I have very specific needs in a living situation. For example, I can't use stairs, share laundry facilities, or be too close to certain types of businesses whose practices could compromise my breathing issues. It was easy to imagine having difficulty finding a place I liked, could afford, and would meet my many physical and emotional needs.

I asked myself, "What's the best that could happen? What if it turned out really great?" Suppose a friend called from a seaside resort and said, "We're going on a very long trip. Could we pay you to stay at the mansion just so we know someone's there? You wouldn't have to do anything; just remind the swimming pool company to use only natural products while we're gone."

Is that what happened? No. But I did find an affordable place with no stairs, laundry machines inside each unit, and a suitable location. And I didn't have to drive myself crazy to get there!

In this moment, I will place trust in my Higher Power and turn over what is troubling me.

July 11

Sometimes, when I'm having trouble letting go of something, I imagine what it would be like if I could manage everything. What if I had that power? It's scary to think what I'd let loose upon the world. Just driving across town, in my mind, I've visited capital punishment for those who drove too slowly or cut me off. What if I had that power at hand? What if we all did?

I have often needed to review the many times in my life when things went their own way and a better scenario emerged—even better than what I tried so hard to arrange. And, as an adult, I manage, the best I can, those things that are within my sphere of influence.

I do this best when I invite a process of discernment into my decisions. I don't do it alone. I ask myself, my Higher Power, and trusted friends if what I'm currently doing is moving me toward more doubt, fear, and anger or toward greater faith, hope, and love.

In time, I'm usually shown what to do. Or, as I wait for direction, the innate way of things resolves the issue. When I don't seem to get an answer and a deadline draws near, I make the best decision I can with the imperfect data I have. I do my best to release the outcome, secure in the knowledge that I did what could be done at the time.

I've learned to say, "I've done what can be done about this today. God, remind me that this is no longer my job alone and that I was not constructed to manage all things perfectly. Direct my thinking to what you would have me do and be, for now." Then I breathe and repeat as needed.

In this moment, I will release my expectations regarding specific outcomes.

July 12

My sponsor kept telling me to practice self-care. It made sense, but I didn't have any idea what that would mean for me. She suggested I make a list of ways that I can provide myself with comfort.

That list has come in very handy. I've learned that self-care has many different aspects. When I practice it, I don't do so with any expectation of an outcome. It is just a way of loving myself.

When the pain is high, I can provide care for myself. I look at my list and see what appeals to me at that moment. Sometimes, it is a hot bath. Or it may be listening to a novel. I know it is an act of care and not an attempt to fix myself, make the pain go away, or feel better. Often, something positive does occur, but for me, that is not the intention of self-care.

In this moment, I will make time for self-care. I will ask my body what it needs and allow myself the time it takes to be met without feelings of shame or judgment.

July 13

When I *Act As If* I am not being inauthentic, I am building my self-esteem.

If I am with an intimate friend or person in CPA, I am open about what's going on with me and available to listen to them, too. I try to talk, as often as possible, about the solution. But the solution grows out of the problem, which sometimes I need to discuss, as do others. *Acting As If* is not about denial or blind optimism.

Sometimes, I may need to *Act As If* I am patient and kind with others in fellowship, even if I'm not feeling that way. Or I may choose not to give my romantic partner or close friend one more rundown on the sorry state of the nation of me, opting to spare them from feeling too much is put upon them. That sort of *Acting As If* feels okay within the larger context of healthy intimacy, probably because it is a choice. I know I can and do share more with my intimate friends over time.

Whether it's as mundane as *Acting As If* I want to take a shower when I'd rather not, or as complex as acting, to the best of my ability, as if I am a full-fledged member of CPA, working my program. *Acting As If* builds my self-esteem and keeps me safely on my given path.

In this moment, I will remember: Progress, Not Perfection. I can Act As If until I have made progress I am proud of.

July 14

Maintaining trust in HP when things look grim is the ultimate spiritual test.

When I feel my trust waning, it's usually a good time for me to deepen my faith. I practice surrendering more deeply than before, letting go of anything I expect, and being present in this moment. It's not easy to build trust or faith in HP, but it helps me.

I have an easier time with anger than trust. I know that HP can handle all of my anger. So, I pray for HP to help me find peace, trust, and accept the unacceptable. So far, HP has answered my prayers, usually in unexpected ways. So, I know HP is out there, and even if the world makes no sense to me, it does to my Higher Power.

In needlepoint, the front of the fabric can have an intricate, clear, and beautiful image, such as a bouquet of flowers. It all makes sense and is coherent. But if you look at the backside, it's a jumble of threads, knots, and colors. All I see is a senseless, tangled mess. But HP sees the order behind the mess—how that jumble of threads is actually a detailed pattern intended to form a clear image on the other side. This story helps me find perspective, strength, and trust.

In this moment, I will have faith. I will Let go and Let God, trusting that HP knows the whole picture.

July 15

This topic is rarely discussed in meetings, but it is an important part of my identity. Facing the changes in this area is part of accepting who I'm becoming and the reality of my situation.

Chronic pain and medical problems have all but robbed me of the desire to engage in sexual intercourse. What can I say regarding having sex? One thing is, "I'm done with that. I'm done with all of that."

For me, intimacy is what matters. My husband and I are intimate, as close as two committed beings can be. This includes spooning, a way that we can still be physically intimate. My husband holding me close to his body is such a comfort and reassurance that I matter to him, that I am still loved by him.

I know in my heart and mind that my husband still sees connecting sexually as important, even after we've been married for twenty-eight years. My husband has not had sexual relations with anyone else because of my infirmity. He has drawn himself even closer to me. We have become more emotionally intimate as well. He shared his fear that I may drop dead at any time because of age and illness. Now, we can face that fear together. We are bound—spiritually, mentally, and physically.

I thank God every day for my dear husband being so committed to our vows and to me. How lucky could a girl be to love more deeply than I could have imagined, even at this time in my life? Despite chronic pain and illness, intimacy continues to be a precious gift in my life with the love of my life.

In this moment, I will make time for intimacy.

July 16

I've always been a very impulsive person—take action and talk later. This skill served me well at times in my life. I wanted things fixed or done quickly. Patience was a foreign concept; I wasn't aware how problematic that could be.

Encountering chronic pain and chronic illness, I realized, after many failed attempts at fixing my situation, that it was only getting bigger the more I tried to fix it. A methodical approach was unknown to me.

In CPA, time and time again, fellow members would say, "Go slowly." I heard it so many times that finally I understood. I could see that my impulsivity made for some poor decisions. CPA is teaching me to slow down and talk things through before taking an action or to wait when no clear path or direction is visible or wise at this moment.

Now, I can see how I was trying to get to the finish line and put myself back to how I used to be. But in the process of being impulsive and rushing, I made many mistakes. I would jump ahead unprepared or put the cart before the horse in my approach. I learned by making these mistakes.

Through CPA, working with a sponsor, attending meetings, and listening, I cultivate patience and slow down the pace of my mind and life. I have been able, with the help of my Higher Power and fellow travelers, to make better decisions. Not all the time, of course: *Progress, Not Perfection*. I've found the more I slow down, the more is revealed to me—things I would probably have missed had I been racing ahead.

In this moment, I will remember to be patient with myself and others. I will stop rushing to get things done and just enjoy the process.

July 17

Sometimes, with chronic pain and illness, it feels like I keep bumping my head into a wall. Being referred to yet another specialist, filling another new prescription, and paying another hospital bill are parts of the game I play. I used to get angry over the rules of this seemingly unfair and endless chronic pain game.

CPA has shown me I am not a lone player in this game. The chronic illness playing field can look much the same for many of us. Certainly, the emotional aspects have commonalities. Working the Steps helped me to acknowledge and accept broader views of the ins and outs, challenges, and triumphs. In meetings and fellowship, I learn tactics from other members. My sponsor helps me recognize how I have grown and encourages me to listen to my Higher Power's coaching. A recent Fourth Step inventory helped me to release some of my resentment toward the medical system, my insurance provider, and a former doctor. This cleared the way for me to be more open-minded and trusting with my medical team.

I think that before CPA, I was a well-informed and pleasant patient. But inside, I felt bitter and helpless because the doctors and treatments hadn't helped much. Now, I see that even though my physical health has declined, I am getting better at playing this chronic pain game. I think this is largely due to acceptance, recognizing and releasing my expectations, and turning over outcomes. These tools were all learned in CPA and are developing with regular practice. I am grateful for my CPA teammates, who help me clear my head and my Higher Power, who guides me on my path.

In this moment, I will realize I don't have to do this alone.

July 18

For me, part of working Step Seven required humility—remembering that it's God, not me, who manages the process of removing defects.

I told one of my early sponsors I wanted to create a spreadsheet or a database to put all my character defects in so I could track them. He didn't think it was a useful recovery idea, but he finally said, "If you really want to do it, go ahead."

I got off the phone and turned on my computer. Immediately, smoke started coming out of it. I'd never experienced that before. I hurriedly pulled the plug. I opened the computer and looked inside. The power supply had been burned up.

I called my sponsor and told him what had happened. He laughed and said, "Well, it looks like your Higher Power didn't want you to do that project."

I said, "My power supply burned up. Now I'm really powerless!"

Since then, I haven't tried to track my character defects. Partly because I realized it's God's job and partly because I don't want another computer to burn up.

In this moment, I will be proud of my willingness to work the Steps. I have made progress in my recovery, and that deserves to be celebrated.

July 19

A list of what I am grateful for helps me become aware of the good that is already present. It helps me change my perspective. Rather than focusing on what I'm lacking and have lost, I acknowledge the abundance in my daily life.

This list can be done at any time during the day. I identify what I am grateful for in that moment. It can be short—three items for the day, or long—using each letter of the alphabet to name one thing I am grateful for. I also keep an ongoing list that I add to regularly. When I'm feeling down, like nothing in my life is good, I can refer to this list and be reminded of what I have to be grateful for. This helps to shift my attitude.

I love this tool because it can be done in almost any situation. Everyone can find what works best for them. It amazes me how quickly my perspective and mood can change by focusing on what I have to be grateful for in life.

In this moment, I will acknowledge what I am grateful for in this life.

July 20

I can set boundaries pretty well now because I didn't have much choice but to learn how. It started, though, with acceptance. For example, I must accept that I'm as ill as I am. I can't be up and about for more than four hours. To do so means resorting to medications that have side effects that are bad for me. Life has set this boundary for me, but I've come to accept it and respect it by acting within my limits. Acceptance, humility, and Step One are a big influence on how I see and use boundaries today.

I still have difficulty dealing with the storm of emotions that follow when I have to decline an activity, a meeting, or even a phone call with someone who does not grasp my condition. I suffer over their hurt feelings. My ego suffers, too. I don't want to be tagged a weakling, malingerer, victim, fool…all the things I would silently label others who seemed, to me, to be exaggerating their problems. Understanding and forgiving myself for my old, ignorant views helps me not blame others when I notice those ignorant reactions coming my way.

The sense of loss I feel when having to set boundaries troubles me, sometimes acutely. As my siblings and I age, I find it especially hard to say to myself, "Well, if they don't get it, then we probably will not know each other very well anymore." There's sadness at what seems to be an unkind obstacle that life is setting upon me.

What can I do? Live as I am. State the truth; don't rush to blame or defend. Don't judge, but ask God for acceptance of possible losses. Make sure my behavior is expressive of love, always hope for the best, and give it to God.

In this moment, I will ask my Higher Power for help with something I am having trouble accepting.

July 21

Years ago, when I was first ill and didn't have any program tools, if I woke in the morning feeling miserable, I gave up on the entire day. I falsely believed the whole day was shot and I was useless. I didn't understand that feeling awful at the moment was not predictive of how the rest of the day would unfold.

Once I found Twelve Step recovery and heard that I could start my day over at any time, I began to pay more attention. I realized that my symptoms waxed and waned throughout the day. I had been tossing out entire days because of how they started. I noticed that some days, I began feeling strong and able to function, but later in the day, I would go downhill. There was no predicting from one moment to the next how I would feel at any point in my day.

When I had a bad night, which was frequent, I would decide that the day ahead was lost, cancel my plans, and not do anything. But once I stopped writing a story in my mind about the future based only on the present moment, I found I was able to start my day over more easily. Sometimes, my symptoms didn't improve, but my attitude did, which made for a saner day.

I've had small moments of spiritual awakening. Coming to see that, at any point, I can start my day over was one of them. It's allowed me to be open to more possibilities than I'd believed existed.

In this moment, I will remember that I can restart my day at any time. How I feel changes throughout the day. I will not allow a negative feeling or situation to ruin the whole day.

July 22

The first part of Step Two, "Came to believe that a Power greater than ourselves[...]" unfolds differently for each of us. Some have had a Higher Power in our lives for a while, so this is relatively easy. Some have had no experience with a Higher Power, so it may take some thought to work this out.

If we don't believe in any kind of Higher Power, we can open ourselves and become willing to identify a Higher Power that we're comfortable with. Some of us use fellowship; others use nature. Some of us even create our own. Another way to work this Step is to *Act As If*. We *Act As If* we have a Higher Power and go forward, using this as a starting point. As time goes on, our own Higher Power naturally develops.

If we're already comfortable with a Higher Power, we can begin to use that Power specifically in the area of chronic pain and chronic illness. We can turn to our Higher Power for guidance as we work through the Steps.

The second half of this Step, "[...]a Power greater than ourselves could restore us to sanity," can bring us real relief. We now have a Power to turn to as we begin to believe that sanity can again be ours.

Sanity can mean having peace and acceptance of our circumstances. Things happen in our lives that are beyond our control, and our Higher Power can help us accept these things. We are not alone; we can trust and surrender. It may be easier for some than for others, but it's possible for all of us if we are willing. Working this Step brings us hope for a better life.

In this moment, I will take comfort in my growing faith.

July 23

I do best when I share with a peer or sponsor how I'm specifically applying the principles or speak freely about not actually applying them.

I may contact fellow members of CPA to vent. Surely, that is human and a necessary part of real fellowship. But I need to report on the solutions I'm engaging in and how they are working, as well as listen to fellow members' experience, strength, and hope.

Here's an example: I am going on about love and compassion, and my sponsor doesn't seem to be following very well because he interrupts to ask, "How is that playing out at home?"

I reply, "Oh, at home? Well, you know my wife has been unhappy of late."

He mentions that when his partner struggles, he consciously treats her with some of that love and compassion we'd been discussing. "Ah," I think, "yes, loving-kindness meditation or some love-thy-neighbor-prayers are in order."

But he just says, "I start by doing the dishes without being asked."

Without being asked? That kind of stuns me. I think, "Wouldn't that be some kind of grave tactical error, especially for someone as truly ill as myself?"

He goes on, "Talking about love is important, but doing the little things that are loving is often what helps."

"No kidding?" I say. I chew on this notion a bit and then say, "Alright, I get it. I gotta go. I have dishes to do."

In this moment, I will do things differently by taking one small action that is in alignment with my recovery.

July 24

Sometimes, a simple acronym like *HELP (Hungry, Exhausted, Lonely, Pain)* allows me to see when I am overdoing. It is in my nature to overdo. I was taught to be a "human doing," not a human being, so I keep pushing until I can do no more.

When I am *Hungry*, I get irritable. When I am *Exhausted*, I am irritable. When I'm *Lonely* and when my *Pain* flares, I am sad and irritable. The truth is, when these things happen, I need *HELP*. I can implement suggestions of appropriate reactions for each. I can try to rest, eat something, reach out, let someone know how I'm feeling, ask for and get support.

I think that I should be able to do it all myself, but the reality is that it's okay to reach out for help. All that stuff I learned when I was able-bodied is simply untrue. There are many people who are happy to help me, like all the folks in the CPA fellowship who listen when I reach out. There are meetings every day that I can pop in on to hear stories of hope. I am not alone any more thanks to CPA.

I learned in CPA, too, that *Rest is an Action*. It makes sense to include rest in my daily activities. On days when there just doesn't seem to be time, I take more time for rest the next day and try to practice good sleep care that night.

Paying attention to when I'm *Hungry, Exhausted, Lonely*, and in *Pain* reminds me to attend to my needs. It takes time to unlearn the behaviors I spent a lifetime using and replace them with the compassion and love my Higher Power promises me.

In this moment, I will take time to check in with myself.

July 25

Am I moving toward or away from being in a place of serenity? This question is a tool that helps me a lot. In any given situation, I ask myself if what I am thinking, feeling, or doing is moving me closer to a state of serenity or further away from it. This gauge helps me put the Serenity Prayer into action.

> *God, grant me the serenity*
> *to accept the things I cannot change,*
> *the courage to change the things I can,*
> *and the wisdom to know the difference.*
> *Thy will, not mine, be done.*

This question helps me shift my attitude. Last week, I was so angry; it seemed that all of the money, time, and energy I'd spent in physical therapy had done absolutely nothing to ease my pain—and may have made it worse. I was mad at myself for wasting money and mad at the therapist for possibly making my condition worse. When I posed the question, "Is being angry moving me toward or away from feeling serene?" I was able to step back and see how I was hurting myself by letting my anger take over. When I asked my Higher Power what would increase the serenity in my life, the next indicated action was clear. I made an appointment to speak to the therapist in his office rather than in the large communal therapy room to talk with him about my worries.

Applying this question and the Serenity Prayer to real situations helps me make sound decisions for my life and well-being.

In this moment, I will put the Serenity Prayer into action.

July 26

I am a new member. I mainly go to CPA's online meetings. I've been unable to commit to in-person meetings as I suffer from multiple chronic pain and illness issues. I'm unable to work outside my home and cannot leave my house in the evenings because my level of exhaustion is too tremendous. I feel isolated and alone. I am tired of repeating my story to every person I cancel plans with. So, I'm grateful for our online meetings!

I used to be like the Energizer Bunny! I just kept going and going. I owned four businesses and ran my home like a business. My three daughters wanted nothing, and I exercised religiously for at least an hour a day. Then, one day, it all came screeching to a halt. I was sitting at a stoplight, and a truck rear-ended me while going forty miles an hour. It left me with chronic conditions.

I fell into a deep depression. I was forced to rest. I had no idea how to do that. I had been working in some way, shape, or form since I was ten years old. I tried to use pain medications but was unable to do so without causing harm to myself and those I love. Now, I choose not to use them.

What works for me has been finally accepting my pain as part of my life. I am always going to have pain. It is part of me. I am a person with chronic pain who needs rest.

It's been a long process to accept the things I cannot change. I cannot change the pain and illness. But I can lead the best life possible, and that includes scheduling rest. It's usually just what I need.

In this moment, I will slow down and listen to my body.

July 27

Step Three is never completed; I do it every day, often many times throughout the day. Early in my recovery, it was not easy or familiar. I didn't see how turning over my will would help me. It wasn't a thought that would occur to me when I was struggling, and I really didn't understand my Higher Power. It took time to develop this new habit. First, I had to remember to do it, and then I needed to see a result to believe it was and will continue to be, worth doing.

When I first worked this Step, I was *Acting As If*. Over time, I experienced the power of this Step in my life and witnessed it work in the lives of my fellowship friends. Sometimes, I shift my attitude, feel relief, or get an answer quickly. Other times, it takes longer.

For example, I turned over the difficulties I was having with someone in my life and asked for guidance. The next day, I heard about a book that had exactly the information I needed to interact with the person in a new way. Another time, I left for a trip in great pain. I turned myself over to my HP, and I could manage the travel and truly enjoy my trip.

Long ago, someone in a meeting told me, "Don't quit five minutes before the miracle." Step Three is where I experienced miracles most often, from small to large. Things have happened in my life that once seemed impossible. So, I will continue to make the decision to turn over my will and my life.

In this moment, I will have faith in my Higher Power to do for me what I cannot do for myself.

July 28

Most often, doing the next indicated thing refers to the process of narrowing down my entire life and chronic illness to what needs attention right now.

What's indicated is governed by the next obvious need. Sometimes, my actual needs, or what needs to be addressed next, are not obvious, or choices of consequence. That's when I turn to my morning meditation practice, which suggests I ask my Higher Power for direction.

I find it helpful to ask, "Is this a Godly thought? If I were my loving parent, would I suggest this? If I go forward with this suggestion, is it my experience that it will lead to greater clarity, peace, or connection with my fellows?" My intuition, or sense of God's will for me, reliably increases as it is matched with a willingness to listen to any answer that might come, including the seemingly harder suggestions. I need to listen, reflect, possibly discuss, and then act and let go of the outcome, whatever it may be. Either way, the experience is helping me develop this way of communicating with God.

Knowing that when I am too spun up with worry to know what to do, I can pick up the simpler tasks of life as they present themselves. When informed by my understanding of God, seemingly more complicated actions become easier to handle.

In this moment, I will be still and ask my Higher Power for direction.

July 29

When I first came to CPA, I felt I had no experience, strength, or hope to share. I was a sponge, soaking up the stories of others who had what I wanted. They were laughing and happy. They thought life was worth living. I was depressed and hated my life.

Thank goodness for all the people who had messages of hope to share. They told me a better life was available—that I still had reasons to be hopeful, even if I couldn't envision life as anything other than miserable right now. They said to keep coming back, even if I struggle to see any changes or question if CPA is the right place for me. And until I could hold hope again myself, they would hold it for me. They shared how they were once miserable and in need of this same help and how working the program changed their lives. They talked about some of the tools that made a difference: prayer, a God box, the Steps, CPA literature, and living *One Day at a Time*. I was told that God did not make junk—that I was a precious child of God. All I had to do was the next indicated action.

Slowly, my attitude changed. My life changed. And then, one day, I finally felt like I had my own experience, strength, and hope to share. I'd not thought this possible; my friends in CPA knew better.

Today, I'm grateful for all I have endured because now I get to pass along my experience, strength, and hope as a lifeline to someone else. When I'm struggling and have lost my way, my Higher Power brings me to a CPA friend who shares their story, and I find my way back to a state of sanity once again.

In this moment, I will Act As If I have hope until I find it for myself.

July 30

I have suffered from chronic pain and illness for almost half of my life. Most of the symptoms are probably the result of childhood trauma and neglect. While I believe this was not God's original plan for me, this is what happened, and my God can work through it. I still oscillate between acceptance and anger when it comes to what they did or did not do to me that resulted in health problems and disability. This has been part of recognizing my powerlessness over past events and people. I'm very grateful I could surrender it all to my loving, caring Higher Power I call God.

While I cannot control the presence of my symptoms, I can still help manage them. I try to keep a balance between surrendering control and taking actions to manage my pain and illness. I take many pills a day, at specific intervals, with specific directions. This requires a lot of planning and intent focus. I also have a home exercise program, pain management therapies, appointments to schedule and keep, dependents' activities to manage, plus home and yard maintenance to somehow work into the plan. And a social life? There's not much time or energy for that.

I have no ultimate control, yet I am in control of how I plan and execute each task, react to each encounter, and approach every day. Thanks to CPA, I am practicing inviting God's presence into each action and moment of planning. I am learning to say, "Thy will be done, not mine," many times during the day. I am getting better and better at attaining this level of serenity.

I cannot control the outcomes, but I can take action.

In this moment, I will recognize that being powerless is not the same as being helpless.

July 31

One of my sponsors told me, "Your character defects are like a big, black beach umbrella. You built it back in childhood to protect you from the storms and have been holding it over you ever since. But now, the sun is shining." Steps Six and Seven are about folding that umbrella up, putting it away, and standing in the sunlight.

I suppose if I ever needed the old, big, black umbrella, I could pull it back out. Or maybe I can get a better one. That is to say, I can always go back to the old behaviors. But I can continue to develop some better responses, should any adverse situations come up. Like one of those umbrellas that folds into a small space, my new skills are easy to carry, pull out and use, and put away again.

That's the kind I carry and use now, thanks to the Steps, fellowship, and program of CPA.

In this moment, I will recognize and release my defects of character that no longer serve me or my Higher Power.

August

August 1

Who are the newcomers in CPA? There are some who have been in another Twelve Step fellowship and others who are brand new to Twelve Step recovery. Additionally, there are those like me who have been around CPA for a while, but a new diagnosis has turned their lives upside down, and they feel like they're back at Step One again.

When I first arrived, I was miserable and could take in very little information. However, I could receive members' kindness, acceptance, and willingness to reach out. The laughter and lightheartedness I saw attracted me. I thought, surely these people were not as sick as me—their lives were not as filled with suffering. I soon discovered that some had situations more challenging than mine, yet they were not unhappy like I was. I wanted what they had.

In time, I became familiar with slogans such as *Easy Does It*. I realized I didn't have to do everything all at once, including my CPA program. Eventually, I felt comfortable at meetings and even braved leading a meeting. A fellow CPA member sat next to me and coached me through it.

When someone identifies as a newcomer, I remember the discomfort I felt when I was one, too, and how the friendliness of other members eased my anxiety. I do my best to let newcomers know I am available; they are not alone. Today, I am so grateful to have found CPA because now I, too, can laugh—life is no longer so serious. I entered CPA with a heavy heart. So, these days, when genuinely able, I do my best to be a ray of hope and light for the newcomer.

In this moment, I will remember the feeling of belonging and make an effort to welcome and extend hope to the newcomer.

August 2

I first worked Step Four by reviewing my troublesome past. I asked myself, "Where was I to blame?" This was my first introduction to looking not at what needed changing in others but at my part in my difficulties.

In CPA, I found focusing on my role in the situation opened the doorway to emotional freedom. Looking at where I was wrong meant admitting not only moral wrongs but inaccuracies in my thinking and expectations, too. Some were less obvious than others, so I asked myself, "Where had I tried to skip over processing my feelings?" and "What traits have I developed because of chronic pain and illness that are harmful to myself or others?"

Before CPA, I'd become resentful. Then, I nurtured and fed those resentments. I was completely stuck in my grief, which led to a severe depression I believed was unavoidable, considering all I had experienced. At the time, I didn't believe resentment played any role because I didn't have any. Resentment wasn't my issue; pain and illness were; I was hurt.

My searching and fearless inventory revealed that while my life was dramatically different from that of my able-bodied friends, I blamed them for not understanding me. They did not intentionally harm me. I also discovered I believed others owed me complete understanding and help in all matters. Getting these ideas out on paper allowed me to see the fallacies in my thinking and, with God's help, to release them.

When I attend meetings, I listen for the principles I need to be reminded of instead of stewing in bitterness. This is just one concrete example of how, though I'd worked the Steps many times prior to CPA, I needed to work them here.

In this moment, I will adopt a teachable attitude.

August 3

Medications can be a difficult topic and one I tend to avoid addressing at a meeting. I avoid discussing them because what works for me might not be appropriate or acceptable to another member.

But that doesn't mean the topic doesn't come up at meetings and that I don't choose, from time to time, to share about medications in a general way. One of the most common things I share, especially if a newcomer is at the meeting, is a quick reminder that CPA has no opinion on medications. I might also share my gratitude that there are medications that help me. I have a sponsor I can speak with directly and specifically about my medications. Together we can address any concerns I may have about how they impact me or my program.

I can listen when others share their experience, strength, and hope regarding medication. I was at a meeting where a member shared a technique she used when deciding whether or not to take medications. I liked this approach and use it now when dealing with my own medication decisions.

I choose not to take medications during a meeting, even a business meeting, where others can see me. It is something I can do to avoid upsetting or triggering another member and to help keep the meetings a safe place for all CPA members.

In this moment, I will choose to have healthy, respectful boundaries when it comes to listening and sharing in CPA.

August 4

Because I live with chronic health conditions, bad days are inevitable. It is the nature of the beast to cycle through good and bad periods. For me, the intensity of time and misery varies. Because it's so unpredictable and uncontrollable, I would be a crazy person if I didn't have CPA to help me navigate through the rough waves.

In CPA, I've learned how to function even on bad days. As I type, I am in pain, and it's unpleasant. The pain rattles my brain, and it is hard to think clearly. Yet, because of my program, I've learned I really can think and function when I feel this uncomfortable. With the help of my sponsor, friends, and Higher Power, I discovered that I don't have to stop everything just because it is a medium-pain day. I accept this is my reality today and make the necessary adjustments, but I no longer believe the entire day is lost.

I also know that I need to pace myself. So, I'll take a break, get a heating pad out, and choose a relaxing activity or nap. Yes, I can function, but I know there are limits, and I care about myself, so I will respect those limits.

In this moment, I will change my level of activity to suit my current needs, with my Higher Power's help.

August 5

As I've continued to practice the CPA program, I've learned more about my fears. My fear inventories show that, beneath the surface, lie these false beliefs: I will be abandoned; I will not be okay; loving anything in life is dangerous because loss and grief are unbearable. Knowing these root fears has been helpful. It reminds me they are only old, destructive ideas and emotions trying to attach to my present circumstances.

I've also found it helpful to write or say aloud which fears have been activated and then refute them. It's as if I'm both the prosecuting and defending attorney. For example, when I feel alone or left out, I counter this feeling by telling myself, "You have not been abandoned unless you've abandoned yourself. Go ahead, throw yourself on the floor, wail, and express those feelings! But you are no longer a helpless child today. You have God, a program, fellowship…You'll be okay."

Ultimately, I've had to rely on God for support, but it's not always that easy. The Twelfth Step has been helping me to prepare for and receive touches of spiritual consolation. I've taken opportunities to try genuinely helping others struggling with their emotional and spiritual journeys. When I've done this, I've been reminded of all the positive things that have been part of my experience, and find that I, too, have been consoled. I can trust my Higher Power to direct my thinking, knowing I'm a member of this fellowship. Practicing the connective language of the heart has been my most powerful antidote to fear.

In this moment, I will face my fears and rely on my Higher Power to console me.

August 6

The slogan, *Progress, Not Perfection*, reminds me that when I am at my baseline and know what to expect from my body, I could probably do anything, but I can't do everything. That is progress. I look back at my too-busy life before chronic illness and realize that this type of perfection—the expectation that I can do everything—doesn't exist. Even if I run around doing stuff twenty-four hours a day, there will still be things left to do.

Life has certainly slowed down for me, and at last, thanks to CPA, I've become okay with that. This slogan reminds me that the progress I make on any day is enough. It also reminds me that there are many ways to measure progress. I am currently recovering from an acute illness, and my doctor's orders are to rest as much as possible. Again, thanks to CPA, I know that resting *is* doing something. Sharing in meetings nurtures me emotionally and spiritually. Beyond the act of participating, it also does something else. It helps me to keep making progress.

Before CPA, I could not grasp the concept of pacing myself. I could not stop hurrying. I was always crashing. I've learned a lot since my first meeting. By practicing new tools and actively making changes, I made a lot of progress in this area. Even though pacing is now second nature to me, I don't do it perfectly, and I don't have to because it's about *Progress, Not Perfection*.

Without a doubt, this slogan is in my recovery toolkit of things that make my life today easier, richer, and more comfortable on many different levels.

In this moment, I will seek to practice Progress, Not Perfection.

August 7

I came to CPA with decades of success applying other Twelve Step principles, slogans, and literature. I knew the Steps could restore me to sanity regarding my chronic pain and chronic illness, so I leapt into action. I then heard a few CPA slogans, like *Rest is an Action*, *Do Half of What I Think I Can*, and *Easy Does It*. Everything I heard was contrary to my action-driven thinking.

The "Set Aside Prayer," which asks me to "[…]set aside everything I think I know about[…]" the Twelve Steps, myself, and my Higher Power became my greatest friend. What if I don't act selfishly and become less self-centered? What if I am enough, have enough, I know enough, and I do enough? What if my Higher Power is tangibly caring and loving? What if self-acceptance, not self-recrimination, is the key? What if self-care isn't selfish? What if self-love is HP's will for me? What if…?

The "Set Aside Prayer" helped me adopt a newcomer's mindset and attitude. By becoming teachable and emptying my cup of what I thought I knew, space was made for my Deeper Voice to speak. Freedom from my distorted thinking allowed new experiences and ideas to take root. I realized I had an obsession to control by using the Tenth Step repeatedly. I also saw my self-loathing and self-abuse.

Now, I apply *Easy Does It* to my relationship with myself. I treat myself with compassion, tenderness, and patience. I am so grateful that CPA has given me the wisdom to know there are many things I don't know and the grace to trust my Deeper Self instead of my distorted thinking. Every day is an opportunity for new beginnings.

In this moment, I will set aside what I think I know about myself, others, and especially Higher Power.

August 8

Working Step Eight in CPA, I thought most of the harm I'd done was to myself. I'd slipped into self-pity and resentment over my predicaments, which seemed only natural. I came to realize that my attitude had caused harm, and I needed to make some amends,

As the main financial provider for my family, I worked while ill and, over time, slipped into a behavior pattern that shouted, sometimes literally, "I am the sick one. You are able-bodied. Handle your own problems! I'm killing myself to support us." I would rage when I felt overwhelmed and thought little of pouring out my desperation on my partner, unaware of how this left her feeling weighed down and alone.

Listening to my sponsor and many shares in CPA helped me realize that "just because I am in pain doesn't mean I have to be a pain," as stated in the "One Day At A Time" reading. It dawned on me that I was not a pain to friends and coworkers, while I completely ignored and stopped caring about how I was behaving at home.

I became willing to make amends, but first, I had to analyze my motives. So I asked myself, "Am I really looking for an opportunity to share my newfound hope and the changes I'm making, or to relieve my guilt? Could I have done things differently at the time, or was my past behavior the best I could do given the circumstances? Am I looking to be excused, or am I willing to listen and take suggestions on how to make things right?'

It was the best I could do. But it was still harmful, and it remained my responsibility to make amends, as best I could. I needed to be willing to go on record about my part in things and listen to what she had to say in response.

In this moment, I will remember "just because I am in pain, doesn't mean I have to be a pain," to others.

August 9

I'm so grateful to the Twelve Traditions for guidance when challenges arise in my meeting(s). A perfect example of this was when we read a book that wasn't Conference Approved Literature in our weekly meeting. This book provided guidance through the Steps for our fellowship before we had our Step book, *Recipe for Recovery*. Many of us didn't realize that the writer of the book, who had chronic illness, catered the language to people with a similar experience. Our friends with chronic pain, without an illness diagnosis, began to feel overlooked. Of course, we had no intention of doing this when we decided to read this book.

The unfortunate problem grew. Another meeting heard we were reading this book and decided to do the same. Now, there were two meetings where some of our members felt excluded. Tradition Four guides us to acknowledge that our choices can affect more than just our small meeting.

This controversy over the book even sparked a few committee meetings where a proposal was written and brought to the World Service Conference. This occurred to protect the message of CPA in every meeting. I'd never want a fellow member to feel left out.

Just like we all contribute whatever we can financially and energetically for our Seventh Tradition so that our meetings and CPA as a whole can continue to function, we also contribute by adhering to all the Traditions. We do this to safeguard the future of CPA so that all who want to find us have an "us" to find.

In this moment, I will turn to the Twelve Traditions for guidance in my relationships.

August 10

For many years, I've had my diagnosis. I tried the medical fixes, accepted what I had to live with, and grieved my losses. I knew my limitations, accepted them, and adapted. The period of constancy that ensued, though extremely difficult, had a certainty about it. I didn't like it, but I knew what to expect, and I could often turn my attention away from my illness.

I came to CPA after new symptoms arose. I felt off-center a lot of the time. I was cycling through fear of debilitation, mustering energy, bouncing between accepting and obsessively managing my health and then surrendering it again.

One concept that helped me when new symptoms arose was that I could work toward a diagnosis and solution slowly, *One Day at a Time*. Very often, the solution has been finding a way to be in the world with the new symptom, using some adaptation found with time and experience as the days are lived.

I've also learned it's important that I do not catastrophize when something new occurs. Either I've found a way to improve, or I haven't, but each time, I discover that somehow my life has been okay—it is okay. And isn't that what causes my terror when a new symptom hits? "Oh God, here it is: the thing that's going to make life intolerable," would get stuck in my head, but I can also recall saying to God, in periods of relief, "Thank you, I did not go under. I'm okay now."

In this moment, I will believe that I am okay.

August 11

Before CPA, I tried to use another Twelve Step program to help me with chronic illness. It was difficult, mostly doing it alone, but I had some program time under my belt prior to falling ill, and I used everything I could. I was grieving my losses, coming to accept my conditions, and learning to adapt and live authentically.

But finally, I was in so much physical and emotional pain that, one day, I admitted that my relationship with God, without the support of others, was no longer working. I did not want to believe this because I didn't think anything could be done about it. I asked my Higher Power for people with whom I could feel a kinship about chronic pain and illness—people with whom I could recover my spirit.

I decided to look for one more self-help book, which circuitously led me to CPA. I phoned into a meeting that very evening. I talked late into the night with a member, taking my first Step One, Two, and Three, as well as a small but vital stab at Four and Five. That long day was my first spiritual awakening in CPA; it was profound and unforgettable.

My spirit's greatest awakening was simply this: I am ill, but it's the only life I have, so I want to try to love it. Most recently, I have begun to suspect that learning to love ever more effectively may be the core task of life. I've also realized it is often the sharp emotional feelings, those little, insistent thorns of light, that spur me on toward the great meaning life has to offer.

In this moment, I will seek to be more loving.

August 12

Setting appropriate boundaries is a helpful way for me to manage the stress that accompanies my chronic pain and illness. When I am exhausted and in a lot of pain, my response to a stressful situation is often different than if I am well-rested, fresh from a CPA meeting, or feeling spiritually connected. This is where boundaries come into play. Realistic boundaries limit the stressors I am exposed to, and I can then creatively implement more resources and program tools to manage the remaining stressors.

When I was employed full-time and trying, unsuccessfully, to manage my pain and illness, I frequently made phone calls to doctors' offices and insurance providers while commuting to work. There were a few spots near my office where cell phone coverage was lacking. I would get so frustrated by the time constraint I had placed on myself and my inability to take notes while driving. I've found I have much more effective conversations when I am comfortably lying in my bed with my computer spreadsheet in front of me to take notes. I don't worry about dropped calls. This is so much less stressful for me!

Many of my boundaries were unhealthy and harmful to my condition. I could not see this until I listened and learned from others in CPA. My condition is unpredictable. Using *One Day at a Time* helps me develop more reasonable boundaries. As a result, my stress is much lower, which helps my pain levels.

In this moment, I will look for boundaries to implement that may help reduce my stress.

August 13

Rest is part of a balanced, healthy lifestyle. I often took my body to extremes, disregarding its basic needs, which may have contributed to my now being in pain and having chronic illness.

For me, learning to be still was quite challenging, especially in the beginning. It went against my basic nature and compulsive need to be productive. I needed to learn that my worth is not equal to my accomplishments. I am so much more than what I do.

The essence of who I am exists in just being uniquely myself and sharing my experience with others. This is my purpose, and I am more than qualified. Yes, this version of myself is much more sedentary than I once was. But in CPA, we find creative ways of being rather than always going and doing.

In this moment, I will seek to be uniquely myself.

August 14

Step Nine has been revealing many things I don't want to acknowledge. It feels difficult to let go of my old ways and try new ones. Instead of going down old roads of panic and depression, I have sought help by coming to CPA. The fact that I continue to do so is part of making Step Nine amends to myself. Sometimes, I've read just one paragraph of another person's story, and my recovery has been renewed.

For most of my life, I had a close relationship with my Higher Power. After I became sick, disabled, and wracked with constant pain, I gave up completely on God. Without that connection, I let out my anger more often and more intensely. Who cared anyway? And truthfully, I judged and punished myself more harshly than others. It was painful to discover the choices I originally made to protect myself resulted in isolation and created a self-fulfilling prophecy.

I'm writing from my bottom. I don't think I have any cool philosophy or teaching to impart, but I can say that instead of going deeper into my loneliness and isolation, this time, I am sharing.

Others' recovery stories really challenged my belief that I was alone in this drama. I constantly asked myself, "How could anyone understand the suffering I experience every day?" I can recognize how making changes from the same logic and habits that I'm seeking to change from probably won't be helpful. That's why I need others and this fellowship. I've forgotten this over and over again, and each time, I went back to isolating myself and having more difficulty with my illness. By prioritizing my recovery, I've been able to find a place, even in these darker moments, to keep working on myself and moving forward.

In this moment, I will keep moving forward so I do not become stuck in misery.

August 15

I sponsor others, as my sponsors have sponsored me and with my Higher Power's guidance over the relationship I have with my sponsee. Over and over again, I am amazed by how the Steps can work without rigid rules or formats. Step work can be expressed through poetry and artwork, writing in journals, sharing it aloud, or taking part in ceremonies, such as one for Step Six, where we burn a list of things we no longer require in our lives. We talk, cry, identify, share, read, pray, answer questions, etc.

I work with people who cannot write, and they, too, can work the Steps. One sponsee recited their entire Fifth Step aloud after becoming clearly aware of each item in their Fourth Step. I believe that where there is willingness, there is always a way if we are open to finding it.

Then comes the day a sponsee asks me if they can be a sponsor. They are usually concerned because someone has asked them to do so, and in turn, they ask if they are ready. We return to Step Twelve in *Recipe for Recovery* and confirm that, yes, the time has come. I am still here for them when questions arise. We can find solutions by praying and talking things through together.

Those I journey with through the Steps change, and our relationship changes as well. Someone I barely know becomes a close friend, confidant, and someone I can turn to at any time. It's a beautiful thing to experience.

For me, the miracles of working this program just keep happening. I truly believe the only way for them to stop would be for me to stop sharing and working with others, one-on-one, heart-to-heart, with Higher Power at the helm.

In this moment, I will trust the sponsorship process and appreciate its rich rewards.

August 16

I used to think about all that was taken from me by chronic illness. But by working the Steps in CPA, I was blessed to be able to look at my life with a healthier perspective. Almost everything I ever cared about, knew, or believed has changed. My life is now lived and loved on at a level I never knew existed.

I always knew the loving relationship I have with my wife was possible, but I didn't think I would find it for myself in this lifetime. I'm happy to say that at the tender age of fifty-something, I actually found that person—that relationship. I'd been diagnosed with a chronic illness years before, but my wife always saw me as whole. Chronic illness was merely part of the details, in her opinion. She helped me to acknowledge this. CPA helps me continue to accept it in all aspects of my life.

After a few years of marriage, my wife was diagnosed with a chronic illness. She's not a member of CPA but says she benefits from it. Chronic pain and chronic illness were, and still are, hard on our marriage. With both of us being sick, well, it's kind of a circus at times. It can feel like we're a house of cards, each leaning on the other, holding one another up. We take turns being the cared-for or the caregiver.

Most of our decisions are now made around our medical conditions. We deal with it all using humor, honesty and sometimes just expressing our frustrations. Through it all, we know how blessed we are, and we're grateful most of the time.

In this moment, I will be supportive of the people in my life regardless of their condition.

August 17

CPA helped me learn how to respect myself by setting boundaries, and I am still learning.

I do this by saying no to negative self-talk and harsh judgment of myself and others, stopping to breathe in the moment, and pausing to connect to my Source. I say no to autopilot, automatic reactions, and lashing out. Instead, I circle inward to calmly appreciate what there is to let go of and learn from at the moment.

I spend time feeling appreciation for the blessings in my life. And sometimes, I need to rest and not feel appreciation for anything other than the sensation of the bedsheets against my skin. Healthy boundaries mean I trust myself and my judgment and believe I know what I need and how to express it. Ideally, this expression comes with kindness and compassion. But if that doesn't immediately happen, I can always choose other words or ideas and try again later.

In CPA, I am becoming better at meeting my own needs. I have accepted that I cannot control unforeseen circumstances or anyone else's actions or tone of voice. I have to turn over that old habitual desire to control. Reaching out to my Source, appreciating nature, and being connected to love all help. So does sharing in the collective wisdom of my sponsor and the CPA community.

In this moment, I will practice boundaries. I am modeling for myself and others the importance of treating myself with loving respect.

August 18

When I first came to CPA, I was dealing with the utter disappointment and despair of having to stop my art career mid-flight. As I got sicker and sicker, I could spend less and less time in the studio. Eventually, I had to give up my space altogether. I couldn't even pick up a paintbrush—my body rejected the motion. I was heartbroken.

My negative attitude almost kept me from staying in CPA. I heard a share about how someone was trying to adapt to their new life and picked up painting to pass the time and express their creativity. I used this story as a way to separate myself from others. "I knew it. They don't understand! They can still paint!" I thought. Jealousy took over; I found it hard to relate. I was busy comparing myself right out the door.

I'm so glad I stayed. When I could look past the details of what a person was sharing, there were always things I could relate to. The next person sharing the joy they found with paint could be an inspiration for me to find the joys that my body will allow. I talked to others and realized I needed to work through my grief about my career. The Steps helped me do just that.

I have begun learning how to make art digitally. I'm an artist, whether I am painting, sculpting, or creating artwork only in my head. My illness and my pain can never take that identity away from me.

I'm learning in CPA how to focus on just being who I am now and not on what I can do or produce. I am learning how to be the best version of myself. All of me is of value, making art or not. Even with my limitations, I can find joy.

In this moment, I will look for the nuggets of joy that surround me.

August 19

I became ill in my early thirties. At that age, I expected to have a strong, capable body. Instead, I found myself living in the body of an eighty-year-old.

Before CPA, I was at war with my body. It did not do what I wanted. It failed me. It was not like other people's bodies. It made me different and unable to keep up with my friends. I was ashamed of it. I didn't want anyone to know how poorly it functioned. I felt guilty, believing this was all my fault. This negative thinking led to depression and despair. There was no escape from my body and all the ways it was unreliable. I didn't see how I could go on living like this.

Through working the Steps and going to meetings, my attitude eventually changed. I was able to see the ways my thinking, not my body, caused me so much misery. I learned that my illness was not my fault; I am not defective. Though there were many things my body could not do, once I opened to a wider perspective, I saw all that it could.

I replaced the rage and attacks toward myself with compassion. I learned that being gentle with myself resulted in feeling more sane. And that everything still gets done without needing to push myself.

The more I turned myself and my body over to my Higher Power, the more I discovered what was possible. Over the years, I saw that my body kept changing. Some things got better, some things got worse, and some new things showed up. So, I also learned that *This Too Shall Pass.*

In this moment, I will be grateful to continue learning, with my friends in CPA, how to love my body and love myself.

August 20

Compassion, for me, is to care about someone's suffering and want to alleviate it. I'm quite good at doing this for other people. However, in CPA, I've learned that I am worthy of treating myself with compassion.

This was a new concept for me. Mostly, what I offered myself was a harsh tone of voice, demands for improvement, and belittlement. I would accuse myself of being lazy, being an idler, and not trying hard enough. I never considered having compassion for the way I was suffering and how hard it was to be so dependent on others.

Over time, I have learned how to stop and notice when I am having a difficult time and to remember that berating myself will not be helpful. Recently, I became bedridden for a few weeks and unable to walk without assistance. I didn't blame myself for making this happen, as I have in the past. I treated myself like a dear friend or loved one. "Oh, sweetie," I'd tell myself, "it's so hard to lose your ability to function. This is not easy, and it's not fun. I am so sorry it's such a hard day." Then, as part of shifting my attitude, I accepted that I was staying in bed until this passed. There was no need to do anything other than rest. This was self-compassion in action.

Deciding to practice self-compassion was part of the amends I made to myself in Step Nine. This is ongoing—a living amends that I continue to make as I live with an unpredictable health condition. So today, I use whatever energy I have available to practice gentleness, tenderness, and warmth toward myself and others.

In this moment, I will practice self-compassion, and when I falter, I shall recognize it and try again, seeking Progress, Not Perfection.

August 21

I used to think that, as an adult, I should be brave, not scared, when I go for a procedure or see a doctor about my health concerns. In CPA, I've learned that all my feelings are legitimate. When I feel like a small, scared child, I don't have to pretend that I feel otherwise.

It takes courage to go see a new doctor, go to a facility for a procedure, hear a new diagnosis, or receive test results. I needed to recognize that I can be afraid and still find courage when I'm in a medical setting.

Turning to other people helps me feel more courageous. I reach out and ask others for support. This reminds me that it's okay to feel scared; my courage will be there when I need it. I'll be okay and get through whatever is scaring me.

Courage means feeling afraid of something and doing it anyway. It's a great concept but hard to do. How can I take care of myself so I feel safe enough to do it anyway? I can bring a touchstone—an item that brings me comfort—into a doctor's office or bring a supportive friend. I can use prayer or meditation as I prepare. I can also plan a reward for myself as something to look forward to.

I am an adult, and I'm human. My mind and body experience fear; courage does not always come easily. Thanks to CPA, I've given myself permission to have a full range of feelings. I let go of the shame I felt when I'd cry or shake in fear. Being authentically me is the most courageous thing I can do.

In this moment, I will face fear, be it small or large, using the recovery tools I've learned in CPA.

August 22

For me, anonymity can mean keeping my mouth shut when I otherwise might speak. I'm usually the talker in a group. We are often taught in recovery programs that it can be helpful to talk to our sponsors, speak up at meetings, and share in fellowship. I was also taught it was necessary to speak truthfully in order to live truthfully.

I come from a family where no one's space is held sacred. In fact, knowing everybody else's business is a competition. I happily took part in such conversations. Thanks to recovery, today, I choose not to do that, not in my home, with my family, or in CPA.

Breaking anonymity in the form of gossip is cruel and destroys relationships. I value the sacred space I'm discovering in CPA. We don't gossip here. We show love for each other through respect, trust, and building a safe community for all to share.

On a spiritual level, anonymity also brings me closer to God. Learning to restrain my negative thoughts about others is teaching me to refrain from criticizing myself, too. Only God hears those thoughts, and with the help of a sponsor and friends, I can learn to speak respectfully and kindly of others and myself in every situation.

There is no need for me to reveal anything spoken in confidence. That only strokes my ego and blocks me from the joy, happiness, and freedom available in the sacred and trusted space we hold for each other in CPA.

In this moment, I will respect myself and others by keeping the confidences shared with me.

August 23

When I am not feeling well, I get grouchy and irritable. My best self is not in charge. When my energy is low, my ability to think is compromised, I'm angry at the world, and it is hard to be a nice person.

The "One Day At A Time" bookmark states, "Just because I am in pain doesn't mean I have to be a pain." This has been helpful. I learned, the hard way, that people—even those who love me—don't want to be bossed around or yelled at when they are doing their best to help. When I feel decent and am in my right mind, it is easier for me to treat others with gratitude and kindness. But when intense symptoms show up, I can forget.

I've not found one perfect way to deal with my inability to be decent at my lowest moments, but there are some ways that help me regain my sanity. First, I recognize that my inner critic is coming out and that I may not have the inner strength to be nice. At those times, I do my best to separate myself from others when possible. I call my sponsor and say all the negative thoughts in my mind so the energy is released. Often, once that happens, I can adjust my attitude.

There are times I make a mess of things despite all my best efforts, and need to make amends. This means accepting myself as an imperfect being. It calls for compassion for the person I harmed and willingness to repair the pain I have caused. Then I let it go and work at doing better next time.

In this moment, I will treat others with kindness. If I harm others, I shall make amends.

August 24

Today, practicing self-compassion meant sleeping until 3:00 p.m. after a rough night of not sleeping. I was awake every hour on the hour until I heard the creak of my neighbor's pipes as she began her day. Then, I slept—maybe from the comfort of knowing I was not alone. This was clearly what my body needed and a gift I could receive without shame, guilt, or remorse.

I've often had difficulty falling asleep, staying asleep, and, subsequently, waking up. In the past, I've sought the help of four specialists, each with their own unique sleep study protocols and devices. I tried every medication prescribed. I tried forcing myself to fall asleep at sunset and get up at sunrise. None of these brought me relief.

In CPA, I found the kindness to forgive myself for sleeping in the day or staying up all night. I developed a nighttime ritual that works for me most of the time. With twelve hours in bed, I get nine nonconsecutive hours of sleep. On nights I can't sleep at all, I often listen to audiobooks. Even if I only sleep a few minutes here and there, at least I learn something from having the audio on repeat. Most importantly, I forgive myself for not sleeping.

With the self-compassion I've learned in CPA, I let my body tell me what it needs. Sometimes, that's a cool day sleeping in the comfort of my soft sheets and cozy blankets.

In this moment, I will appreciate the rest and sleep I have been given.

August 25

Fear is my primary character defect that drives most all the others. When I was very young, I learned (incorrectly) that I was the only one I could trust. Any security to be had in this world, I would have to provide. I became an excellent planner. I possessed responsibility and prudence. I also lived in fear, and honestly, I still live with it.

With that background and the financial costs of living with chronic pain and illness, it's understandable that I would find finances especially scary. My fear of financial insecurity goes through a cycle. For example, my spouse is showing signs of memory loss; I don't see our savings being able to meet their long-term care needs. I cannot be indifferent to the fate of those I love. Yet, would I have chosen to miss love to avoid the dread I have now? No.

So, what do I do when I'm afraid about money issues? I remind myself how irrational it is to think I could ever have enough cash to cover every bill possible in the future or that doing so in the way I imagine would be the best solution. I would still imagine horrific outcomes for my partner, no matter how much money we have.

I can no more be my spouse's Higher Power, than I can be my own. I must return again and again to the God of my understanding to gain a more balanced and hopeful perspective, the ability to let go, surrender and know the emotional and spiritual consolation that always follows.

In this moment, I will turn to my Higher Power when my brain is concocting negativity.

August 26

When I first became sick, I would compare living in my body to having an abusive partner. It was unpredictable, caused physical and emotional pain, and ignored my protests to stop hurting me. Looking at my body this way was triggering; it brought up a history I thought I had worked through.

While working Step One, I discovered that, although my body is in pain, causing difficult circumstances, it was also doing a lot of things correctly. It was digesting food, getting fuel, pumping blood, breathing in and out, and absorbing oxygen. My body was doing all these things without any direction from me. It was a softer approach—to see my body as working for me rather than as the enemy.

I still wake up not knowing how I will feel. I can't predict what my day will look like. My body, pain, and illness can all shift on a dime. I can quickly go from feeling okay to wretched. Even with the unpredictable nature of living with chronic conditions, I now feel like my body is on my side. I see it as a strong warrior withstanding the most difficult of circumstances. I'm proud of my body for being so determined to keep me alive.

One tool I have developed to keep my head in the most helpful space is listening to my body's messages and warning signs. I pause and ask several times throughout the day, "How am I feeling, and what do I need?" Along with asking Higher Power for guidance, I can get through those really tough days, knowing that this too shall pass.

In this moment, I will pay attention to the messages I am being given from my body.

August 27

Over time, my description of God has evolved. When I arrived at CPA, God was a "Good Orderly Direction" and the "Great Out Doors."

Several years ago, a surgical procedure went awry, leaving me in pain for the rest of my life. I was devastated. I felt alone, angry, and fearful. About that time, my husband was having procedures to correct his own medical issues. While he was in the hospital, I was pacing at home, scared that something might go wrong. The what-ifs kept going through my mind. What would I do if he didn't recover and come home? How would I manage on my own?

He is my best friend, full of love for me, and my main support system. As I was pacing, I received a message from my Higher Power, as clear as if someone in the room had spoken to me. The voice said, "Do not be afraid; you will never be alone. I am always with you." I was stunned. Immediately, warmth and love flowed through my body, and I was comforted. I fully trusted those words.

From that moment to now, I know those words to be true. I feel God's love and support every day. I take time every day to nurture and deepen our relationship. I'm not much for formal prayer. Rather, I talk to God throughout the day, asking for guidance to do the next healthy thing. I ask to align my will with God's.

In CPA, by connecting with others and hearing their stories, my attitudes about pain are changing. I'm becoming a much more accepting, compassionate, understanding, and loving woman. My definition of God is continually changing. I see God everywhere I look.

In this moment, I will go about each day, asking for guidance to do the next healthful thing.

August 28

In the past, I've acted dishonestly by lying to myself, and subsequently others, about the true nature and daily experience of living with my illness, disability, and chronic pain.

I was told by medical providers at a very young age that children do not have migraines. My first symptom of chronic illness came at age five after I'd been injured while roughhousing with my friends. I was just stitched up and sent home.

I was taught to minimize my symptoms, and minimizing can be a type of lying. Dishonesty has consequences. I started searching behind my parents' back for relief from the pain. I turned to drugs and alcohol, which are not a fit substitute for genuine medical care. At twenty-three years old, I gave them up so I could face the reality of my condition.

Then, I obsessively sought solutions for my medical conditions. By being honest, I found that some medical care was available, and it was my responsibility to seek it out.

Since coming to CPA, I have been able to drop a lot of blame. I blamed myself, my parents, and the world. *One Day at a Time*, one hour at a time, I try to check in with myself by asking, "Am I being as honest as I can right now?"

The consequences of hiding my symptoms to please others had devastating effects on my body, self-esteem, and spirituality. I've even tried to please doctors by diminishing my truth. I no longer do that. Today, I get better medical care, I have a loving sponsor, and working the Steps in CPA is setting me free of the guilt I carried for far too long.

In this moment, I will choose honesty with all those caring for me.

August 29

When I came to CPA, I had recently left an abusive relationship that closely mirrored my childhood experiences. I don't identify with the word "victim." I am one of millions of people who have experienced emotional, physical, and sexual trauma in life. What I wasn't aware of was how those experiences intersected with my life-long chronic illnesses and pain. In a meeting, I heard the term "medical trauma," and it instantly connected. Currently, I have ongoing symptoms likely from the multiple negative, even traumatizing, experiences in medical settings, like a life-changing diagnosis and being dismissed and called names by a provider.

Simply put, I've got some medical trauma to manage. The solution has been practicing the CPA program. I've faced many medical providers who don't understand. They are not malicious, just ignorant. Most haven't been trained to treat the complexities of multiple diagnoses like my body endures. Oftentimes, treatments have had ineffective or surprising side effects. My providers can get just as discouraged as I do. When I cannot cope, I turn to the CPA friendships I've developed through regular attendance at meetings, working with my sponsor to apply the Steps, reaching out to others, and doing service when I am able.

I never thought I would look in the mirror and love the person I see as is, but I do. Every day, when I wake up in this body, I come into it slowly. I check the date, time, and weather on my phone. Then I text with another CPA member as I wait for my foggy brain and stiff jaw to start to coordinate. I ask for direction.

Not everyone needs to know the specifics of what caused my trauma, but the kind words, gentle suggestions, and program of CPA have comforted and carried me through, and continues to do so.

In this moment, I will notice the comfort I receive from applying the CPA program.

August 30

Step Two has been called the hope Step; whenever I lose hope, I come back to Step Two. This Step was my springboard to first identify and later trust my Higher Power. I don't question the unrestricted existence of a spiritual force, as my experiences have proven this beyond doubt.

At first, this required a monumental change in my thinking. One thing I had skipped over in early recovery was the word "care" in Step Three. Today, I am grateful to feel cared for despite chronic pain and illness. I try to relax in the caring arms of my Higher Power. At those times when my spiritual connection fizzles, the care expressed by CPA members, warms my heart and soothes my pain.

Love, connection, and understanding are things greater than me that delight my Higher Power and myself. I can't do these things alone. I share myself with another person and spiritual guidance sparkles in the air. With CPA and my Higher Power, I know there is always a helping hand, there is always a solution, and there is always hope.

In this moment, I will look for hope by connecting with my Higher Power and CPA fellows.

August 31

Having an obsession means being constantly preoccupied with something, such as an idea or desire. For decades, I spent a lot of energy obsessing about my pain and what I could do to stop it. I lived in fear, trying every kind of modality imaginable.

Should I see another doctor? Take a different medication? Or possibly have another surgery? Even the smallest movements could trigger symptoms that lasted weeks. I responded with anger, sadness, and the idea that something was terribly wrong with my body.

I have a very strong faith in my Higher Power, and I consistently surrendered my life over to God. I prayed for help with my pain, turned it over, and put it in my God box. Then, I found Chronic Pain Anonymous and my life changed.

My attitude and relationship with my pain changed when I started going to meetings, reading the literature, and working the Twelve Steps with my sponsor. This attitude shift was transformative and profound. I started practicing self-compassion. I learned to honor my body; I accepted pain as normal for my chronic condition. My anxiety and obsession decreased when I stopped battling my chronic pain and chronic illness. In fact, my pain even decreased and became more manageable.

I am finally learning to live peacefully, joyfully, and comfortably with myself and others. I still have many limitations and challenges due to my illness and need a lot of rest. But now, I can do so much that I never thought would be possible. Today, I live with serenity and hope.

In this moment, I will find acceptance so that I may live peacefully, joyfully, and comfortably with myself and others.

September

September 1

When I first came to CPA, I didn't understand that my life was unmanageable. Before I became ill, I managed many different areas in my life, and I was good at it. I was sure I could manage my illness, fix it, and get back to my "real" life. The concept of being powerless over chronic illness made no sense. Of course, I could find solutions and have control over my body.

I didn't recognize that no matter what I did, I was not going to get rid of my illness; I was not going to return to what I believed was normal. Even though this reality was in my face, I did not see it. I was obsessed with trying to control my body, the people around me, and my healthcare providers. I was sure I just hadn't looked under the right rock yet, and I desperately kept digging.

It was an awakening to finally understand that my life was unmanageable. My relationships with family and friends were filled with tension. I had the erroneous belief that if they just didn't ask so much of me, held a party at the time of day I wanted, or didn't open windows, I could prevent symptoms from showing up. It was exhausting and ineffective.

It wasn't until I came to CPA that I saw how this was making my life unmanageable. Once I did, it was a huge relief. Learning from my sponsor and hearing others share in meetings showed me my life was unmanageable. And not only that but that I wasn't expected to manage it alone. The skills from a lifetime of managing work and my busy life were not the skills I needed to live with chronic illness.

In this moment, I will be patient with myself as I let go of my past and unrealistic expectations.

September 2

Today, I have a dreaded project I need to tackle that I wish I would have completed a year ago. It requires concentration, and I can only work on it in increments. I could be irresponsible and not do it all, or push myself to work until the task is completed, and I am a total wreck. I don't believe either of these options would bring me feelings of serenity. As a person who loves being productive and getting things done, I don't like how long it is taking me to accomplish this task.

How am I applying my CPA program to address this task? I have turned this project over to God numerous times and practiced Step Three. Today, I will tackle another piece: remembering to take things one moment at a time. I don't have to finish it today. I only need to achieve *Progress, Not Perfection*. I will do what I can and then rest. *Rest is an Action,* too, after all. But I do need to continue to take the next step. So, I try to *Keep It Simple.* That is all I need to do each day: take the next step. I have enough, I know enough, I do enough, I am enough.

In this moment, I will turn to CPA slogans to reduce my anxiety and dread.

September 3

In Step Nine, I first made amends to myself. Before I could approach others, I had to acknowledge the ways I had harmed myself and make amends by relating to myself differently. Then, I would be able to speak to others from a healthy mindset.

After doing my Fourth Step inventory, I understood that kicking myself when I was down was no longer acceptable. Beating myself up had to stop. I would think things like, "Why did you eat that food when you knew it would make you sick?" and, "You stupidly went to that party, and now you are paying the price!" The harsh voice in my head caused me much harm. Part of making amends was to begin speaking to myself as I would with a dear friend who was suffering.

I now use a tone of voice that is gentle, with an attitude that is loving and kind, and I shower myself with lots of forgiveness. I've learned to forgive myself for choosing to push beyond my limits. It's okay to make this choice at times. Now, I know to treat myself with extra compassion when the time comes to pay the cost of that choice.

After making amends to myself, I proceeded to make amends to others. It was done with a relaxed attitude, forgiveness of my imperfection, and not laden with shame, blame, or guilt. It was a slow effort, guided by my HP, to behave and speak in new ways. Some amends to family and friends were a change of behavior—a living amends—that required no words or explanations. My HP, my sponsor, and I knew what I'd been doing, and that was good enough.

In this moment, I will begin the amends process by forgiving myself and adopting compassionate self-talk.

September 4

In the past, I believed if I wasn't busy doing something productive, I was being a lazy slacker. People rested when they went to bed at night; rest was not a daytime activity. My narrow definition of rest didn't allow me to do the exact thing I needed to take care of myself.

When I first heard in CPA that I had permission and was encouraged to rest during the day, I was surprised and delighted. It took me a while to adjust my thinking and begin to truly accept that it was okay to rest, go to bed in the middle of the day, and do nothing. At first, it felt like I was going to get caught, that I was somehow being naughty. I had to let go of the judgment that said I was doing something wrong and should be ashamed of myself.

As I began to include rest in my daily life, I experienced the benefits and realized it was not a bad thing but actually a very good thing. I felt better when I took periodic rests throughout the day. I found I had less pain and more energy when I was active for a short time, then returned to bed or the couch for a while. This pacing—alternating action with inaction—made me less cranky and, much to my surprise, higher functioning!

Today, I am a pro at resting. Sometimes, this means I take thirty minutes in my lounge chair watching TV, and sometimes, it means I spend three days in bed, barely moving. I've learned that taking the time to rest is a gift to myself and to those around me.

In this moment, I will remember I am not being rebellious when I rest.

September 5

CPA and all that it offers—like members who fully understand what it's like to live this way—changed my life. Sharing openly at meetings and with CPA members takes strength and shows faith. Reading and hearing others share what lifts them and how their prayers were answered gets me through the day and gives me great hope for the future. We, as CPA members, may have different health issues, but when we come together and share our experiences, it is clear we have so much in common.

Living with chronic pain or illness does not mean our lives are void of all happiness. We may struggle physically, mentally, emotionally, and spiritually, but we can also have times of joy, fun, and peace. In CPA, we are learning how to live our lives to the fullest—to the best of our abilities.

Believing in a Power greater than myself—one I cannot see—helped me in this more than I could ever have imagined. When I took that leap of faith and started trusting in my Higher Power, I let go of my control. I began believing in what cannot be seen. When I need help and am unable to take physical action, I can choose to take spiritual action and trust fully in my Higher Power. As time went on, my faith became trust. I saw tangible results of the Great Unseen taking care of me in ways I never dreamed possible.

Previously, I was on my own; now, I have fellows, friends, and my Higher Power, who is only a whisper away. From being alone to belonging, CPA holds my hand as I take life *One Day at a Time*.

In this moment, I will celebrate my participation in CPA and consider taking spiritual action to deepen my conscious contact.

September 6

To prepare for a procedure, I began to turn over my anxiety about it at my regular CPA morning meeting. I brought up the procedure in fellowship and asked members to share their experience, strength, and hope about how they had managed their fear, anxiety, and different aspects of this procedure. Connecting with others who had used CPA tools for this same thing helped me enormously. I learned it would be a good idea to rest the day before, take sunglasses for the bright lights, and bring my own earplugs for the very loud machine.

The day of the procedure, I said the Serenity Prayer a number of times and practiced breathing exercises in the waiting room. I messaged my co-sponsor and asked for her prayers. I was nervous about using my own earplugs and asked the technician if it was okay. He said I didn't need them, so I put them in my locker and went in. I again said the Serenity Prayer a few times as I lay on the table. The noise was awful; the headphones the technician provided were not enough. I got through it without panicking by asking my Higher Power to be there with me. I felt surrounded by loving light.

Afterward, I talked with my CPA fellows about the experience and was able to let go of any frustration about the noise level that had been so agitating. I made a mental note that next time—and there most likely would be a next time—I will bring and use my own earplugs. Now I know that's the best option for me, thanks to my willingness and my Higher Power's guidance.

In this moment, I will recognize all that I am doing to support my well-being in trying situations.

September 7

Before CPA, I spent decades in other Twelve Step fellowships. I utilized techniques learned from sponsors and program friends. I sat quietly with my indecision and asked Higher Power for guidance. I used my emotions to interpret my HP's will. If irritation was overwhelming me, that was not HP's will. If I felt calm and had a sense of ease, then I was aligning with my Higher Power's will.

In CPA, this hasn't worked for all things. Often, I've been faced with choosing between one painful action and another. Neither decision felt all that calm or easy. So, I added another step in my process. I would pray:

> "HP, help me welcome these difficult emotions. Help me to stop struggling against things that scare me or cause me discomfort. Help me learn to be in harmony with my feelings and honor them as valid."

I understand that life hasn't always left me feeling great. I became extremely frustrated when my doctor didn't have anything else for me to try. I got upset when my medications didn't curb my pain. Those feelings were valid, but I didn't stay there.

I found I could get through difficult, painful, and irritating times by doing three things.

1. Acknowledge my emotions and sensations with validation. Step One.
2. Ask HP for comfort and guidance. Step Two.
3. Listen for and take appropriate action, even when challenging. Step Three.
4. Repeat, if necessary.

In this moment, I will experiment with prayer and the first three Steps.

September 8

The Doctor's Opinion in *Recipe for Recovery* speaks of CPA's role of "listening to suffering individuals with compassion and understanding, offering hope and support." I want to be there with the loving hand of CPA for every member and give back what was so freely given to me, but some days I just can't.

It has taken many hours of trial and error with my sponsor to learn how to make self-loving boundaries. In the beginning, I believed I had to pick up every call and respond to every text. If I didn't, I was somehow being selfish. Also, I was afraid they would pile up. I was overwhelmed and had forgotten that I was among the suffering individuals of CPA too.

Today, I can give members the space to express what they need without any direct response from me. Thanks to CPA, I can reply to a twenty-minute message by text. "I love you. You're not alone, and I just can't talk now." Or send a heart or praying hands emoji. And as if by magic, all my CPA friends still love me. We have an unspoken agreement not to take things personally. If we don't respond, it is not because we don't want to. It's because it would cause us harm to do so. I constantly remind myself that others have a Higher Power, and I'm not it. I even tell my sponsees to call on their HP first and then call and let me know what HP said. When I pause and ask my Higher Self, I find previously unknown resources of cognition and energy.

In this moment, I will honor my energy and respect that I must care for myself before I can care for others.

September 9

Regarding the Ninth Step, it can be a good idea to vet my amends with a trusted advisor so I can be prepared before proceeding. I've done this in writing and by role-playing. My experience has shown, both as sponsor and sponsee, that it is very easy to slip into something other than acknowledging my part in past behaviors, along with my willingness to change.

My sponsor or trusted friend might help me by asking, "Are you really trying to get the other person to somehow acknowledge their part in things?" "Are you trying to rekindle an old, inappropriate romance?" "Are you looking for an opportunity to shine as the new, improved Captain Spirituality?" and "Do you wish to take the fact that the person is willing to have an intimate conversation as a chance to offer them some advice or to talk about your illness and pain, once more trying to get another to understand it fully?"

Although the Ninth Step is about my part only, it's certainly not another opportunity to turn things back into "all about me." It's devoid of any subtle insinuation that the other played a role in how I behaved, nor indulging in windy explanations about my illness, my new spirituality, my new requirement to make amends, and so on.

With care and the help of my sponsor, I prepare myself properly. Making amends focused solely on my part, I am unburdened and so able to move forward, free to meet the world, once more, squarely.

In this moment, I will commit to reflecting on my words, actions, and choices. I will continue to learn and take responsibility.

September 10

Finding the best time to do a daily Tenth Step inventory has been a process for me. By the end of the day, I am often tired and foggy. In addition to not having an accurate memory of the events of the day, I'm also harder on myself when I'm tired, which is not so productive.

I've recently started to take short inventories throughout the day, especially when I've just finished something that usually brings out my character defects. For example, when I've had dinner with family members, while on the way home, I'll take a quick inventory of the time I spent with them.

Taking inventory of shorter spans of time has helped me to not become overwhelmed by trying to remember details from the day. It's also helped me to identify when I need to surrender something to my Higher Power.

I've found it very important to take an inventory when I'm uncomfortable. When feelings of shame, fear, or anger start to come up, I'll try to pause and track down what thoughts or behaviors could be behind these feelings.

In this moment, I will honor my physical and emotional states by being as creative as I can with my Step Ten inventory process.

September 11

As strange as it sounds, it's been easier for me to accept my life when I've been mostly bedbound. That's when the internal wars between my mind, body, and chronic illness reach some kind of peace arrangement or truce. With me, acceptance grows and then plateaus when I know what to expect each day.

The war begins again during the weeks when I feel much better. It's like having a little taste of normalcy that, in turn, activates an intense longing for things to be different.

Oscillating between fighting and accepting my life, it can seem as if I am constantly at odds with myself. But on a deeper level, I know they can coexist. I can keep fighting to get better while simultaneously accepting my reality.

People in CPA recovery share that some days, they have to take it one minute at a time. I relate to the unpredictability they speak of since I don't know what condition I will wake up in each morning.

I no longer think of acceptance as a final destination. For me, it is a tool or a practice I keep circling back to at different stages of my illness and healing. Acceptance is always available to me, right where I am at this moment.

In this moment, I will accept being here, right where I am, in this body, as it is right now.

September 12

I found CPA through other groups. I was in recovery, but deep down, I knew there had to be more. One of the support groups I was in started a CPA meeting, and I went along for the ride.

I have many angels in my life who often show up as people in my meetings. One convinced me to get a sponsor and work the Steps in *Recipe for Recovery*. So, I opened my heart and got a sponsor. I started Step One again. And this time, it was different.

The decision to act and become a member of CPA eventually brought me some peace. The fellowship I feel so connected to was something I didn't know I was missing until I had it. With my fellow CPA members' support, I worked the Steps every day and incorporated them into my life. I have learned to forgive myself and my crumbling body. I have discovered that I have a huge heart, soul, and mind. I have found a place for regeneration and a continuation of that process. I have joy, love, kindness, and mindfulness thanks to being an active member of CPA.

In this moment, I will express my gratitude for CPA by sharing information with others who are interested.

September 13

Having boundaries is an important aspect of my self-care, especially as it relates to living with chronic pain and chronic illness.

My boundaries are situational and contextual. Creating them starts with me becoming aware of what I need and understanding what's important to my self-care in a given situation. Then, I express this to others in a respectful way, remembering this is a two-way street. I need to listen to others and respect their boundaries, too.

My boundaries can be emotional, physical, or mental. They're guidelines that keep me safe. They outline the ways I will behave toward others and what is acceptable in how they behave toward me. They can be rigid or flexible. Boundaries allow me to establish what's important to me so I do not ignore my own needs or let others control me. Moreover, I am not being self-centered and insensitive to the needs of others by dominating the situation. This is a balancing act and takes practice. I have specific boundaries and those that are more open. I give myself permission to say "No" at any time.

For me, setting boundaries in a relationship is a collaborative process. It often requires flexibility, self-awareness, and willingness to practice this skill—knowing it is *Progress, Not Perfection,* that I seek. Identifying my boundaries and having the self-agency to communicate them is empowering. Ultimately, they lead to mutual trust and respect in my relationships, whether with friends, family, or healthcare practitioners.

In this moment, I will honor my boundaries and try to express them clearly and compassionately.

September 14

I was frightened by having a procedure, and I wasn't sure I wanted to go through with it. With the help of CPA, I became empowered to allow myself to stop the procedure at any moment, even up to the last minute. Giving myself permission to say "No" and set a boundary in the moment was liberating.

I need to set boundaries with myself and others. It helps me to set limits on how much energy I expend daily. This means scheduling time each day to rest, including not answering the phone or working at my desk.

I also have to set limits with my spouse. For example, I've asked him to respect this boundary: "When you are ready to get out of bed, please try not to wake me up by looking at your phone."

I have to set limits for interacting with my friends, too. "I can't go out at night, so can we make plans during the day?"

Sometimes, my boundaries are set in advance, and sometimes, in the moment. My flares are unpredictable, and it takes self-awareness to not harm myself. For example, sometimes my daughter phones me, is upset, and wants to talk. If it's been a long day and I don't have anything more to give, it's important to give myself permission to say "No" in a respectful way. I can tell her I am sorry, that it's been a rough day, and I wish I had more to give. Alternatively, I can say, "I can listen for five minutes," or "I can't listen now, but maybe in an hour I'll be able." I can even say, "I love you, and I want to hear about it, but I just don't have it in me to give you the attention and comfort you deserve," which is what I really want to say every time.

In this moment, I will remember that saying "No," can be a loving action.

September 15

When I'm feeling poorly, I can get irritable and easily blame others. I'm learning to express boundaries using "I" statements, not "you" statements.

My boyfriend puts our dirty dishes straight into the dishwasher. I'm often too tired and just put them in the sink. When I have more energy, I deal with them, which might mean they don't get loaded until tomorrow. This drives him crazy, and I can get nasty in response. I say things like, "Stop bugging me! If you want the dishes in the dishwasher now, you can do it," But, thanks to CPA, I now say, "I'm tired. Thank you for your patience with me. I will put the dishes in the dishwasher as soon as I am able." And wow, his whole attitude shifts to one of understanding and compassion. When I use "you" statements, he immediately goes on the defensive. When I use "I" statements, it becomes clear to him that I'm not shirking my responsibility, just honoring my pain and fatigue. Nine times out of ten, not only does he load my dishes, he asks if there is anything else he can do to help me.

Boundary setting is an ongoing and imperfect process, no matter how it's done. It has taken me years to understand that I can take responsibility for my own safety and ask for what I need. *Easy Does It* and *One Day at a Time* are slogans I try to keep in mind, always.

In this moment, I will commit to using "I" statements in hopes of communicating more effectively with those I love.

September 16

When I found CPA, I had no previous Twelve Step experience. Some of the Twelve Step language and the different meeting styles and formats felt strange to me. But I felt welcome and understood. It was refreshing, and I felt hopeful. I heard working the Steps was beneficial, but I couldn't grasp what was impressive about them. For a while, I just attended the meetings and enjoyed the support and fellowship I found there. After a number of months, I began working the Steps with a sponsor. I learned this is a program of action, and to discover the positive impact of the Steps, I would have to practice them.

For me, Step One was about honesty. Admitting powerlessness made me face my denial and accept that I couldn't make my illness go away. Trying harder wasn't working, and wishing didn't help either. I blamed myself for somehow causing my illness. To acknowledge my powerlessness, I had to let go of that self-blame.

My life had become unmanageable. I often ignored what my body was telling me and pushed ahead, resulting in an endless cycle of fatigue, pain, and stress. I frequently set unrealistic goals and felt defeated because I couldn't reach them. I wanted to be in control, keep everyone around me happy, and get all my work done.

CPA suggests that to find peace, joy, and comfort in our lives, it is helpful to accept change as a part of the program and life in general. We may have to do things differently, which can be difficult and frightening. We don't have to go through these changes alone. Some changes came easily, but with others, it took time for me to become willing to try something new. With guidance and support from God, my sponsor, program friends, and applying the Steps, I was able to change. For me, working the Steps led to deep insights, personal growth, and maturity.

In this moment, I will be grateful for my honesty, open-mindedness, and willingness.

September 17

I was explaining Step Two to a sponsee once, and an idea hit me: restoring my sanity and clarity wasn't a one-time thing but a process requiring continual upkeep and renewal.

I use CPA's meetings, fellowship time, Steps, and service opportunities as ways to help maintain my sanity. If I get away from one or more of these, my thoughts become increasingly unreliable. At first, I begin tracking my symptoms in detail, sometimes down to the minute, trying to discover triggers and eliminate them. I'll think I've found the magic trigger—the one causing all my symptoms. Then, a few days later, I'll think it's something else. In this next phase, I think I will get better, and I won't need CPA anymore. Leading to the notion that I'm not qualified to be in CPA because my symptoms aren't severe enough. And finally, somehow, I convince myself of the exact opposite. I know I'm worse than other people here; nobody understands me, and there is nothing left to live for. For me, this is the definition of distorted thinking and insanity.

Add a touch of grandiosity, resentment, and codependence—all of which I struggle to manage—and I truly begin acting in destructive ways. I know it, and everyone else can tell, too!

It's time again for Step Two! "Higher Power, restore me to sanity. Give me clarity of thought, word, and action," is a prayer I return to again and again.

In this moment, I will ask my Higher Power to restore my sanity, clarity, and humor.

September 18

Just for Today has brought me closer to the ideal of living *One Day at a Time*. It's taught me that no matter what I've experienced, it will be okay, even if it's *Just for Today*. More so, those three words have invoked a sense of connection with my Higher Power every time I've used it.

During my first years in CPA, my concept of a Higher Power was one that got credit for my successes but disappeared when things got difficult. Somehow, saying, *"Just for Today,"* reminded me that I was not alone and could get through any day with my Higher Power.

Recently, while working on a complicated project for CPA, it became too much for my brain to organize that day. It was already due, but deadlines in CPA are generally flexible. I called the committee chair, acknowledged it would be late, and that I'd done all I could, *Just for Today*. As a fellow member of CPA, they understood and helped me to remember I hadn't failed. I was simply done, *Just for Today*, and would continue when able.

Because I acknowledged my limitations and trusted things would be done in Higher Power's time, I didn't push myself too far. A few days later, I was able to work on the project again. I told myself, "I am only doing what I can, *Just for Today*." It was amazing to me how things got done this way, little by little, step by step. *Just for Today*.

This slogan has become a reminder that all things change. And that with my Higher Power, I am capable of addressing whatever comes my way.

In this moment, I will experiment with using Just for Today in my life.

September 19

When I need help, I'm often unable to see the kind of help I need, at least not right away. Taking quiet time in the morning and reviewing what will happen that day with my Higher Power helps me see where I would benefit from assistance.

I have an aide two days a week. There are always lots of things that need doing, and I can't always think of them on the spot. So, I take some quiet time to compile a task list. If it does not seem complete, I visualize the house, going room by room to see what needs to be done.

On the days without an aide, I consider what I can and cannot do, given the state of my body. I accept I may only do half of what I plan, and trust my Higher Power will make sure the key things get done. If I am stressed and frozen, I ease into those feelings to see if they will pass. If they don't, I reach out to a CPA member. I may not share the specific issue I'm facing, but just reaching out relieves some of my stress and reminds me I am not alone, even if I am physically by myself.

In this moment, I will remind myself that, with my Higher Power and the CPA fellowship, I am not alone.

September 20

The most influential discovery of my life is that my Higher Power loves me. In turn, I've learned the most powerful thing I can do is let someone know I love them.

I ask HP, throughout the day, "What would you have me do?" I hear lots of things. Some are my own thoughts. Then there is a warmer thought that feels like being told "I love you," by my Higher Power.

My family knows how much I love them, although it is still important to say. I also tell them I appreciate them and am grateful for them. When I know a person is leaving my life, I try to make sure they know how much I love them.

My family and relatives all say, "I love you" at the end of every call. I tell people who might not expect it from me, like doctors and my mailwoman. She kindly puts packages on a table outside the door so I do not have to bend to pick them up. I like to show my gratitude for this seemingly simple act that saves me so much energy. When I express my appreciation, they tend to smile or tear up. I smile, too. And just like that, I feel that same warmth and love that my Higher Power sends me every day.

My life can still feel dark as pain and illness continue to change its course. HP's love helps me through. Having more moments of joy in life, I can now understand the value of taking the time to say, "I love you."

In this moment, I will commit to expressing love to people and creatures every chance I get.

September 21

CPA has defined recovery as the ability to live peacefully, joyfully, and comfortably with ourselves and others. Joy does not come easily, especially when physically miserable. But it did help my spirit when I'd take a moment to find some. At some point, I decided that when all my thoughts appeared to be rotting, I'd ask myself, "Where is the good?" By doing that, I've discovered that something good can always be found.

I have not bypassed my suffering or sugarcoated it by using this tool. Looking for the good has broadened my perspective. I can now see the suffering but not become completely focused on it. Being able to see beyond my pain has helped me to stop obsessively tending to my body every moment of every day.

I've found that joy can come in many flavors and varying levels of intensity. I've also noticed that joy brings a smile to my body, along with a moment of relaxation and ease. For example, I was in bed the other day with the kind of fatigue that doesn't go away by being prone and resting. So much needed doing, and I wasn't going to be able to do any of it. My eyes and head were hurting, so I couldn't read or watch TV—my preferred form of entertainment. So, I listened to a podcast someone had told me about on my cell phone. It was just what I needed. Grateful, I stopped and reminded myself to take a moment and recognize the good. Because this had been good. The huge relief I'd felt in my body by doing something that didn't hurt, had been not only satisfying but a distraction from my discomfort as well.

This has now become a habit, finding the good. It's helped me see that everything in the world is not terrible like I used to believe. Even on my worst days, there have been moments that fill my heart with joy.

In this moment, I will endeavor to find something that fills my heart with joy.

September 22

What is my relationship with my body? For many years, the answer would have been, "What body?" Before I had chronic health conditions, I had no awareness of my physical sensations or connection to my feelings. I was a head, floating around, with no contact with my body.

I did not begin making contact with a kind attitude. I was always fighting with my body, trying to force solutions. Even when I was not feeling well, I ignored the pain, fatigue, and cognitive lapses. I did not know how to listen to the communications being received from my body.

Through working the Twelve Steps, I identified how I treated myself. During this process, it felt like I was being held and gently guided toward a mindful relationship with my physical self. I'd put the many ways I had abused myself on my Step Four inventory, and, in Step Nine, I began making amends. This meant I had started to show compassion toward myself, treat myself tenderly, and learn ways to practice self-care. I had finally begun resting when my body was tired. Such a novel concept. I'd also learned it was alright to say no to an activity, particularly if it strained my physical resources.

Taking good care of myself always seemed like such a basic concept, but also vague, mysterious, and complicated at the same time. I'd never been taught self-care or had it modeled by anyone. But after coming to CPA, I have learned what it looks like in practice.

In this moment, I will open my mind and heart to a more mindful relationship with my body.

September 23

I have an autoimmune disorder that manifests in poor sleep. Some days, I awake exhausted and ill. Other days, I awake refreshed and function very well for about three, sometimes four, hours.

Prior to CPA, I took medications that allowed me to override my dysfunction and let me regularly push past my limits. The medications did not bring me energy from another source; they sapped my innate reserves and, over time, accelerated my decline. After I came to CPA, it was suggested, and I decided to try to accept my condition. I stopped the medications that were harmful and accepted I would have much less energy. The great upside would be not getting sicker every day. After I accepted the need for change and followed through, I felt more grounded and in touch with life.

I discovered that there is a direct correlation between exhaustion and distorted thinking. I find it especially helpful to do a random, spot-check inventory of my thinking. When my thinking becomes skewed, I take steps to amend it.

Sometimes, I say aloud, "These things don't just happen to you. Remember, your life is meaningful and filled with opportunities for love, purpose ,and beauty."

Then, I lay down and rest.

In this moment, I will remember that my life is meaningful and still full of opportunities for love and purpose.

September 24

Just do the next indicated action. When my mind is spinning, trying to solve future possible problems, this saying comes to mind. I don't have to figure out the rest of my life at this moment.

Whenever I ask myself, "What is the next indicated action?" I usually find a manageable answer. A chore I despise needs to be done—I can reward myself afterward. I am feeling poorly—I can rest. I've fallen into a dark emotional hole—I can pick up the phone and call my sponsor. When I live life in each moment, guided by these words, I don't feel overwhelmed by the thoughts swirling in my head. I am no longer paralyzed by fear and doubt. I can manage to take just one action.

The other day, I woke up exhausted; I was powerless over this situation. There were many things on my to-do list. I was awash with feelings of disappointment, anger, and confusion. I tried to plan the rest of the day, but that just made me feel worse. Then, I remembered all I had to do was the next indicated action. At that moment, it was to get out of bed and go to the bathroom. That, I could manage. I kept repeating this process and got through the day. I moved slowly and dealt with each moment.

Focusing on just the next indicated action reminds me that I can only live in this moment, and I always find the next right action, eventually. Little by little, and impacted by each choice, the next indication appears. The cycle begins again. This is how I live now., For me, the result is a life of serenity and ease.

In this moment, I will do the next indicated action as slowly as needed.

September 25

I always felt smart, capable, and strong. I had fear, but I also had plenty of resources to face my fears and take action. When I fell ill, I responded with a nothing-to-lose attitude. I followed my passions and did things I'd have never risked doing when I was well. I did whatever made me happy. I thought I was a poster child for how to cope with chronic illness!

After many years of pushing on, ignoring my body, and frequently disregarding signs of harm and strain, I finally had to face my deteriorating condition and physical limitations. I fell into a major depression. It was profound, and it took a long time and a lot of work to learn to manage my mental health and the associated emotions. Subsequently, I felt my depression worsen whenever I had too much going on and was overwhelmed.

The need to carefully allot my limited energy resulted in a constant, persistent underlying fear that made me feel weak and afraid of life. My go-to way of dealing with fear was diving into action. That had become and continues to be, impossible.

So, what helps me now? First, I acknowledge the fear is there; I have lived with it for many years, and it has not taken me out. Then, I ask my God for the courage to get through this day. I am somehow always granted this when I ask. I "came to believe," as Step Two puts it. I also believe that my friends in CPA are direct expressions of God, so I often seek their company and sometimes their counsel, but always their spirit.

In this moment, I will accept that fear is normal, and not too big for my God and me to handle.

September 26

I spill a lot—most recently a liquid supplement on my bedspread—because my hands are weak and painful to use. Each time, it's a brutal reminder of the things I can no longer do, and that makes me angry. My mind viciously responds with negative self-talk. I lash out against the parts of my body I feel are betraying me.

CPA is teaching me to recognize and address negative emotions. First, I identify and name the feelings: I feel frustrated that my hands are weak and it hurts to use them. I feel isolated. I am sad that I am unable to do my job and resentful that I'm not healthy. I don't accept help because I feel ashamed for needing it.

Next, examining these difficult emotions, feeling them, and giving them to God clears the way for more helpful emotions to come in and rebuild. Self-compassion is key for me to be able to do this. I know from my CPA friends that these kinds of destructive thought patterns happen all the time! It's normal. I bet healthy people get upset with themselves when they spill something on the bedspread, too!

It takes effort, but I try to regularly take a self-compassion break, which includes supportive and caring self-talk. Sometimes, these words originally come from a friend, my sponsor, or God. Eventually, though, they come back out of my own lips. Aloud, I console myself by saying, "Dear, you are doing okay. Your hands are tired, but they are still beautiful. You can spill things all over the house, and I will still love you. It's okay to feel weak, and it's okay to feel pain. You are not a failure; you are capable, and you are competent. This one event does not define you. It illustrates your common humanity. You can set it aside when you are ready. You are loved just the way you are."

In this moment, I will face my feelings with creative, compassionate, and comforting self-talk.

September 27

The first time I read the Twelve Steps hanging on the wall of a CPA meeting, I balked at the word "God" in Step Three. Fortunately for me, the program itself certainly qualified as "a Power greater than." So, I tiptoed in, with a tiny bit of willingness, and set my fears about God aside. Frankly, I didn't feel too much of anything, just awkward and uncertain.

My perception of a Higher Power has evolved since I joined CPA. I started to notice the word "care" in Step Three. The spiritual richness I gained by asking for and accepting guidance while in the care of God was profound. I felt like I had a new purpose. I felt serene, at least until doubt or fear crept back in. I am only human, after all.

On high-pain days, I learned to picture myself being comforted and enveloped by my Higher Power. This new practice replaced my old behaviors of self-deprecation and neglect. My caring Higher Power made these changes possible. I am grateful I was in the care of CPA.

Step Three became the backbone of my CPA recovery. I made turning over my will, thoughts, life, and actions a regular practice. I was blessed to do this with other CPA members. Often, I found that others turned over the same things as I did and recognized even more that I could put into God's care.

In this moment, I will remember one of the ways I can come to believe I am in the care of a loving Higher Power is by listening to other members' experiences.

September 28

I love Step Eleven because it helps me to keep in touch with God. I like to spend time on this Step in the mornings. It helps me start the day feeling grounded, organized, and open to God's guidance.

There's a notable difference between the days when I just plow ahead without thinking and the days when I take the time to contemplate and ask God to be in control. If I do not purposely do this, I easily slip back into obsessively trying to control and direct everything. My morning ritual does not have to take long or be complicated, but I do like to take a few minutes to start the day this way.

This Step instructs me to pray—only for knowledge of God's will for me and for the power to carry it out. I communicate with God about other things, but I try to always come back to God's will. God knows more than I do. I'll be honest: I don't always want to know God's will. I want what I want. But experience has shown me that when our desires differ, I am better off in the long run following God's will instead of my own.

Step Eleven is a Step that regularly adds a lot to my life for a relatively small investment of time.

In this moment, I will make time to improve my conscious contact throughout my day.

September 29

Some say that the opposite of fear is faith. This saying has become a vital tool for my recovery.

There are different kinds of fears. Some are solely in my mind, like when I fixate on worst-case scenarios. What if my eyes get so bad I can't see anymore? What if my hands get so bad I can't write or hold things? I face these fears with program tools. I call my sponsor, pray, and get to a meeting.

Then, there are fears that physically overwhelm my body. These are quite challenging. Attitude shifts don't seem to alter them. I'm unable to think clearly. I experience a clenching in my gut, shortness of breath, shakiness, and instability. This is when faith is all I have to grab onto. Like a scary roller coaster ride, I just have to sit in my seat until the ride comes to a stop.

The upside of having fear in my life is that my program and recovery are strengthened every time I handle it in a new way. Facing everything means I observe my body, my emotions, and my thinking. I am a compassionate witness to my suffering. In CPA, I am learning how I can experience this fear and keep living my life at the same time. I reach out to my Higher Power constantly and have faith that I'll be given strength and courage. I remind myself that *This Too Shall Pass*. Faith that my HP is there is what keeps me sane and able to stay on the roller coaster until the ride ends.

I am powerless over fears arising, but my HP can handle them. All I have to do is to keep turning them over. When I keep my HP close, my recovery deepens.

In this moment, I will notice my fears and turn them over to God.

September 30

I woke up the other day in greater pain than usual. My first thoughts were about what hurt, how much it hurt, and how it would impact me. Then, I imagined all the things that would be harder. My thoughts were spiraling away.

Suddenly, I realized that I hadn't started the day with my usual routine. Normally, when I wake up in the morning, I thank my Higher Power and share some gratitude. So, I paused, smiled a little bit, and said, "Hi," to my Higher Power. I thanked my Higher Power for giving me this day to live. I remembered that part of being human is to adapt and overcome problems. These are challenges, not barriers, that I am called to face.

After my morning practice, I decided I needed to cancel a planned excursion and use the time for some necessary self-care. I declared it a day of compassion. As I pampered myself, my obsession with why I was in more pain or whether I was the cause of my pain melted away.

Throughout that day, I went to several CPA meetings. I was safe to be my authentic self. I shared this miraculous story of how my day started on a slippery slope and how my Higher Power gave me traction. With help, I stopped and chose a different route for my day.

In this moment, I will declare today as a day of compassion.

October

October 1

When it was suggested I attend a recovery program, I thought that meant recovery from substance abuse. I immediately felt like my experience, as someone who has suffered with chronic pain for nearly twenty years, was being denied. My attitude immediately shifted to the polar opposite of acceptance.

I worked hard in my career, and then I started having to leave periodically due to my health. By increasing or decreasing my medications, and with discipline and focus, I improved enough to return to work. I did this many times. I was constantly fighting for my old life. I thought I was in control. In fact, my pain had never been completely managed and controlled by me, my doctors, or anyone else.

My career counselor kept suggesting that I come to CPA, the aforementioned recovery program. Eventually, I did. I learned, after a few days, that it wasn't as I'd feared: a call to give up all hope for improvement and just give in to my illness and pain. Working Step One in CPA, I learned to accept that I do not have total control over my pain. I never did and never will.

My spiritual path has always been about seeking peace, and yet my body has been in chaos. I've learned that it is a choice how much my mind contributes to this chaos. Also, choosing acceptance is not about buying into a concept but being able to let go enough to see the truth. Through all this, I discovered that acceptance seemed the most courageous and spiritual approach to truly living.

In this moment, I will ask how I can apply Step One to the circumstances of my chronic pain and illness today.

October 2

I am not good at setting boundaries, but thanks to CPA, I am learning. I am learning to tell people no, and it's not easy. However, saying no does not bring the world to an end. I have to make adjustments at my job and with my role in my family, especially regarding babysitting grandchildren and providing holiday dinners. I worry about what people will think. I want to please everyone, but I am beginning to practice setting boundaries for myself in a way that is loving to all.

I have an illness that is not visually apparent a lot of the time. Others do not realize the physical struggles and pain I have because they can't see it. I fear being judged as lazy or unwilling to do my part. When these thoughts come, I remember the notion that what others think of me is none of my business. That expression is enormously helpful for me. When I set boundaries, I remain thoughtful of others and compassionate with myself.

Sometimes, I choose to overdo it and push past my usual limits, and that is okay, too. It is my decision. If something comes up that I know will cause me extra pain, I can still choose to do it. I don't want to live my life only to prevent extra pain; I want to find a serene balance between doing and not doing. CPA gives me tools to help me set boundaries when it is appropriate. I am gifted the freedom and wisdom to not let my fear unnecessarily narrow my way of living.

In this moment, I will set boundaries that are thoughtful and compassionate towards others and myself.

October 3

I thought I was committed to faith and that CPA's Step Two would be simple for me. It has proven more difficult than I imagined.

In my chaotic childhood, I was determined to fight for independence. I took great responsibility for my siblings and myself. As an adult, I wanted to be the creator, controller, and hero of my life's story. One tool I used was a heady, academic faith.

I always prided myself on staying calm and strong when facing crises in my career and personal life. Then, I became chronically sick. Consequently, life became confusing and disordered. I couldn't figure out how to be "well," and I couldn't muscle my way through problems without physical repercussions.

Practicing Step Two taught me to stay open to a less intellectual spiritual path, and I encountered a loving, caring Higher Power. Instead of depending on self-sufficiency, I found humility in releasing my idea of how life should be. At first, letting go felt like giving up, but it was actually the first act in making room for a Higher Power's involvement. By remembering to make space for my Higher Power and stay out of the way, I've discovered sanity inside the truest part of myself.

When I find myself triggered, activated, or struggling, I take a pause. Often, I receive spiritual guidance. In this process, I have learned to cherish myself and find purpose—releasing myself into the ocean of wisdom always present in a Power greater than myself.

In this moment, I will let go and give my Higher Power space in my life.

October 4

My chronic pain and illness exacerbated innumerable fears that existed long before I came to CPA. Nearing the top of the list was fear of economic insecurity. I clung to my career. Retrospectively, I would have left my job much earlier. Fear blocked me from making a change. I had surgeries, received workplace modifications, and shared some of my tasks with others. These actions kept me functioning for a few years, but I knew it was unsustainable. Fear held me hostage in a job that was very fulfilling but physically beyond my capacity.

It wasn't a coincidence that my last day of work was ten days after my first CPA meeting. The willingness to face this problem was simply not available before. CPA gave me tools to face what I previously could not.

While applying for disability, I faced my anger and sorrow over the loss of my vibrant body that used to fly up the office stairs two at a time. I reviewed the overall situation and then turned the outcome over to my Higher Power. I shared my emotions with CPA friends who had traveled this path before me. Over time, recovery seeped in and displaced the former fear.

My sponsor accompanied me throughout this entire journey. I am so grateful for the insight I gained through Step work, and the support of many co-travelers. Using the acronym *FEAR: Face Everything and Recover* helped me learn to live peacefully, joyfully, and comfortably, thanks to the care of my Higher Power.

In this moment, I will remember that nothing is too frightening to face with the help of my Higher Power and my CPA community.

October 5

One of the gifts of recovery is the practice of taking the focus off others' faults and putting it on myself where, with God's help, I can address my part in things.

In Step Ten, I no longer ask, "Where am I wrong?" Instead of using one general question that only assigns blame and results in feelings of guilt or shame, I use more focused and practical questions that encourage self-reflection and change. These are some that I like to use: what's inaccurate and unhelpful in my thinking and behavior? What thoughts, emotions, or behaviors are distorted, exaggerated, or obsessive? Is my ego seeking power of some kind? Am I indulging in my negative emotions rather than letting them arise and pass? Am I repeating to myself things that make me miserable and that, upon close examination, are distortions caused by fatigue and pain? Where have I strayed into obsessing over things I know are beyond my control this day? What is it I'm unwilling to accept? What do I need to let go of? And my personal favorite: what do I need to do to promote deeper trust and surrender?

In CPA, making amends is a helpful way for me to treat the debilitating effects of chronic pain and illness. Most often, it is in these ways that I harm myself and then others. Awakening to them is facilitated by the Tenth Step.

When I examine things that are vexing, I look for how my perspective may be contributing to the problem. I amend my attitude where needed and promptly make amends to anyone I may have harmed while I was stuck in the problem rather than moving to the solution. I'm grateful for this Step. It allows for the fact that in CPA, I'm engaged in an ongoing process of self-evaluation and change.

In this moment, I will remember Step Ten helps me reflect honestly on my thoughts and actions.

October 6

I arrived at CPA bewildered, despondent, and in despair.

Prior to CPA, medical appointments filled me with guilt and shame. I felt too sick to bear the physical requirements of a medical visit and feared encountering another dismissive and shaming visit with no solution. As a result, I tended to wait until I was in crisis before I went to a doctor for help. I would then overwhelm them with information and repeated requests for help. It was unreasonable to expect anyone to see the horizon while being hit by a tsunami. In other words, I had an unreasonable expectation that these doctors could address all my issues at once while my body was in crisis.

My growth in CPA has given me a new relationship with medical professionals. I now know the serenity I feel from preparing, in writing, what I need them to know and pausing to pray before appointments. I cannot overemphasize how helpful this has been for my doctors and me.

With the help and loving support from a Higher Power, a sponsor who guided me through all Twelve Steps, daily meetings, literature, tear and laughter-filled conversations with members, and following practical suggestions, I am finding a stronger, shameless, blameless voice in every area of my life.

In this moment, I will search for ways I can make difficult situations easier to manage.

October 7

There's a saying I heard when I first arrived in recovery: don't quit five minutes before the miracle happens. Although I was working the Steps, going to meetings, and reading the literature, it didn't seem like anything was happening. My life was not getting better. My prayers to my Higher Power were in my God box, but they weren't being answered. Everyone kept telling me to "*Keep Coming Back*" and that the program "works if you work it." Well, I was working it. So, why was I still so miserable?

Impatience and the desire for immediate, dramatic results hindered my ability to see the progress I was making. Someone in a meeting reached out to me, and we began to talk on the phone. It helped to talk to a caring person who was a good listener and understood the challenges of living with a chronic condition. I'd been isolated for some time; now, I was no longer alone.

That was my dramatic miracle, but looking back, I now realize how many small ones I missed along the way.

In this moment, I will not quit five minutes before the miracle happens.

October 8

I love working the Twelve Steps with another person as a shared journey. Although each person's path is unique along the road of recovery, I often find there are some common wonders and obstacles many of us meet along the way. I enjoy sharing what I've learned, as well as guiding someone through their own unique exploration and discovery. We're not in a hurry; the pace is up to our Higher Powers.

My sponsor has helped me to trust, making it possible for me to learn to trust others. She modeled how to communicate clearly and directly while taking care of her own needs. I was afraid to call when I was struggling, but when I called, she let me know she had fifteen minutes or that she could not speak at that time. I learned it was safe to reach out—something I'd not experienced before. And it is this experience, strength, and hope that I, in turn, get to share with the people I now sponsor. I can be a mirror in which someone else can see their strengths, successes, and inner wisdom. These are some of my closest relationships because we share our minds and hearts with honesty, vulnerability, and courage.

In this moment, I will be grateful for the shared joy and growth I receive in sponsorship.

October 9

It was always easier for me to talk about willingness than to practice it in all my affairs, as suggested in Step Twelve. Until I admitted that a life based on self-sufficiency wasn't working, I couldn't become willing to depend on a Higher Power. For me, this has often meant depending on my CPA home group.

I was not thrilled about working the Steps. I needed the gift of desperation to prod me into doing so. I realized that those practicing recovery shared about how they worked the Steps; they talked about reliance on a Higher Power.

I qualified for membership because I had "a desire to recover from the emotional and spiritual debilitation of chronic pain and chronic illness," as Tradition Three asserts. But the willingness to get started eluded me. After a period of complacency and duress, I was motivated to learn what living life as fully as possible could mean for me. So, I became open to the emotionally and spiritually healing parts of the CPA program experience, like the Twelve Steps and Conference Approved Literature.

I needed to leave behind hanging around CPA and become willing to be a part of CPA as much as my body and mind would allow. I needed empathy. I needed to be heard and understood. And most of all, I needed to reconnect with a God of my understanding. For that, I needed the Twelve Steps.

In this moment, I will choose an attitude of willingness that turns the key and opens the door to recovery.

October 10

I've heard that Step Ten is the first of the "maintenance Steps." Having worked Steps One through Nine, I have seen beneficial changes in myself, my relationships, and how I react to my chronic pain and chronic illness. But I'm human and imperfect. Step Ten acknowledges that I may fall back into old habits and can make mistakes. The good news is none of that is problematic. There is a solution. I can become aware of my thoughts and actions. And when I notice that I've been relying on old, unhelpful habits, instead of my new recovery tools, I can take action to repair that.

CPA's "Step Ten Inventory" shows me ways I may be waning from my program. One question that stands out for me is, "Did I project negatively into the future?" This habit gets me into trouble. Fear stokes my active imagination, and my mind generates stories of horror and doom. Why make myself miserable about something that has not happened and likely never will? As I await tests and treatment options, I remind myself to live in this day and not project my fears into the future. I choose, instead, to have faith and trust that my Higher Power is in charge and that whatever happens, I have all that I need to get through the day. I don't want to waste the joys of this moment by living in an imagined scenario in the future. Practicing Step Ten helps me maintain my serenity.

In this moment, I will remember that although my conditions and humanity can knock me down, it is possible to get back up by applying Step Ten.

October 11

My body is incredibly unpredictable. I find that disconcerting and frustrating, to say the least. When I'm having some more manageable days, I get tempted to put off the things I need to get done, like paying bills, and do something I want to do instead. So I do some fun things, like going out with friends, and then BAM! My symptoms change. Consequently, so do my plans. The time I thought I would have to get certain things done now has to be spent caring for my health. Logically, I know that I can have fun and enjoy myself even if everything due in the near future isn't finished yet. But when I don't, and high symptom days come, and I miss a deadline, I can feel like such a loser. As a result, guilt and shame become associated with having fun.

Sometimes, when more difficult days happen, I begin to feel more depressed. If it lasts longer than I expect, I begin to experience fear and believe it will never get better. After all these years in CPA, I can still forget to use my program! Again, more erroneous guilt and shame.

But, at some point, I remember I have tools from CPA I can use. I have literature I can read. I can visit the awesome CPA website. I have people I can text, email, or call. I can go to a meeting. Most importantly, I remember my Higher Power is always there, waiting for my prayers. This is one of my favorite things to do on any day.

In this moment, I will remember all that is available as a CPA member to help me get through the harder days.

October 12

I have lived through situations where I felt completely disconnected after an unkind word or action from someone. I default to a trauma response where I feel unsafe and lose trust in my intuition and sanity. An old belief looms large that I'm in this life alone and can't trust anyone.

For much of my life, I vigilantly controlled and directed everything and everyone. I believed that if I did that perfectly, I would be safe. Step One in CPA was easy because I had decades of evidence that my best efforts to feel safe had only made my life more unmanageable. I had turned myself into a chameleon to survive. It was suggested that the Twelve Steps could restore me to my Authentic Self and give me refuge from the volatility of others. I asked for the courage to change the things I could and found a sponsor—one person I could share the real me with.

Thanks to my sponsor and a spiritual awakening while working Step Twelve, I am finally living as myself for the first time in fifty-five years. The sense of freedom and well-being is indescribable. I love myself exactly as I am at any given moment. I can accept life and others peacefully and comfortably. When I'm the object of someone else's ire, I don't get completely frazzled or derailed anymore because there are trustworthy and supportive people I can go to if my feelings are hurt. Thanks to CPA, I can now reflect on the wisdom that traumatic life experiences may have to offer me.

In this moment, I will remember that other people's unskillful words do not minimize my truth or compromise my emotional safety.

October 13

It takes courage to say, "I need help." It takes courage to say, "I'm sorry, I can't." It takes courage to just lie in bed. It takes courage to go to yet another medical appointment. It takes courage to accept help using the bathroom. It takes courage to cry, let alone laugh. On my own, I struggled to find that kind of courage. I had to find something greater to internalize that it wasn't up to me alone.

CPA and the Twelve Steps taught me to release and change the harmful thoughts society had conditioned into me. The primary example of this was accepting I could not handle everything by myself; I needed help. I gained the necessary courage and learned how to ask for help. Part of what gave me the courage was attempting to set aside all I thought I knew about myself, my abilities, and my life.

Now I can recognize the profound courage it takes for me to say, "Help," or "No," or "I can't," but most importantly, when I say "Yes!" It means I am willing to try something new. Because today, I believe it when I say, "Yes, I can be extremely creative and adaptive," or "Yes, I will use the Steps," and "Yes, I will ask for the courage to change the things I can."

In this moment, I will remember just how courageous I am.

October 14

Before I worked Step Four, it loomed over me. I thought it would be a lot of unpleasant, hard work. I don't know why I had these negative ideas. I think, sometimes, Step Four gets a bad reputation.

One thing I had correct was that Step Four was definitely work—not something I could do quickly if I wanted to do it justice. I did a little at a time, working slowly and using my chosen method. I just needed to get started, and then I continued spending time thoughtfully working through it when I could.

My sponsor and I did Steps Four and Five concurrently. I learned I was carrying blame for things that were not my fault. These were things I had not been able to recognize in myself. However, my sponsor could see past my emotions to the truth of the circumstances. It was a relief to be rid of unwarranted guilt. A greater sense of self-awareness grew. My weaknesses and strengths became more apparent. This awareness came into play while working subsequent Steps. Because I had faced and identified my faults, I was better able to notice them when they were activated. This, in turn, made it easier for me to let go and allow my Higher Power to remove them.

I also learned to recognize my strengths, which was beneficial and increased my self-esteem.

I am grateful that I had a wise and loving sponsor who guided me through Step Four. It's an important part of working the Steps, and it is right where it belongs in the process.

In this moment, I will remember that the Twelve Steps are an amazing resource and that Step Four can be a great gift.

October 15

When I was working my Steps, I discovered I had caused harm to myself. When it came time to make amends, one of the ways I did this was to practice self-compassion. This meant there were new behaviors and new attitudes for me to learn. This took time; none of it came naturally at first.

When I've had a hard day, rather than berating myself for believing I'd done something that made my symptoms worse, I'd find a way to soothe myself. It didn't make the discomforts go away, but it allowed me to be kind and loving to myself. A cup of tea, a call to a friend, putting on music—these were ways I acted compassionately and began making living amends to myself.

There were times I got stuck in my head, continually writing stories of disaster that never had a happy ending. With kindness, I would let go of the story I believed to be true and return to the present moment. I would focus on the question, "What do I need right now?" and on caring for myself.

Being kind to myself and treating myself the way I would a friend who was in pain were new concepts for me, but they have become reliable tools in my recovery. I used to think being easy on myself was just letting myself off the hook and avoiding taking responsibility. I thought that I always needed to push myself as far as possible. I've found that just the opposite is true. Being compassionate and tender toward myself is what truly gives me strength and courage.

In this moment, I will be compassionate with myself when my mind tends to become obsessive.

October 16

The CPA "One Day At A Time" reading states, "One Day At A Time—I will ask for help when I need it. I will accept assistance graciously and be thankful. I will appreciate the people in my life who support me."

Before I came to CPA, I was not able to "accept assistance graciously and be thankful" for that help. I was frustrated that there was so much I could not do myself. I was generally unhappy with how those helping me did things differently. I was a demanding perfectionist—with myself and others. In CPA, I realized this was an area in which I had to make many amends, and I still do.

For example, during the years I could no longer manage the family finances, and my spouse took over these responsibilities, instead of being grateful they were paying our bills with whatever system worked for them, I criticized them for what was missed, what was wrong, and how the files weren't up to my standards. I was anything but gracious!

Today, there are still moments I slip into old behaviors. I can be in bed, unable to make something to eat, and my partner will bring me some toast. Many times, it isn't the bread I want, or there is too much butter on it. I feel that twinge of frustration, but I can usually catch myself these days and choose to say, "Thank you," and gratefully eat what is provided. This is an act of humility and gratitude. It increases my sense of well-being and that of my relationships as well.

In this moment, I will accept help. I will find a simple way to graciously express my appreciation.

October 17

In CPA, the parts of me that were neglected and pushed aside for many years have become the focus of my spiritual work. Before CPA, I disregarded how I felt—physically and emotionally. I did not even consider feelings to be relevant in my day-to-day life. I was focused on, and struggling with, trying to keep up and somehow fit into a lifestyle that was becoming increasingly impossible—and actually threatening—to access.

Since childhood, I have had problems sharing how I feel with others. There was no room for my grief and all the other painful emotions and mental anguish that accompanied my physical problems. I tended to be quite stoic. I would focus on others and put their needs first, as I'd been brought up to do. My own needs were uncharted territory. By taking responsibility for my feelings and doing the work I needed to allow my spirit to heal, I've learned to share myself fully in the fellowship of CPA.

These days, I can easily reach for the phone, send a text, email another member, or go to a meeting. I also call my sponsor on a regular basis. Being able to genuinely share myself with another has become an invaluable part of my healing process. Some of the most important people in my life today are members of CPA. We may have vastly different personalities, interests, or opinions, but we have so much in common elsewhere that the differences don't seem to matter anymore.

In this moment, I will remember that sharing my pain and difficulties may be exactly the thing that helps another member. Every part of who I am has value.

October 18

In making "a searching and fearless moral inventory," my sponsor helped me see that Step Four was the dawn of having a real relationship with myself. This was when I first started showing more pieces of myself to others. I started sharing experiences I wouldn't have previously. I came into CPA with a wall I'd built around myself that was so thick and strong that no one could hurt me again—emotionally or physically.

In CPA, I was gently given space to be honest with myself and others, which is now how I like to live every day. It was and still is, okay to be vulnerable. I can now recognize that I am powerless and always was, but I now also trust that I'm going to be okay, regardless of the outcomes. However, it took a lot of guidance, support, and patience from all those involved, including myself, to get to that point. Retrospectively, it all started with willingness.

The time I spent on myself seemed counterintuitive at first, but then I began to see an old friend—a version of myself that I enjoyed being. I had lived under the impression that knowledge, success, outward appearances, and living on others' terms were just a part of life. Then, my goals were crushed by chronic pain and chronic illness. I felt like all that was left was the option to surrender.

All of this helped me see that my figurative wall needed to come down. Fear of knowing myself was keeping me from being able to move forward. Now, after learning to manage that fear with the help of CPA, I am able to sit with myself as I am; I like who I am, and I feel blessed to be who I am.

In this moment, I will release my protective walls, trusting that I know enough, I have enough, I do enough, and I am enough just as I am.

October 19

I used to think of my body as something separate from my real self. I saw it as a sort of flesh prison that my mind had to live in. I treated it badly as if to punish it for the way it was. I wanted no pain, so I wanted no body. I used to self-harm and use small, acute injuries as a distraction when I hurt too much; I used to yell at and insult my body parts. I didn't understand that by yelling at my body and treating it poorly, I was actually yelling at myself—treating myself in that same manner. After all, my body is not just part of me—it is me.

In CPA, I'm learning to be gentle with myself. Myself includes my body. I'm learning to say, "Hey, legs, you're not feeling great? Okay, we will rest today. And I will use my cane. Would that help?" Instead of screaming, "You useless legs, I hate you," as I did in the past. I'm learning to say, "You worked hard today, back. Here is a heating pad," when I've done a little too much instead of thinking, "Why must my back punish me like this?"

By accepting that my body and I are one—that I am different and that I have different needs—I can have a more harmonious and serene life. Existing as a human means having a body; the great human illusion is that my mind is separate. Rather than hoping my body will feel better later or planning for a life in a body I don't have, I am learning how to live fully, just as I am, and *Just for Today*.

In this moment, I will reassure myself that it is acceptable for my body to be different, and to have different needs.

October 20

My sponsor shared with me how she uses code words to communicate with loved ones when she's not okay. She suggested that if the code is funny or silly, it can lighten the moment.

I broached the topic with my children. I've been telling them for years, "Mom doesn't feel very well today." How could they possibly differentiate between times when I'm a little unwell and very unwell? Or when it's physical, and I can't go somewhere with them, or more emotional, and I need some time alone and can't be available for a little while? My younger son suggested a code for the hardest times when I am barely functional: the fox is in the box. I laugh every time I think of it.

This code reminds me that it's good to laugh, and I don't have to take my illnesses so seriously. It gives me a warning, too, reminding me to try to be considerate of others, too, in those moments.

Just the other night, I was exhausted and in pain. My son did a magic trick and wanted to do many more. I knew I could not watch even one more. To avoid hurting his feelings, I said, "The fox is in the box." He quickly accepted what that meant. There was no long argument with him not understanding, me getting frustrated and speaking harshly, and ending with both of us feeling bad afterward, which would have happened in the past. It's been a miracle that I'm learning to laugh about my situation. I find that the more I accept my situation and my needs, the easier things get.

In this moment, I will learn from others and not take myself too seriously.

October 21

In CPA, I was taught that we share our experience, strength, and hope. It was noted that we don't share unsolicited advice, medical, legal, or otherwise. We don't push our political opinions, dispense marriage or psychological counseling, or give recommendations as a professional. Even if I were certified and qualified to provide some service, that's not my role here. As a member of CPA, I'm only qualified and free to share my experience, strength, and hope. I usually like to include how whatever I'm sharing has evolved from my time and active participation in CPA.

This distinction saves me from a host of pitfalls. It saves me from feelings of grandiosity and making some, possibly grave, errors. If I'm chatting with a CPA friend and sharing complaints and talking about medications, specific therapies, or whatever else we may know about, as trusted friends, we are, of course, free to do so privately.

In meetings, I share what drove me to CPA, what has happened as a result of my participation, and what my life is like now. Basically, I try to share my relevant experience. When a newcomer, peer, sponsee, or member reaches out for help, I share what has happened. My life now has a Twelve Step program that is a continually reliable source of support, in fair weather and in foul.

If I have no program experience with something, I say, "My experience with that is limited." When asked for help, before giving my answer, I ask myself, "Am I sharing my actual experience, strength, and hope from working my program, or something else? Am I practicing patience and compassion with myself and others?"

In this moment, I will be mindful of how and what I share in CPA.

October 22

I have lived with chronic conditions most of my life and accepted the chronic nature of my illnesses long ago. What I hadn't done was look at the cruelty I continued to use on myself. I was even doing it while using recovery language, taking fearless moral inventories, being of service to others, and more. I denied this behavior through dissociation, diversion, and distraction.

These made things seem easier and less painful for me. Sometimes, blaming and shaming myself seemed easier than being vulnerable and powerless over things that could hurt me.

While working the Steps in CPA, I became aware of this added layer of denial and self-abuse. I accepted it and became able to take the next indicated action. *One Day at a Time*, I've arrived at a deeper level of acceptance, surrender, self-compassion, and freedom than I've ever known before.

In this moment, I will be aware and try to change the things I can.

October 23

In CPA, what I'm powerless over is always with me. I cannot physically separate myself from it. That's because what I am powerless over is my body and the pain I feel. What I can do is recognize my powerlessness. I have an illness that is not curable. This was a hard pill to swallow and difficult to accept. I relentlessly sought the right doctor, procedure, pill, or miracle supplement to cure what I had and relieve my pain.

Today, my powerlessness is evident. I cannot control the pain. But I can look at myself with compassion. I can rest, eat right, and take my medications responsibly. I can take advice from doctors or other practitioners and apply what makes sense for me. So, while I may be powerless in ways, I am certainly not helpless. Today, I find the strength to help myself from a supportive and loving God who wants me to live with peace and security.

Step One is a challenging Step. I know now that I can't do it perfectly and will continually return to it throughout my recovery journey. I need to take this Step every day, sometimes every minute, and pray to God to give me strength. My life is getting better because of CPA. I am so grateful for this program and the people who support me along the way.

In this moment, I will remember I am powerless over my body and my pain, but I do have power over how I relate to my God.

October 24

Working Step Seven in CPA, my sponsor helped me see that I do not have to remove my defects of character. I only need to become willing to let go of my defects of character, issues, behaviors, and beliefs that are blocking me from experiencing serenity and joy. I only need to be willing to let go and be changed by something greater than myself. I humbly request the willingness to engage in something different and new.

As I look back at my story, I can see that my Higher Power has been helping me the whole time. Humility sets in when I ask my HP what's next and follow the breadcrumbs or little clues and signs in life I believe my HP uses to communicate. I trust my HP to do for me what I cannot do for myself.

My Higher Power cares about me deeply, and that includes my hopes and dreams. When I work Step Seven, I humbly wait for what is next to keep feeling joyous and serene.

In this moment, I will believe that my Higher Power is doing for me what I cannot do for myself.

October 25

Before CPA, I suppressed all feelings. I suppressed joy because I knew it couldn't last. I suppressed anger, terrified that, once released, it would be all-consuming. I tried to force myself not to be sad. With an unskillful Pollyanna routine, I pretended like everything was always perfect and denied any emotional pain I experienced. Thanks to CPA, I now know that suppressed feelings only increase stress and anxiety, exacerbating my physical pain and, therefore, my emotional turmoil as well.

After experiencing a spiritual awakening as part of working Step Twelve, I have been able to live more peacefully, joyfully, and comfortably regardless of my physical condition. But a new, unexpected health challenge has thrown me for a loop, and I don't have any idea how to handle it. I am angry and can feel myself fighting reality. I am done! I am back at Step One. But even in the midst of this misery, I am still able to love myself.

Thanks to working on surrender in CPA, I know that hope exists and that the clarity I once had can be restored. For now, I am honoring my struggle and anger by practicing outrageous self-care. Today, distracting myself with bad TV while staying in my room with my door closed and phone off is self-care. And I try to keep in mind that what works as self-care today may be inappropriate or harmful tomorrow.

Today, I can honor all that accompanies my reality with self-love and compassion. I remember that *This Too Shall Pass* and comfort myself however I am inspired to do so.

In this moment, I will acknowledge that acceptance gives me the ability to love myself exactly as I am.

October 26

CPA tools have taught me how to proactively start my day over any time I think it would help. Living with chronic illness and pain, this ability to start over throughout the day has become very useful.

More often than I'd like, things come at me so fast that I can't comprehend what's happening. I am trying to notice and learn from my behavior. And I am trying to help myself grow by changing some of them. I've learned to take breaths and quiet myself. I now know I can take a moment to try to understand, problem-solve, or just process. And a moment of gratitude doesn't hurt either since it brings me into the present.

Being able to check in with myself and reflect on my conduct as the day goes on has been an effective coping skill and doesn't add to my illness and pain. I can start my day over at any time; it's up to me to use the tools of CPA.

In this moment, I will open my CPA toolbox and apply what is needed to begin my day again.

October 27

One of the first impactful things I heard in CPA was that I have value, and my Higher Power loves me, even if I can't get out of bed. I immediately teared up and thought, "No way, they can't actually say that!" I certainly was not raised to think anything like that. But I immediately felt in my soul it was the truth. This led to new beliefs like resting is okay, helpful, healthful, and often the thing I need to do. At times, my Higher Power has supported and guided me towards resting.

Recently, I had a major flare, and my symptoms were overpowering. I ended up needing to rest the whole day and became angry with my Higher Power. I didn't have the energy to attend my child's baseball game. Then, my other kid came home from school and wanted to talk. I realized that if I could put my problems aside to listen and validate their concerns and needs, I could truly be of service that day. Resting and subsequently accepting my situation provided me with the patience to listen to my child.

I've learned in CPA to stop viewing my pain as a punishment from my Higher Power or as a sign that I am "less than." I know now that I am no more or less worthy than anyone else. I don't know why I have this pain, but I do know that we each have our own journey. I am a good and loving person. I deserve good things, to take time for myself, and to have fun.

In this moment, I will be grateful for the many lessons I've learned in CPA by being still and willing to feel and hold my pain.

October 28

Over the years, I've written fear inventories about surgeries, appointments with new doctors, finances, and more. Recently, in my Fourth Step work, something arose that I was afraid to look at—grief. I grieved my formerly healthy body and active lifestyle, the loss of my career, and the ability to be independent. I prayed for willingness and gave it time, but I was making little progress with my Step work, so I asked my sponsor if she had any suggestions. Her suggestion was a fear inventory! So, I wrote my answers to a series of questions: 1) What am I afraid of? 2) If that came true, what am I afraid of then? 3) Repeat question two until there is no more fear.

Doing this simple exercise revealed why I was afraid to look at my grief. I might find I am still grieving...which might cause despair and depression...which might cause me to not be able to function...which might cause me to give up. Wow. I had been afraid of what was hidden beneath the menacing tip of my figurative grief iceberg. It was too scary for me to face the feelings I had denied for so long, and I balked. Doing my inventory using those three questions let me see my deeper fears clearly. And, as is often the case, I saw that they were not entirely based in reality.

There are many unknowns when living with chronic illness and pain, and I am grateful to have this powerful inventory tool to break through my fears and restore my sanity.

In this moment, I will humbly request the courage to inventory my fears.

October 29

It's not always simple to find sponsorship, but it can be done. And for me, it is necessary.

Why? Because, after all, CPA is a Twelve Step program designed to produce a spiritual solution. Most spiritual traditions advocate connecting with others in community. I can't effectively work the Steps in isolation. It is one thing to speak in general, ethereal terms about spiritual matters, but another to try to live a spiritual life without discussing the specifics of how I practice that spirituality. This is difficult and takes ongoing presence of mind, willingness, and courage on my part. I need others on this path.

I get and give this fortitude as a peer, co-sponsor, or as a personal sponsor. I share at meetings that some moments in the sponsor-sponsee relationship are necessary. Also, I think of my sponsor as special, as the one to whom I tell all and the one who may speak freely to me without hesitation when that's what I need.

I've heard it said, "You have to give it away to keep it," and, "The spiritual life is not a theory. We have to live it." It's in sponsorship that I've found the sure way for me to experience the warm feeling I get when I know I have truly helped another. I worked in a helping profession and know that I helped people there, but in sponsorship, I've been certain of it, and for me, there is no finer feeling.

In this moment, I will be grateful for all my fellows traveling the CPA road to recovery.

October 30

I am grateful. The weather is cool, I have two beautiful puppies, and my home is a cozy nest where my body can relax and soothe itself. In this space, I feel held and warm through uncomfortable moments.

My thoughts are racing. I'm in pain. I can't breathe. It's been six years with no solution. And yet, amid this suffering, I can stay home. I can take a break. Thanks to CPA, I'm learning to communicate my needs, express my difficulties, and ask for help in effective ways.

Amid the chaos of my illness, there's peace and quiet around me. I have found sanctuary. Supportive people and friends remind me to breathe or urge me forward when I don't think I can move. They try to empathize with my situation rather than fix it.

Amid the chaos of my illness, there's peace and quiet around me. I have found sanctuary. Supportive people and friends remind me to breathe or urge me forward when I don't think I can move. They try to empathize with my situation rather than fix it.

In this moment, I will relax and feel the gift of serenity surrounding me in the stillness.

October 31

My holidays are celebrated differently now compared to how they were before I became ill and chronic pain became a part of my life. One thing that helped me to begin enjoying holidays again is practicing acceptance, more specifically, the *Three A's: Awareness, Acceptance, Action*. I am A*ware* that my capabilities are reduced from what my family and I were accustomed to. I *Accept* that, and I take the appropriate *Action*. The holidays are not what they used to be, but they can still be joyful. Accepting this has not been easy for me, especially not at first, but the more I practice having acceptance, the more it enhances my life.

I'm very fortunate that my partner is willing to do the majority of the work for holiday celebrations. Not everyone has that help. There's still a bit of a problem with this, though. I have to let go of how I think everything should look and be willing to accept something different from what I would have done. That can be a struggle for me. When this problem comes up, I remember my program and apply the things I have learned in CPA. I don't always remember to do this right away; I usually start by attending a meeting, going through online posts from the fellowship, or reading CPA literature. By doing this, I am reminded that I have tools to help me recover.

In this moment, I will be grateful for all the practical sources of help in my life, and see the value of applying spiritual principles.

November

November 1

I love that, in CPA, a Higher Power gets to be my Higher Power. No one gets to tell me what it is or what I have to believe. I alone get to determine what it entails. And I appreciate that my relationship with this Power develops over time. I don't have to know exactly what it is right now in order to work the Twelve Steps or to be a member of CPA.

I think each of us has our own Higher Power. And, I believe there is an Ultimate Higher Power, greater than all of us, which I call UHP. I call my HP "Higher Power of Love" and "Spirit of Kindness and Compassion." My Higher Power is available to handle whatever the Ultimate Higher Power brings into my life. I may not know exactly what my HP is, but I am discovering what it wants for me.

My Higher Power:
- wants me to feel safe.
- wants me to feel loved.
- wants me to love myself.
- wants me to accept myself exactly as I am.
- wants me to live with ease.
- wants to know me.
- wants to be here for me.
- wants me to believe that there is nothing wrong with me and there has never been anything wrong with me.
- wants me to feel proud of myself.
- wants me to be kind and gentle with myself and others.
- wishes I had all of these things when I was a kid, growing up scared and alone.
- wants all of this for me and so much more.

In this moment, I will accept what HP means to me.

November 2

The actions of the first three Steps—admitting, coming to believe, and making a decision—make me think of that wonderful brief description: I can't, God can, let God. That "let God" part sounds pretty simple, and I think it might be, but it can surely be daunting, too. Turn my will and my life over to something other than my own control? Whoa, there.

I find it challenging to let go of control and find peace by just trusting my Higher Power, but I'm told it can be easy. The easy times are when things look hopeless when running my life has ended up causing more pain and maybe even a big mess. That's when I'm ready to wash my hands of it all and give my Higher Power a chance. A lot of the time, it's not as easy because I want to be in control, to be sure things turn out the way I want them to. Experience has shown me, however, that being in control often does not guarantee I end up with the desired result.

A thought that helps me is the idea that I can try turning my will and life over, and if I don't like the result, I can always take my life and will back. Often, I find I inadvertently take it back. In reality, I turn it over and take it back often. This decision is growing and evolving as I continue to work the program and the Steps.

Yes, I have worked Step Three, but that does not mean my understanding and application of it in my life will never change. I remember that it is *Progress, Not Perfection*, I seek through working the Steps, and I will keep doing my part.

In this moment, I will let go of control and turn to Higher Power.

November 3

I put the first three Steps into action, using the phrase, "I can't, You can, I will let You." I identified my defects of character in Step Four and shared them with my sponsor in Step Five. Now, all I have to do is become willing to have them removed. I'm told Step Six is a gentle Step.

In Step Seven, I will be giving my defects to my Higher Power. But in Step Six, I'm merely getting ready to ask. CPA's program of recovery has built-in baby steps—all I have to do in Step Six is get ready.

I needed a physical action for Step Six to be transformative. I got ready by writing down all the things I was going to give up for removal. These were mostly old habits; I was ready to release them. They're like a sweatshirt I've had since college, filled with holes, threadbare, and ready for retirement. It no longer keeps me warm, but it's familiar and comfortable, and I wear it anyway. The day eventually comes when I decide it is time to let it go. It does not serve me anymore. I need to get psychologically ready to let go of my old friend, filled with many memories.

I do the same in Step Six. I get ready to let go of old behaviors that are no longer serving me or may be harmful. Step Six prepares me to let go and ask for my Higher Power's help.

In this moment, I will ask for help in letting go of all that does not serve me.

November 4

I've been ill for decades. For many years, I considered all my days bad days. I was often overwhelmed, and that intensified the suffering I experienced.

What I find helpful is to separate, when I can, my physical pain from my emotional and spiritual maladies.

On days I acknowledge as extra tough, I vow to use the tools of the program so that, at day's end, I can say, "Well, it was a good day. I did not succumb to hopelessness. Perhaps there is something to learn from this experience in the future, even though it may not have felt that way today."

CPA asserts that my emotional and spiritual issues are treatable. I decided to trust the process and believe it might work for me. The more I can separate my physical pain from any emotional distress about that pain, the more my day improves. Certainly, I wouldn't choose to have this pain, nor do I have to like it, but I can accept it, be open-minded, and be teachable regarding my response to it.

For sure, there are times when I'm so ill that I can't see anything of value in my day, yet I choose to stick to my CPA practices. My experience is that these practices pay off eventually. The great adventure I've embarked upon is a spiritual one. These are now the guiding principles of all my good days.

In this moment, I will focus on all that is positive.

November 5

Before CPA, I obsessively tried to maintain control over my health conditions to a problematic degree. I was sure that if I found the right doctor, treatment, or procedure, my problems would go away and I wouldn't have to deal with them anymore. I spent years focused on this search for an answer or cure. Despite all of my efforts, time, money, and research, my situation did not get better but worse. In Step One, I recognized I had been operating under an Illusion of control and needed to surrender and let go of the belief that I could control my condition.

Step One invited me to do something differently. It suggested I admit my desire to change my body and my desperate need to fix my body. It was also suggested I examine my powerlessness in the situation. In Steps Two and Three, I identified a Power greater than myself who could help me, and I turned my life over to this Power. I started to give up obsessing and fixating on things. But I didn't give up hope or stop engaging in helpful activities. I gained confidence and trust in the guidance of my Higher Power. Then I practiced following the guidance rather than my self-will. Surrender allowed me to become open to the idea of living in a different way and, possibly, even adopting a new belief system.

That was all I needed to do to begin my recovery journey. Acceptance was not directly asked of me in the Twelve Steps. Acceptance happened as a result of working the Steps.

In this moment, I will continue to have faith and work the CPA program.

November 6

Am I moving toward or away from a place of serenity?

Serenity is such a fine place. Sometimes I feel like I'm there, just for a moment, and sometimes I get a few moments. Other times, I wonder if it's even possible.

Today, I'm imagining this serene realm as the tip of a pin, a very tiny sphere with a huge amount of space around it. I imagine myself moving away from, then closer to, but then away again, from the tip of the pin, where serenity is accessible.

But I don't experience serenity itself as a destination or a goal—it is a moment-to-moment experience. When I work the Steps, I acquire tools to help me experience serenity. I can think more of others and be more honest with myself. I can ask for spiritual guidance. I can ask for others' help, and I can do service. I realize that though I might be powerless, my Higher Power is more than enough to get me through today regardless of how much serenity I feel at any given moment.

Just knowing this moves me toward the tip of the imaginary pin. I don't have to beat myself up if I am not in a serene place. I can turn to my program tools, and I will move closer to it. I don't think it is possible to force myself to be serene, but there are things I can do to move toward it.

As with anything, serenity comes and goes for me. All things pass. I think this is natural, and when I can accept this, I find myself even closer to that I seek—serenity.

In this moment, I will accept that serenity can fluctuate.

November 7

Step Two suggested that I consider how my emotional and mental processes were skewed. I realized that I was not thinking clearly or effectively. I'd arrived at CPA in a dark place.

I was demoralized, depressed, and afraid. On some level, I knew my resources were not up to the task of coping. I could feel that I needed to be "restored to sanity." I didn't understand then, but my desperation brought with it the gift of humility.

I discovered that many in the fellowship had found ways out of their own dark places; they had what I wanted. It seemed logical that if I could bring myself to try what they suggested, I could also find my way out. However, I was nervous about the role of God in the program when I knew, without question, that I could only trust myself.

I was wisely told once to avoid thinking too much about a Higher Power. It was explained that I didn't need to understand this Power to decide if my sanity could be restored. Rather, participating in this program of specific action would allow that Power to flow, and for me to have a spiritual experience.

I needed the experience of finding this Power. My sponsor suggested I just get started and assured me that if things didn't work out, they would be there to help.

Today, I thank God for such forthright, kind, and sensible CPA members who supported my spiritual journey. It became the great experiment of my life.

In this moment, I will appreciate the support and wisdom of CPA members.

November 8

When I came to CPA, I became aware of just how broken my body, mind, and spirit were, as I never was before. I was defeated, licked—I could not deny it any longer. The process of accepting this was painful and difficult.

Surrender of body, mind, and spirit continues to be an important element of my spiritual growth. I have to counteract the dictates of my ego daily by opening my mind and heart to a spiritual solution for my problems.

In CPA, I've learned how to open myself, just as I am, to be useful to my Higher Power. The Twelve Steps help guide me on my spiritual path, and as I travel them, I am never alone. I have been given companions to walk with me along this spiritual path. We meet, share our ups and downs, and help each other on the way when we become confused or weak. We offer each other spiritual nourishment and comfort as we journey. We all make our way through the path of the Twelve Steps with the help and support of others. Then, we can come together; that is where we find our safety and our strength.

In this moment, I will go to a meeting or connect with a friend in my CPA program, knowing that our coming together yields comfort, nourishment, safety, strength, and spiritual growth.

November 9

Medications provoke an internal battle: the little child inside me doesn't want to swallow any stupid pills! When I first came to meetings and learned that CPA has no opinion on medications, it helped me feel safe. I've had to make some difficult decisions dealing with medications, but there are so many wonderful people in CPA to speak with privately about making these choices.

There was also an external battle for me to face. Because of shared past experiences with addiction, my partner had strong opinions about medications I should avoid. With the help of working the CPA Steps and talking to others in the program, I have been able to have honest conversations with my significant other about my choices. This is all really difficult for them, yet I know how important it is to include them in my recovery. CPA has made it so that they still feel involved, but I'm not relying on someone who, in this situation, is incapable of giving me the support I need.

Now, when new medication recommendations come from my doctor, I feel prepared to deal with the proposition. I have a new way to make decisions because of the meaningful experiences I shared in CPA. I take my time to make decisions about new medications and treatments. And I always pray or meditate when I'm feeling any doubts. I feel so grateful to have a community to help me through all these difficult decisions. This support leaves me feeling better about my choices and my life. I'm no longer alone on this journey.

In this moment, I will use the resources and fellowship of CPA to support me in making healthcare choices I feel good about. I can involve my loved ones, as needed, with grace, ease, and honesty, knowing I have all the support I need.

November 10

My experience with Step Ten is that I easily forget about it, which results in not receiving its benefits, like helping to maintain my spiritual fitness.

After I completed the Steps, I thought, "Okay, I'm done." The truth is that I am never finished working the Steps if I want to keep them active in my life. Step Ten is crucial because when I continue to take a personal inventory and admit my wrongs, I stay updated on areas of my life that need improvement and those going well.

I use the Steps in my life, often applying them outside of CPA. Step Ten is a clear way to continue to work my program. If I stay aware of my weaknesses and strengths as they come, I'm reminded to turn them over to God so they can be removed or used.

When I realized I was not using this Step to its full potential, I thought about ways to make it more active in my life. I decided to find a Step Ten partner. We agreed to email or phone each other once a week to discuss our Tenth Step. Ideally every evening—but actually a few times a week—I reflect on my day. I become aware of character defects that show up and notice my strengths. Checking in with my Step Ten partner gives me the accountability and encouragement to follow through. Not everyone needs that accountability, and I may not always need it, but for now, it's working well.

In this moment, I will remind myself to take a personal inventory and reflect upon it.

November 11

When I practice Step Eleven, I experience serenity.

My daily practice consists of morning meditation and prayer to ask for guidance on my day. I also ask for my defects to be removed, and to clearly hear my Higher Power. The evenings are for journaling, reflecting, and praying about my day. I ask for the power to continue carrying out my HP's will.

The more I practice, the more love, joy, calm, and self-compassion arise in me. This, as well as keeping things simple, has improved my mental stability and emotional maturity. When I meditate, I feel peaceful and connected with my HP.

I find, as I've come to forgive and love myself, that I am more able to give away what has been given to me. My relationships with those I love have grown. I can see that my emotional sobriety is growing, too, as I connect further with myself and others.

I quiet myself when things come too quickly; I pay attention to my breath during difficult situations. I gain a sense of serenity by being present in the moment. Presence is my power. There is a relief in finding acceptance of myself.

I've also discovered I am more than my chronic pain and chronic illness. I look at my past now and can admit how I was powerless in my life and that my HP was always there. Practicing every day helps me to recover.

My behaviors have been gradually changing as I work the Steps. Finding my inner power through prayer and meditation has changed my life. Today, I humbly ask to be used for the greater good of our fellowship and of the world.

In this moment, I will turn to prayer and meditation.

November 12

Just for Today is an important slogan and coping strategy for me. Often, a full day is more than I can handle, so I experiment with breaking it down into smaller chunks.

Sometimes, *Just for Today* becomes just for this moment, just for now, or just while this is what I am feeling or experiencing. Reducing my perspective to just for now helps me stop feeling overwhelmed—trying to figure out how I'm going to cope with a set of symptoms and circumstances for an indefinite period of time. When things cannot be fixed and are out of my control, using my recovery tools—such as spiritual coping strategies—becomes essential for strengthening my resilience and improving my quality of life.

Basic meditation practice helps me. I use breath as the anchor for my meditation. It is the focus I return to, again and again, after the mind inevitably wanders elsewhere. Suggestions I tell myself, such as, "There is nowhere else to be, nothing else to do," help me return to the present moment. I prefer engaging in a meditation practice that has a beginning and an end. I find it relaxing and more approachable. There was a period of time when I needed to set a timer for four-minute increments. Even though my goal was to meditate for twenty minutes, that was an inconceivably unendurable amount of time. So, I gave myself permission to go for shorter periods. Within those meditations, my days were four minutes long.

Just for Today helps me cope with living with chronic illness and pain in skillful ways. I don't have to figure out how I am going to manage five, ten, or even twenty more years of unknown (but anticipated) additional challenges. Using this slogan, I can let go of that uncertain future and focus on the life I have now.

In this moment, I will appreciate the wisdom of CPA slogans, especially Just for Today.

November 13

Sex is out of the question in my romantic relationships. Before CPA, I viewed this as yet another source of pleasure I'd been robbed of. My body had betrayed me with illness and pain. Later, someone I was dating experienced similar losses—pain, medications, fatigue, limited movement, and difficulty breathing. Not being able to have sex was a blow to their ego and self-image.

Going through that experience with them helped me realize that I no longer look at my life through a dark and desolate lens. I see now that my body has not betrayed me. In reality, it works very hard to keep me alive and able to love, live, and connect with others. There are laws of nature, and illness is part of that law. It's a fact of my life. Accepting that fact has given me the freedom to choose how I will live the rest of my life. Instead of being angry about how I think it should have gone, I can now trust in its process.

Today, I believe things are unfolding by divine standards, not mine. I find this comforting.

Life and love have meanings I could not grasp before experiencing chronic illness. To be clear, it isn't the illness that gave me all I have today—it's the spiritual program I continue to work due to that illness.

Connection and honest communication encourage intimacy in all my relationships, particularly my romantic ones. Touch is more meaningful and important to me now that sex is not pleasurable for either of us. Romance is sweeter. I know, without a doubt, that I am loved, my touch is desired, and I am building a meaningful connection. I could be with my new best friend and long-term lover. I never thought I would have this experience or this kind of hope for my future. I only have this hope because I know, no matter what happens, I have the support of CPA. I know I will be okay.

In this moment, I will receive and give love to myself and others.

November 14

When I am feeling especially grateful, I realize that there are more things that work right in my body than things that malfunction. I have come to recognize and live by the fact that my body works very hard for me. When I first got sick, I saw the situation as one where my body broke down and was constantly disappointing me. Now, I realize that even while the laws of nature cause some of my body's malfunctions, the rest of my body works very hard to compensate for those malfunctions.

I didn't change these beliefs overnight! CPA has never suggested I ignore feelings of sadness or concern. That is not a compassionate or kind response. I have to grieve my losses. Two of the hardest things I continue to grieve are my changing physical abilities and social life. Grieving is necessary. Also, it is necessary that I understand and accept that, for this chronically ill, disabled person, grief comes and goes. Gratitude for what is good in my life helps balance the grief; it carries me through the grief and onto the other side of it.

I am constantly grateful for the fellowship of CPA. I do not have to grieve alone, but I don't have to be grateful alone, either.

In this moment, I will accept my evolving grief and the support of the CPA fellowship.

November 15

When I first came to CPA, I struggled to understand the idea of surrender. I didn't want to give up. I was in my early forties, and my children needed me. I was their homeschool teacher. I was fighting for my health so that I could be a mom and a wife. I was also involved in advocacy for people with my illness, which I found very rewarding.

In CPA, surrender doesn't mean we stop medications, treatments, or therapies. We don't have to stop advocating for ourselves or others. It took me a while to understand that surrender doesn't mean giving up. In the past, when one of my doctors recommended a new medication, my hopes would soar. And if the side effects were too much or the medicine didn't help as much as I had hoped, my whole attitude would plummet. I would become depressed and overwhelmingly disappointed. It would affect my whole life, including my relationship with my family.

After working through the Steps and adjusting my attitude toward my pain and illness, I have found some freedom. The difference for me now is that I'm not so invested in the outcomes. My spirit no longer lives or dies based on them.

I have given up the struggle. I'm proud of my body and all that it does correctly, especially with all of life's obstacles. I don't know what scientific advancements may come or what limitations might improve or go away. Today, I surrender; I accept myself, my body, and my illness exactly as I am right now.

In this moment, I will let go of outcomes and practice acceptance.

November 16

My Fourth Step began with some dread. I expected it to be hard and unpleasant, but that turned out not to be true. Step Four, for me, was taking a methodical and careful evaluation of myself. I discovered things that were hiding, and I recognized things that were in the open. I spent time relating to myself in a way I don't think I would have otherwise.

This Step helped me to know myself, and to acknowledge my weaknesses and strengths. Step Four was a building block which helped me prepare for the next Steps. Becoming aware of my weaknesses was important when I got to Steps Six through Nine. Spending time exploring these helped me to recognize when character defects were in action. This gave me the chance to turn them over to my Higher Power for removal at the right time.

I think the Twelve Steps are wonderful and that they're in this order for a reason. Step Four is in the perfect spot. Step Four has given me invaluable knowledge and insight.

It's suggested we find an accessible way to work the Steps; there are several to choose from. It's also suggested that we work them at our own pace. It may seem like a big job, but how do you eat a large, nutritious meal? One bite at a time. I learned to take my time, enjoy the process, and let my Higher Power guide me. Working this Step with a sponsor's guidance and support was essential for me. It kept me on track. Working this Step has been a wonderful blessing in my life.

In this moment, I will recognize my own courage in working each CPA Step.

November 17

When I first came into CPA, I had recently resigned from the position that financially supported both my wife and myself. I thought letting go of my high-powered job would allow me to get better. I had an enormous fear of financial insecurity but enough savings to cover a year's worth of living expenses. I assumed I would be able to work again.

My wife had retired ten years prior. She had taken over most of the household duties and was renovating our fixer-upper house. After three months, I'd gotten worse physically; it became clear that I wouldn't be able to work anymore, even from home. I figured applying for disability was pointless, as I had no clear diagnosis to explain the daily debilitating fatigue I was experiencing. I told my father we were going to lose our home soon, and he began to financially support us. At first, I felt shame, but I began to see that as my Higher Power stepping in to keep a roof over our heads.

I am now able to work a few hours a month, and my wife is making a small income, too. I've been able to let go of shame and gracefully accept food every week from our local food bank. We are by no means financially secure. By working the Steps, I've moved from fear of financial insecurity to trusting that my Higher Power has a plan for me. I don't know how that plan fits in the bigger picture, but so as long as I focus on today, the here and now, and God's will for me, I know I am okay. God is my employer.

In this moment, I will turn to my faith in a Higher Power, especially when I feel afraid.

November 18

It's a blustery fall day. The apartment is cold. My will today is to stay in bed, my head wrapped in heat and ice at the same time, and wallow a little in the frustration of my chronic illness. I have things to do. I'll be moving soon to a more accessible apartment which meets my physical and emotional needs. I want to wallow in the sadness of leaving and grieve that my body cannot maintain this rural lifestyle through another winter.

I have a service commitment in CPA today; I want to be present for that commitment more than I want to stay in bed. This is an example of recognizing God's will for me.

Today, I try not to get caught up in word choices for my Higher Power. I'm okay with slipping between "God" and "Higher Power," whom I find most strongly in nature. But, for me, God is everywhere.

When I resist God's will, I feel, live, and experience the consequences. God wants me comfortable and rested, not emotionally, physically, and mentally depleted from pain and illness. I'm learning how to align my will with my Higher Power's will, a day at a time, an hour at a time, a minute at a time, a second at a time.

Right now, that means being kind to myself, spending a couple more hours in bed before coming face-to-face with friends, avoiding loneliness and isolation, and letting God work through my fellow members and me.

In this moment, I will rest and take the time I need.

November 19

As soon as I was made aware that I needed a surgery, I contacted my sponsor. I knew three months ahead of time when it would happen. I asked for support in my various recovery communities, locally and internationally. I also sought assistance from the religious institutions I am a participating member of. A woman younger than I intersected these circles of support, organized a flow chart for rides to and from the hospital two hours away, and made a regular schedule of visitors and helpers, including a soup train.

At the hospital, I arrived perky and ready for surgery. I tried my best to be kind, considerate, and generous with my thoughts and actions, even during the more trying times. This surgery had only been performed there twice that year. There was a lot of confusion once I left the operating room. I spent a lot of time breathing and hiding my swollen head under the sheets to protect myself from the bright lights and frequent intrusions of nurses and doctors. I prayed and prayed some more.

I turned the entire experience over to my Higher Power and asked for help. I received what I needed.

In this moment, I will be strategic about who I ask for support and then turn this over to God.

November 20

Before CPA, it felt like I was just trudging through misery, waiting for it to end. Everywhere I turned, there were new problems, diagnoses, and pains. Looking into the abyss of ever-increasing illness, I saw no joy, just suffering.

Then, I came to CPA. Now, I laugh a lot. I can share my experiences in meetings and fellowship. In meetings, I share generally; when I'm hanging out with the friends I've made, I share more specifically. Since I share things with people who really get it, I feel lighter. Not only have I begun to enjoy my life, my outlook for the future has become more joyful also.

For me, joy occurs in fleeting moments. And when I am in one of those moments, I soak it in. I remember how it feels and put it away for a sad, rainy day. To be honest, there is sadness every day, but there is also joy every day.

Even though I have pain and illness, I have a good life. I have an active social life. It doesn't look like the lives of most people in the world. It looks like my friends and I getting together online and hanging out. We have virtual watch parties, where we can watch TV as a group. We laugh and joke, and we share deep, painful truths.

I don't have to do everything alone. And with the people I've met in CPA, I've learned that having a community isn't so bad at all. That's where much of my joy comes from.

In this moment, I will appreciate my connection with CPA members and using humor as a tool.

November 21

I used to think I had to do everything perfectly. I'd feel bad if I turned one problem over to my Higher Power today only to obsess over and try to fix another tomorrow. If I had a period of serenity and was then miserable and in a dark hole a week later, I'd think, "What's wrong with me? Why am I not getting it?"

My sponsor pointed out that I'm human. I'm never going to work a perfect program. It's not possible to be serene twenty-four hours a day. I had an unrealistic expectation of myself and of what defined a successful program. So, I kept feeling like I was failing. The old thoughts that said, "I am never good enough," kept appearing.

It took time and practice for me to become gentler toward myself. I learned slowly and made mistakes along the way. I attributed my success in life to working hard and being perfect. It was astonishing that I could not do my program perfectly one hundred percent of the time.

I've come to understand that my recovery is about small changes and not quick, major overhauls. My harmful patterns didn't disappear. I became more aware of how and when they occurred and noticed them sooner each time. This gave me freedom to make new choices. When I feel depressed, I cycle out of it just a bit quicker when I remember to use a few of my program tools. It took me years to consistently remember I have a Higher Power to turn to when I'm struggling, unhappy, or confused.

Perfectionism still appears, but today, I notice it and remind myself that I'm okay just as I am; nothing needs to be perfect.

In this moment, I will accept that I am perfectly imperfect.

November 22

I use Step Eleven on a daily, sometimes hourly, basis now. At first, though, each part of Step Eleven challenged me.

Prayer and meditation were not skills I had when I first arrived in CPA. I thought prayer meant telling God what I wanted. I thought meditation meant sitting in an uncomfortable position, making my thoughts stop. Now, I have a broader understanding. Today, I regularly speak to Higher Power. Just knowing I am not alone—that HP is always there—helps me. I've learned many methods of meditation. A favorite is focusing on my breath, feeling it flow in and out of my nostrils. This shifts my mind and helps me to pause and redirect my attention.

No one in CPA tells me what my HP is supposed to be. I don't have to follow any religious traditions or use the word God, a male pronoun, or any other description someone else believes in. This is personal. It's like in any relationship—sometimes I move away and then come closer again. I have to put some effort into maintaining it, hence the "conscious contact" part of this Step. As I deepen my connection, my love and trust in HP get stronger.

"...praying only for knowledge of His will for us and the power to carry that out" was so hard for me at first. What about my will; what I want? Being so ill, I didn't like what seemed to be HP's will. What I've found is that, often, my HP's will for me was better than what I'd imagined. Other times, it's a gift I'd rather return. That's when I pray for "...the power to carry that out."

The miracle has been that HP always gives me what is needed.

In this moment, I will focus on my breath and deepening my trust in HP's bigger plan.

November 23

Anger is an emotion I find challenging. I want to suppress or push the feeling aside. When I do, it can leak out in ways that hurt others or myself. In recovery, I've learned that anger is just a part of being human.

Angry feelings are often triggered by unmet needs, but I'm not always aware that's happening. If I can stop and identify the root of my anger, I can more easily determine how to move forward. For me, anger can be a reaction to fear, unmet expectations, an increase in my pain and symptoms, or frustration from a situation not going the way I want it to. When I feel helpless, anger can show up. I'm learning that blaming others and trying to force a solution is not productive.

When I feel anger, I can practice *First Things First*, beginning with self-care. I may call my sponsor or a friend, which often calms me down as the energy gets vented. Then, I can think more clearly and discover the next indicated action. I've learned that anger is useful if I use it wisely, not destructively.

When I'm angry, I am not rational. I tend to raise my voice, say things I later regret, attack or try to control others or turn the anger inwards. I discovered these behaviors in my Fourth Step inventory.

My practice today, which I do not do perfectly, is to pay attention to my anger. Usually, it's a clear message that something is needed. With the guidance of my HP, I can focus my energy toward effective and appropriate action.

In this moment, I will pay attention to and honor all my feelings, especially anger, when they arise and then turn to HP.

November 24

Giving others the option to say "No" without explanation, conditions, or hurt feelings has taught me to allow myself the same privilege. I can say, "No," "Not now," or "Not today." Some requests are easy to decline. There are some situations where I have nothing to offer. I gently direct them to others who might be more qualified to meet their needs.

Because speaking is physically difficult for me, I manage the amount of energy I put into speaking daily. I encourage others to reach out to me via text first. Then, we choose a time that mutually works. I am not an emergency crisis helpline. I can only listen attentively for so long before I become emotionally and physically exhausted. In that situation, no one is getting my best attention. I like to set an approximate end time, so we can best use our limited energy and time together.

Within a conversation, I listen and then gently stop and ask questions about solutions. I'll ask, "What solution might work for you right now, in this hour, in this day?" "Is there anything about tomorrow that needs to be handled today?" or, "Can we pray together on finding a solution?"

I have reached out to several others to create a support circle within CPA that I can go to when my sponsor is not available. Not everyone is responsive. I don't take this personally. In addition to managing conflicting healthcare requirements, it takes effort to set time boundaries, establish the best hours to communicate, discover what form of communication works, and then to actually open up. Taking the risk to reach out, as well as setting and honoring healthy limits for myself and others, takes time and attention and is fully worthwhile.

In this moment, I will set limits when I need to, releasing any lingering guilt.

November 25

FEAR: Face Everything And Recover. Reading these words triggered feelings of inadequacy. There is still a part of me that feels like I have to push beyond my limits, that I have no right to say or even think, "No, I can't do that." One of the most challenging things I've learned to face is suicidal ideation. For me, remembering the distinction between experiencing suicidal thoughts and acting suicidal is very important. Being suicidal involves taking concrete actions toward ending my life. Suicidal ideation refers to having thoughts and feelings related to wanting to die or ending my life. As I've faced such thoughts and feelings, I've spent time learning about how and why they occur and how I can respond differently than I used to.

Thoughts of suicide often arise when I'm feeling overwhelmed. Noting how frequent, fast, and intense such thoughts are aids me in understanding that my inner world got shaken, and I am experiencing the aftershocks. This recognition cues me to review what has happened and identify the trigger.

Depending on how overwhelmed I feel, I can take a break for self-care. This may mean taking three deep breaths. It may mean praying to my Deeper Power for love, care, help, and guidance. Meditation has significantly helped, both in the moment and over time.

Life always comes from unexpected directions; it's constantly surprising me. Learning how to better navigate those bewildering times is a worthy endeavor. Part of that is learning how I respond and react. Facing difficult issues and engaging with them directly and courageously has deepened my understanding of what works, makes sense, and increases my quality of life.

In this moment, I will recognize that facing my greatest fears and my deepest moments of suffering have helped me recover.

November 26

Prior to CPA, gratitude was not something that I thought of often.

I'd been in pain and sick for twelve years before finding CPA. I had allowed my condition to take over my life, wellness, sense of self, and zest for life. All of this led to hitting a dramatic, life-altering rock bottom. I'm lucky to have escaped alive.

This bottom was the direct result of not working on the emotional pain and turmoil caused by a life with chronic pain. I was broken. I was a far cry from the person I once was. At that time, I felt that I had nothing to be grateful for.

When I found CPA and began attending meetings regularly, I started to have hope where I'd once thought my life was over. I saw a light at the end of the tunnel; I started to believe I could have a joyful and fulfilling life by following these Twelve Steps.

That's when my—now immense—sense of gratitude began to bubble to the surface. I started being able to pick out things in my life to be grateful for. I perceived situations differently.

I came to realize that the day of my rock bottom was actually something to be grateful for. I escaped alive and was given a second chance at life!

The worst day has now become the most influential day of my life and the basis for the role gratitude plays in my life.

With the help of CPA and an attitude of gratitude, I have found a life of hope and possibility.

In this moment, I will express gratitude for the blessings in my life and all around me.

November 27

I thought that, in CPA, I'd stop making unrealistic, self-imposed demands of myself. The stark fact is that, at any given time, I have a deficiency in my intellectual needs, exercise needs, artistic needs, social needs, sleep needs, etc. I began to think I should have all these things perfectly managed now that I had a program.

Because I started comparing myself to those I most admire in CPA, I was unable to accept my situation or focus on working my program. I was too concerned with others, always thinking, "He is doing this, and she got to do that. What's wrong with me that I can't seem to do so, too?" In turn, my old motivational style—tough love—took over.

With time and effort in CPA, I'm learning that my chronic pain and illness "normal" is mine; yours is yours. I'm beginning to refuse to compare myself to others. When a CPA member tells me, "Here, I don't have to explain. You get me," I take it to mean, "I don't know your specifics nor will I question them. If you say, 'I can't,' I don't doubt you." Everyone in CPA accepts it when I have to do less than I'd hoped. If they remark, it's out of concern rather than judgment.

Of course, as I move forward in recovery, I slip back a little, too. Sometimes, I have to take a moment to lightly say to myself, "Just snap out of it!" This helps me to stop comparing and accept myself as I am while I look forward to my next CPA meeting. I know they'll understand.

In this moment, I will notice when comparing myself to others is harmful, and offer myself compassion instead.

November 28

Since joining CPA, I've found I am more at peace when my symptoms are unruly. When my symptoms flare up, and I have already done the things within my control, like taking my medication or supplements, applying ice or heat packs, or whatever therapy is indicated, all that is left for me to do is rest and wait.

Before CPA, I was not good at waiting. I didn't have the ability to rest and let those indicated actions take effect. Instead, I would panic; I had no tools left to help withstand the flare. So, five minutes into it, I would decide that what I'd done wasn't working and then try other medications or treatments. I would run around, changing my mind over and over again about what was going to work. This just put my body through more stress.

Now, I find that, during a flare, I no longer panic after doing the indicated actions. I trust that the treatment will work, whether it's quickly or slowly. In the meantime, while I wait, my body calls for rest, and I do my best to honor my body's needs.

In this moment, I will rest and patiently consider and accept the next indicated action.

November 29

There are times when I get lost in misery and self-pity. I forget that I have a choice about my attitude. Focusing my attention on the obstacles I face and what I don't have makes me unhappy, depressed, and angry. I want to live serenely, and focusing on discontent in my situation does not cultivate a space of peace or serenity.

When I remember to practice gratitude, I find what is working well in my life, what blessings there are, and all that I have to lose. It doesn't mean I ignore the challenges. What works, what is good, and what I do have in my life far outweighs what I believe to be lacking.

I have a roof over my head and running water in my home. Although some of my senses are diminished or absent, I stop and give thanks for the ones that work. I remember the people I interacted with recently: the mail person, the checkout clerk at the grocery store, and the friend who dropped off a meal. I take time to notice the natural world around me: a blue sky, trees in the wind, and birds singing.

This practice of noticing the good parts of my life fills me with joy. Making the conscious decision to become aware of all the ways in which my world is filled with support, kindness, and beauty means I am not spending that time fixated on the pain in my body, the anxiety about a procedure next week, or that person who let me down.

Gratitude is the attitude that allows me to choose how I live. It is not the external world that makes my life happy or miserable. It's viewing my internal world through the lens of gratitude that makes it possible for me to be happy, no matter the situation. This is freedom.

In this moment, I will notice what I feel grateful for.

November 30

I was once shown a method for discerning if I am lost in my own will or moving toward God's. I used it when I was struggling to understand if a medication I'd been taking successfully for many years was still a good fit. I used it to decide if I should stop spending my time in a way that had, for years, been conducive to my life with chronic pain and illness but no longer provided the same benefits. It most recently helped me move away from a dear relationship that had become irrevocably toxic. The following are some general guidelines I use to evaluate my actions:

What I am doing may not be God's will if it:

- drains me of hope and weakens my motivation.
- prompts me to give up on activities that were once very important.
- pushes me to focus more and more on my negative feelings.
- increases self-centered actions.
- diminishes or erases the spiritual and emotional milestones I have experienced.
- draws me away from my fellows.

It may be in the direction of God's will if it:

- inspires new ideas.
- helps to balance my emotions.
- reminds me of times I was led by my Higher Power.
- sparks a new flame in me, reigniting my motivation.
- realigns my focus to that which is beyond myself.
- refreshes my spirit.
- opens me to the heartaches and joys of others.

Referencing these lists when I'm struggling to make a decision helps guide me.

In this moment, I will use the tools that help me discern my will from God's will.

December

December 1

Anonymity supports recovery. It helps me feel accepted instead of feeling different from others.

Some of the titles and roles I had before chronic pain and illness don't apply to me anymore. CPA has taught me how to release my past and process the emotions that come with letting it go so that I'm free to define myself in a new way.

Anonymity has helped me to see my inherent worth as a human being. Importantly, it has helped me become aware of when I am being judgmental and need to release my preconceptions. When sharing in a meeting, I no longer get stuck on details of my illness or treatments. Instead, speaking in general terms about these things focuses my attention on my feelings and actions as I learn to adapt to my reality and apply the Twelve Steps of CPA. Experience, strength, and hope are what we have in common.

Learning to speak in general terms took practice. Before, I was very caught up in details and oftentimes unaware of the bigger picture. I am trying to grow and change my attitude by listening to everyone and without letting my opinion of their situation, which is definitely incomplete and inaccurate, block any messages of experience, strength, and hope. Anonymity supports unity and equality, two principles that I strive to practice in all my affairs.

In this moment, I will apply the CPA principles of anonymity, unity, and equality in all my affairs.

December 2

I've had maybe four or five days over the past several months where I am just well enough to dress and sit in the car for a drive or maybe go for a very short walk. These are my good days, and their frequency is declining.

In my new life with chronic pain and illness, the times I've been able to get ouhave felt miraculous. I felt full of grace, gratitude, and love—I experienced a lightness of heart about being and staying alive. But, most days, walking outside for a couple of minutes is all I can do before I get too dizzy and weak and need to come back in and lie down. Not accepting that limitation and desperately wanting the ability to do more has been nothing short of excruciating. I need the support, wisdom, compassion, and understanding of my fellows in CPA. They have helped me slowly build a new relationship with faith and hope.

I thank my fellow CPA warriors for answering my call for help and giving so much compassion and love, which was sorely missing in my life. My prayer today is that I will continue to learn and grow into the whole-hearted person God has always intended me to be.

In this moment, I will find gratitude where I can, accept all that I can, and relax when I can.

December 3

Lately, I have been practicing Step One every day.

It has been difficult to admit that I have a chronic illness. For years, I denied the fact that I was living with it. I was mentally detached from my body and the signals it was trying to send me. I fought against the diagnosis and never allowed myself to believe, let alone accept, my powerlessness over the situation.

Admitting powerlessness didn't come easily, but today, I know I am indeed powerless over my pain and illness. Reading some of the CPA literature provided to me at my first meeting helped me recognize that my life had become unmanageable.

By working Step One, I have been able to admit I have a chronic illness; I am powerless over it. I realize how unmanageable my life becomes when I try to control or ignore it. I've begun listening to my body again and using self-care when needed.

In this moment, I will find courage to listen to my body's wisdom and respond with loving self-care.

December 4

A long time ago, I asked three fellows what it meant to surrender, to truly take Step Three. All three said, "You just let it go." Well, that wasn't very helpful to me. But then the third person added, "...and sometimes you have to walk away." Well, with my physical limitations, I can't always just get up and leave the room, but as another fellow pointed out, I can distract myself. I can choose what to focus on. I can switch gears and do something else.

I am currently working Step Three in CPA. My sponsor suggested that I start by practicing with something easy and safe to surrender. For example, choosing when to brush my teeth or which shirt to wear—something seemingly inconsequential. I was thinking about practicing on which TV show to watch next, but an opportunity presented itself. As it turns out, I am practicing on my breakfast. I have about six different items on my breakfast plate. I turn over what order I am going to eat them in. For someone who craves routine and sameness, I would have always eaten them in the same order. But now, I let Higher Power guide me in my selection, and I am often surprised at HP's choices.

Now that I have practiced with something safe and easy, I look forward to trusting HP with more meaningful decisions in the future.

In this moment, I will ask HP for the next indicated action, then pause and wait for an answer.

December 5

Coming to Step Two, over the years, I've always said to myself, "Oh, sure, a Power greater than myself—yeah, yeah, yeah, I got that. I believe in God." Then I'd focus on the second part, "...could restore us to sanity." I knew my life was insane, and I needed to find some clarity.

When I think about Step Two today and reflect on its deeper meaning, it's not just about finding a God. It's about finding a God and believing They have the ability to do something for me. In Step Two, They are restoring my sense of clarity.

What does having clarity look like for me today?

- God is there for me, holding my hand, tangibly showing me support and care.
- I have stopped the endless search for the right treatment, pill, therapy, doctor, and procedure. I no longer expect perfection in anything or anyone, especially myself.
- I think before I act and calmly make decisions, understanding the benefits and the consequences.
- I take care of myself—totally guilt-free.
- By accepting that I have chronic pain and illness and by making peace with that fact, I am inviting joy and serenity into my days.

As I continue to pray and listen, God continues to reveal Itself to me in new and powerful ways.

In this moment, I will come to believe that I can be restored to a place of clarity and serenity.

December 6

What I learned about rest in CPA was life-changing for me. I was raised in an atmosphere of always completing everything that had to be done before I did anything relaxing or fun. I was considered bad if I wasn't being productive and there were tasks waiting to be completed. When chronic pain and illness became part of my life, this mindset no longer served me. I found myself pushing until the pain increased to the point where I could no longer continue because I thought these things absolutely had to be done. I overdid it, and that resulted in me needing more time to recover.

Rest did not come naturally to me. I always felt guilty. It took effort to change this, but I taught myself that rest is doing something important. Resting is not being lazy. I learned that taking the time to rest is being a good steward of valuable assets, like my energy and the ability to function in day-to-day life. Once I understood rest as a wise use of time—a way to extend my energy, and increase my capacity to have a more pleasant life, it became an extremely attractive activity.

It has become helpful for me to review my task list with self-compassion. I ask myself, "What will happen if they don't get done for a few hours, or tomorrow, or later?" I've learned to let things go and have developed a more laid-back, lenient mindset.

I've accepted resting as constructive and learned to not let guilt and shame control me. I discovered that taking a break actually gives me more time in the long run. Resting has become an accepted and pleasant part of my life, something that improves and enhances it significantly.

In this moment, I will view rest as a constructive and productive activity.

December 7

I thought my life had shrunk down to the size of my house. So much of the time, I was unable to leave the house or even my bedroom. I believed I would never have fun or play again. It was a dark time. All I could imagine was a dismal future ahead.

One day, I realized that the world is wherever I am. It doesn't matter that I can't travel to the grocery store, let alone to Paris. Wherever I am is my universe. I can always only be right where I am. And at that time, it was in my home. When I became willing to be creative and see the abundance available to me, I discovered many ways to play and find enjoyment.

I live in the desert, and there are many creatures that come to visit. At first, I adored just watching the coyotes, javelinas, bobcats, lizards, and birds. Soon, I had a stack of books about desert life and a new pair of binoculars. I could sit at my big picture window and be entertained. I learned about wildlife and felt soothed by nature.

This shift of attitude and perspective opened many new avenues of play and creativity for me. I started to write and found writing to be a wonderful way to channel my creative energy. Soon I found opportunities to travel the world online. Without leaving my bed, I visited a museum in another country. I made close friends with people all over the world through virtual gatherings.

Given the technology available to me, I know today that the only thing that keeps me a prisoner in my house is my mind.

In this moment, I will find creative ways to enjoy life.

December 8

This year, we had to once again cancel our annual holiday gathering. We would share our music, home, and festive spirit with many people in our communities—singing with friends, playing instruments, and going for all hours. Last year, its loss seemed yet another way the world was punishing us. This year, what has changed is that we have been using CPA recovery tools to face the holidays. Instead of counting the things we couldn't do anymore, we decided to refocus, and our holiday was simple, pleasant, and one of the best in many years.

It can be hard to hear people talk about missing our once-great parties, but we try to focus on the essence of those gatherings—connection. These days, though gatherings need to be smaller for us to handle, smaller gatherings aid intimacy. We aren't wasting all our energy or saving it for one big blowout each year. We get to connect with loved ones more frequently now, build stronger relationships, and enjoy the loving atmosphere. Through using program tools, those connections stay alive each day.

In this moment, I will make a list of the things I most value during times of communal celebration; I will take a moment to notice where those things already exist in my life.

December 9

After my divorce, finances were a big concern. I was not able to work. I was very careful with money, spending the least amount I could as I figured out how to survive.

Somehow, the funds I needed always came in. A family member paid for a large repair. Someone offered to cut my hair for free. A loan I thought would have to be paid was excused. This is how I learned that my Higher Power is in charge of my finances, along with everything else in my life. I had to do the footwork and manage my funds responsibly, but I didn't need to spend sleepless nights worrying.

Then, an old friend asked me to work at his company. I didn't think I was dependable enough because of my chronic illness, but I needed the money and decided to take a chance. I thanked him for the offer and said, "Yes." To my surprise, I was able to do the work. I worked from home on my own schedule. The job grew, and my ability to do it grew as well. The service work I'd done in CPA had given me the confidence to accept his offer, as I had been able to take on tasks I'd thought were impossible for me. I was able to support myself for the first time since becoming ill. It was in a field very different from the one I trained in, but I was good at it.

This was a blessing from my Higher Power. Being asked to work just when I needed the money, being able to actually do the job, and earning enough to support myself was a miracle.

In this moment, I will consider that service work in CPA may have unexpected, miraculous ripples.

December 10

I arrived in CPA mostly relying on myself. I used my natural gift for prudent planning until it became an obsession. I had to have plans for every possible outcome. I needed an infinite series of safety nets. It was, literally, a sickening endeavor.

This self-imposed obsession to control only led to more pain when the plan did not match my specifications. My expectations, unmet, caused my disappointment and fear to grow. Overwhelmed by my false beliefs that I can and must control everything, I'd conclude, and use my feelings of despair to confirm, that there is no hope.

This is my emotional and spiritual debilitation. And it's treatable.

If I trust in the wisdom of the Serenity Prayer—changing what my God directs me to change, accepting what I can't change, and trusting the wisdom to discern the difference—I can save myself much physical and emotional wear and tear. I come into the present, where I can learn to live as I go. I can take appropriate action, trust I've done what can be done, and accept that the world will do what it will. I can now regard the rest of my life as a mystery to be lived rather than a problem to be solved. Today is my given day, and it's worthy of my best care.

In this moment, I will accept that my ultimate powerlessness is the portal into moving out of the problem and into living, even savoring, my daily emotional and spiritual recovery.

December 11

"Just do the next right thing." Early in recovery, I didn't know what that meant. How am I supposed to judge what the next right thing is?

When I came to CPA, the literature and members said, "Just do the next indicated action." That was something I could grasp much more easily. In CPA, I've learned I have to let go of the obsessive thoughts I have about my illness to understand things more clearly. Often, I just have to take a step back and listen to the experience, strength, and hope of others to fully comprehend this concept.

I came into CPA with a compulsion to overdo everything in order to fix my health problem. I thought micromanaging my life would heal my pain and illness. What I found was something very different; I had to heal from my emotional pain to recover.

Today, I listen to my intuition and consider suggestions based on recovery and reason. When I'm struggling to find the next indicated action, I go to a meeting, talk to my sponsor, and reach out to those in my support system for guidance.

In this moment, I will continue to take the next indicated action, and I will trust my intuition and gut feelings. I know that if I continue to follow the voice of reason, I will maintain my recovery One Day at a Time.

December 12

The journey that leads to Step Twelve is amazing. In hindsight, I realize I have changed dramatically. Others noticed, too, and seemed to appreciate the changes.

Who am I now? Well, I no longer resent or fear my condition. Neither do I deny it. It is part of my life. All the fear-based questions that used to live in my brain have subsided or become fleeting. My brain was barraged by questions like, "How do I fix this?" "What is my purpose?" "How will I live like this?" or even "Am I faking this?" These have mostly fizzled out and are no longer overwhelming. I've found purpose in every day and gratitude for each sunrise.

This is certainly not how I came into CPA. An amazing transformation happened. My sponsor helped me to work each Step until I felt they were really a part of my daily life. Now, I no longer fear a newcomer reaching out to me and asking, "Would you be my sponsor?" I welcome the request.

At one time, I feared the number of people I might be asked to take through the Steps. But today, I trust that my Higher Power will not overwhelm me with too many requests. I trust my Higher Power will guide me to those I am meant to help. With each sponsee, I take a new journey through the Steps. I did it once, and I can do it again. Now, I get to do it with someone new.

In this moment, I will remember that as I sponsor, I, too, am journeying through the Steps.

December 13

Recently, I needed a fairly common procedure, but I was scared. I prayed and asked God for courage and strength. I contacted my sponsor and shared all my fears. I worked Steps Six through Nine with her. As an amends, I gave myself permission to be scared. I didn't have to pretend when I was not feeling brave.

On the day of the procedure, I bookended the experience with my sponsor. Before I left the house, I called and shared anything that was blocking my faith and trust. Then, I contacted her again afterward. I felt held by her love and compassion while I was at the facility.

My prayers that day included asking that the medical staff be guided by God. I prayed for serenity and turned myself and the outcome over to my Higher Power. I was surprised at how calm I felt. I felt the presence of my HP every step of the way. Although there were a few unexpected complications, I just kept reminding myself that I was safe. No matter what happened, my God was there.

The outcome was not what I expected, but my worst nightmare did not come to pass either. My sponsor reminded me to keep surrendering and that my HP would show me the next indicated action. I went home and did nothing. I didn't even answer the phone. I simply rested and focused on my gratitude for having a loving Higher Power and sponsor who support me in times of fear.

In this moment, I will share my feelings with a trusted CPA friend and turn my fears over to the loving care of my Higher Power.

December 14

As I continue this journey in CPA and practice the Twelve Steps, my daily obsession with pain and illness has physically, medically, emotionally, and spiritually transformed in ways I did not think possible. Friendship, hope, sanity, and peace are so freely given by reading the literature and connecting with others living with chronic pain and chronic illness. I was exposed to a new way of life. I felt connected by hearing others describe experiences and feelings I also have. I was shown a set of principles and tools for living life effectively. Learning these tools has become—and continues to be—part of my CPA experience.

Utilizing what the program offers has changed my day-to-day life for the better. As I listen to others share in meetings or talk over phone or text, I identify with their thoughts, feelings, diagnoses, and even actions. That is what connections feel like to me. It takes away the loneliness I've felt for a very long time.

My desire to rely on my spiritual connections enables me to continue evolving while utilizing the tools of CPA. At any time, I can feel a surge of joy and notice I am just in love with life itself. I finally have the confidence to know that what I do, I do to the best of my ability.

It can feel challenging not to identify myself as a deteriorating body. Then, I remember it's truly just a vehicle for consciousness. It knows nothing of death or my deep feelings of loss. I rely on Step Eleven to help me realize that feelings do not define who I am. By watching CPA members, I have learned that when I identify with and support others, my life also benefits. I experience the selflessness of having interest and concern for another. My internal journey progresses; I grow, surrender, and deepen my awareness of the present. Evolution, awareness, and consciousness continues. My life transforms.

In this moment, I will value all that each member has to offer.

December 15

When I'm tired, things seem more overwhelming than when I am rested.

Recently, my email went unchecked for a couple of days while I was taking care of a family member who'd had minor surgery. When I returned home, I had a long list of emails to return from CPA, my job, and other things. I felt vulnerable and frustrated as I read through all of these and perceived them all as demands. I found myself feeling resentful and like I wanted to quit. There was no way I could do all of this.

These feelings created more stress and exhaustion. When I used the slogan, *HELP*, I realized what was happening. I wasn't *Hungry, Lonely*, or in significant *Pain*, but I was *Exhausted*. It was helpful to become aware of that; it helped me put things in perspective. I realized I did not have to respond to everyone right away. When I looked at it logically instead of emotionally, I found that I did have time; I could and would do it. I would schedule the tasks in an order that made sense.

HELP reminds me to notice when I am tired and, therefore, reacting with unhelpful emotions. Then, I can more easily discern this may not be the best time to manufacture solutions. I take care of my *Exhaustion* with rest. Then, I'll be able to do what I need to do. I turn the moment over to my Higher Power and give myself a break.

In this moment, I will ask myself if I am Hungry, Exhausted, Lonely, or in Pain? If I answer yes to any, I will address those self-care needs immediately. First Things First!

December 16

I am so grateful that the slogan *Just for Today* seems to be one of my CPA sponsor's favorite slogans, which means I hear it a lot, and it's starting to seep in. For me, it has created a major shift in my sanity and serenity. Today, as the holidays and an upcoming move approach, I have a lot of fear. I can look around my house, see how everything is settled and orderly, and think, *"Just for Today,* I get to enjoy that everything is settled right now—just for this moment." Next week, when the house starts to look chaotic with all the packed boxes and such, I can tell myself it's *Just for Today*; it's not forever. I can get through it, *One Day at a Time.*

If the moment starts to become overwhelming, I can choose to shift my focus onto positive things, like the excitement of being with my children. In the past, my only thoughts would be worry, fear, and negativity about the chaos to come during the move and stress over having enough energy. There was so much fear that very little serenity could be present during all the chaos.

Today, I can enjoy what is right in front of me with faith that God will help me deal with what is to come. And if I can hold on to my sanity, *Just for Today,* then perhaps I can have some serenity the next day as well, just for *that* day, and so on.

In this moment, I will shift my thinking and live Just for Today, One Day at a Time.

December 17

From the day I was born, my mother said I ate twelve hours and slept twelve hours, and this was true. Then came chronic pain and illness. My appetite disappeared, and nighttime became my most symptomatic time of day. I began to dread the sun going down, as I knew the discomfort and pain would be coming soon.

I found moments of sanity and serenity in CPA's Step Seven when I asked my Higher Power to give me a new relationship with food and sleep. My part was to stop the obstructive thinking and detach from dedicating twelve hours each to food and sleep. I was helped by repeatedly saying, "Thy will, not my taste buds', be done," or "Help me not to judge this night before it even happens." I became open to new experiences by setting aside all I thought I knew about myself and asking HP to change my beliefs, thoughts, and actions regarding self-care.

Through experimentation and with this new, open attitude, I've found that when I stay in the moment, I am able to accomplish HP's will, regardless of the number of hours I slept or meals I ate. Step Four really showed me the damage I was causing by labeling things as "good" or "bad." For example, it was only a "good" night if I slept for twelve hours. My HP and CPA have freed me from this self-imposed, harmful type of thinking and opened me to a life of peace, joy, and comfort. I've found freedom in being me and letting go of who I think I am or should be.

In this moment, I will open my mind and become willing to have new experiences that may challenge my current beliefs.

December 18

CPA has returned the wonder for life I once had that my chronic conditions had robbed me of. My vision of the world was gray, bleak, and dull, but CPA taught me that wonder can be cultivated by experiencing gratitude and noticing beauty around and within myself. CPA, and meaningful dialogue with my sponsor, help me do more of that. Now, *One Day at a Time*, I try to cultivate that awareness and deepen my connection to Source.

And the more I foster that connection, the more peaceful I am. If I'm not feeling peaceful, which can happen to humans living with chronic pain and illness, I use a coping strategy where I pay attention to my five senses as much as I am able at the moment: the warm mug in my hands, the soft fur of my cat, the sound of her dinner howl, the little yellow buds on a plant I'm managing to keep alive, the refreshing taste of my mint tea, the smell of the lavender growing in the yard, and so on.

In this moment, I will explore with wonder the pleasant things my five senses can experience amidst my pain.

December 19

I am grateful I released my resentments against the healthcare system when doing my Fourth and Fifth Steps. I had a chance to vent about the many exhausting surgeries and bemoan the extra conditions I now have. It was good to get these feelings out and not be judged for them. It was also extremely helpful to examine the only part I could change—my attitude about these past experiences.

I am chronically ill, in pain, and must continue to interact with modern medicine. I plan to continue using the Steps and program tools to deal with unpleasant issues that are common to the healthcare system. I will often do a Tenth Step to review my fears and the part I play in my distress. Sometimes, I refuse to accept that all persons and systems are imperfect. I have unrealistic expectations that doctors can fix all my ills and all medical staff will be loving, kind, and patient all of the time.

If I have a major procedure, I will bookend my visit with a call to my sponsor before and after the appointment. I commit to keeping my interactions simple while talking to the doctor and try to avoid spilling out all my emotional angst. Nor will I be overly nice or neglect my own needs in the process. I reaffirm the knowledge that I can't control outcomes. I express appreciation when appropriate. I ask God to direct my thinking before each appointment, and my experience is consistently less stressful and more productive.

In this moment, I will be grateful that my time in CPA has changed my attitude, outlook, and ability to experience life in a new way.

December 20

All manner of physical issues impact my sexuality. Pain, medication side effects, limited movement, fatigue, and headaches are just a few examples. My list goes on and on.

Emotional concerns also tax my ability for sexual expression. My unresolved anger, fear, and erroneous shame are often tangible. Because I never learned how to safely manage or express my emotions, I developed a flat affect and a sharp, brittle persona that can unexpectedly take over. I know my softer, gentler, genuine self is in there and desires romance, but these emotional blocks can make it difficult to get into an intimate mood.

The CPA program is effective because it is "real." I am encouraged to privately "get real" and be 100% open and honest about intimate, delicate topics with my sponsor and trusted friends. Talking about physical intimacy, sharing our experience, strength, and hope in a place where we know it's safe helps open us to fresh possibilities. Have I found adaptations to meet this need? Have I let go of any old ideas that stymied my chances of experiencing touch? Have I offered to help my partner adjust?

I am so grateful I was granted the courage to explore this area of my life that I believed was gone forever. I love how "real" I am encouraged to get into CPA recovery!

In this moment, I will pray for the courage to investigate what I fear the most, with people I trust the most.

December 21

The tool of rest is a significant resource in my life. I get cranky and irritable when I overextended myself. My ability to function and think decreases. I feel like a wind-up doll that conks out. I lose my ability to speak. When I am in energy debt, I can feel like a sixteen-wheeler truck running with the engine of a compact car. There's just not enough energy available.

Rest comes in many forms. It can look like pacing my activity throughout the day: I do an activity for twenty minutes, and then I head back to bed for as long as I need to recharge. I do that throughout the day. It can look like staying in bed for an entire day, including eating in bed and only leaving to go to the bathroom. It can look like spending the day away from the computer and cell phone, not having contact with other people. Interacting with others can be draining, and a day of rest can be a day of quietly being at home alone.

In CPA, I learned that only I can give myself permission for all these different ways of resting. I used to feel guilty and believed I should always be doing something. I accused myself of being lazy if I wasn't accomplishing something each day. Now, I know that nothing gets accomplished if I don't take care of myself. If I get overtired, my symptoms will increase, and then I can be in bed for days, weeks, or months. I learned this the hard way over many years.

In this moment, I will know that being kind to myself means I rest my body and my mind until I am able to return to the world.

December 22

It seems like self-care would be easy. It's logical to take care of myself. However, this simple skill is one I had to learn in CPA.

I have great compassion when someone else is struggling; I listen to them share their emotions and thoughts without judgment. But on my recovery journey, I realized I did not offer the same empathy toward myself. When I was feeling ill, I would blame, attack, and judge myself as inferior, lazy, and irresponsible. I practiced self-violence rather than self-care.

Using the tools I've learned in CPA, I now stop and practice kindness. I speak to myself in a soothing tone and might even wrap my arms around myself and say, "Oh, sweetie, you are having a bad day. I am here for you." Then I do something nice for myself, like make a cup of tea or listen to music that calms me.

As it turns out, it was quite simple to practice self-care once I had the proper tools and support. It feels so much better than berating myself or believing I did something wrong. I have the trust that all I need to do is the next indicated action. I try to do this with a gentle attitude toward whatever I am experiencing at the moment. If I'm cold, I get a blanket. If I'm hungry, I get food. If I'm lonely, I reach out to someone. And I do it all with tenderness.

When my symptoms are making life miserable, I use my "self-care cheat sheet"—a list of inner and outer resources I find most helpful. I need this list because I can't remember all of the different ways I am able to care for myself. Who knew there were so many?

In this moment, I will turn toward actions that will soothe and comfort me.

December 23

I see so many miracles happening daily now that I am on the lookout for them.

Before CPA, my obsession with every physical sensation and uncomfortable feeling ruled my every waking moment. I could not get comfortable with myself or others, and Higher Power seemed so far away. I could not see beyond my misery.

When I made the decision, in Step Three, to turn my thoughts and actions over to the care of a loving God as I understood God, I was introduced to the concept of investigating the "caring" nature of this Greater Power. I began looking for miracles. To my surprise, those miracles abounded: that perfect parking spot for my doctor's appointment, finding the last one of an item I needed at the store, a phone call from a CPA friend just when I needed to talk, and having the energy to help a loved one. I began making a note of each one. Journaling my miracles brought me closer to trusting my Greater Power to provide and care for me.

Today, when things are tough, I practice actively looking for the wisdom and possible benefits from what is occurring instead of narrowing my perspective to only what is painful or uncomfortable. Changed attitudes and perspectives can aid my recovery. If I can't see any good, I return to my miracle journal to be reminded that I am always in the care of a loving Greater Power.

In this moment, I will shift my perspective from obsession to searching for miracles of ease and comfort.

December 24

I used to believe that showing kindness to myself was a selfish act. If I did even the smallest thing for myself, like a quiet cup of tea or painting my nails, I felt I was wasting time I could be spending serving others. I couldn't figure out why I felt so depleted. Part of it was my illness, but part of it was how I was constantly doing for others and neglecting myself.

In CPA, I learned about self-compassion. I have begun practicing it. Not just physically, by allowing my body to rest and not being angry because it needs extra rest, but also emotionally. My inner critic, the voice that always tells me how terrible I am no matter how hard I try, is so much quieter now. It used to be the loudest thing in my head—it told me I was a failure. That's not true. I have challenges others don't, but I am no less of a person. I'm learning to love myself regardless of my bodily limitations. The more I do it, the easier it becomes. Sometimes, I'm compassionate with myself without even realizing it.

Self-compassion was the missing piece for me. It taught me I can love myself just as I am. Today, I am kind, I am gentle, and I love myself. I don't care if people call me selfish; it's okay to be a little bit selfish. I have to take care of myself, or I won't have anything left for anyone else. Most of all, I want to take care of myself because I love myself. That is such a gift.

In this moment, I will kindly care for myself as I would a friend or a child.

December 25

When I first came to Twelve Step recovery, I thought anonymity meant that I didn't tell anyone my last name. Over time, my understanding of this spiritual principle grew to encompass so much more. Tradition Twelve states, "Anonymity is the spiritual foundation of all our traditions, ever reminding us to place principles before personalities."

Anonymity helps our meetings to be inclusive. My diagnosis doesn't include me or exclude me as a member of CPA. In fact, according to Tradition Three, "The only requirement for CPA membership is a desire to recover from the emotional and spiritual debilitation of chronic pain or chronic illness." We connect over shared experiences and feelings. We can relate to how chronic pain and chronic illness have altered our lives in profound and challenging ways and the resulting emotional and spiritual turmoil of facing those challenges. I can share about how I judge myself as lazy for resting or how sad I feel that I can no longer go to the gym.

Anonymity creates an atmosphere of safety—a place where I can expel my dark thoughts and share my joys and blessings. Articulating my vulnerable, raw, and sometimes scary thoughts and feelings helps me become aware of my reality. Sometimes, it is in the safety of a meeting where the first glimmer of that reality comes to light. Then, awareness can lead to acceptance.

In this moment, I will be grateful for my growing understanding of anonymity and its value in my recovery journey.

December 26

I love that "The CPA Declaration" is written as a set of twelve affirmative, positive statements about envisioning a life that is happy and worthwhile. They are about what can happen when I work the program. They are not necessarily statements that are true today; they remind me of what is possible through the gifts of recovery.

When I first came to CPA, I couldn't imagine a life that was not isolated, filled with self-pity, focused on suffering, and steeped in resentment and blame. Yet, as I worked the Steps and turned my will and life over to a Power greater than myself, I found my life was altered in profound and positive ways. I love sharing this opportunity for joy with others and letting them know that, even if they are feeling miserable and stuck, there is hope.

From the "Declaration," I learned that, even with my conditions, I am lovable, and I can love others. Even on my worst days, there is usually something I can find to be grateful for. Even when my functioning is limited, I can give to others and find purpose in my life. Even if today looks bleak, I know I am never alone, and I have a Higher Power that will be there for me. My life will never be perfect. However, "The CPA Declaration" reminds me that my imperfect life can still be one that I love.

In this moment, I will reacquaint myself with "The CPA Declaration." I am willing to experience all the tools of the program.

December 27

I made the decision this year to not visit my parents for the holidays. They live on the beach in the southern United States, and I am in the Mid-Atlantic region. I am a summer girl, so why would I opt to turn down a beach vacation in mid-winter? My chronic pain makes traveling difficult in many ways. The prolonged walking, uncomfortable seats, and trying to manage luggage exhaust me. Plus, I often pick up a bug from the close confines of the airplane. The bed at my parents' home is uncomfortable, and the humidity flares up my condition. For many of my visits, I spend more time lying in bed than lounging on the beach. Looking at the costs and benefits of this journey, I didn't feel I could manage it.

The holidays are difficult for me emotionally. I feel guilty for not seeing my parents and sad about time passing by so quickly. I have learned, in CPA, that the emotional parts of my pain are something I can safely examine. I have become less afraid of my pain; therefore, it has less control and influence over me. I worked with my sponsor to let go of the complicated feelings that came up from not seeing my folks. I hope I'm able to visit them in the spring when my pain is typically more manageable.

I make my best-educated guess at what my body and my mind can handle at a given time, and I enjoy the ways I can be present. Surprisingly, I truly feel that I navigated the holidays in a manageable and pleasant way this year.

In this moment, I will honor my limitations realistically, regardless of calendar norms and expectations.

December 28

In Step Six, I worked with my sponsor to determine my list of character defects and character assets. I am changing the things I can and accepting the things I cannot change. I cannot control my feelings, but I can control my behaviors and actions. During difficult situations, it takes courage to choose to act and behave in new ways. I try hard to keep my focus on the positives and fill my moments with the gratitude I feel. Each day, I turn my mind to what kind of day I would like to have and let my Higher Power do His job of removing my defects of character.

When I engage in regrettable behaviors and the situation starts to become unmanageable, I find it's often due to my character defects. In these moments, I count on my Higher Power to give me strength to breathe and bring myself to a mindful place. Then, I can reflect on how to choose a peaceful way forward and do my best not to act in ways that are harmful to myself and others.

Living in the solution is easier for me than letting things get out of control. Being honest with myself and others helps me choose to take esteemable actions. I feel so much better about myself when I do. I like myself much more. I'm able to let the part of me that feels guilty or ashamed be in my Higher Power's hands. I try to live in the moment, *One Day at a Time*, and focus on what really matters. For me, Step Six is an ongoing, daily practice.

In this moment, I will trust that my Higher Power will remove my character defects when the time is appropriate.

December 29

I enjoy being in the presence of people who are serene. My personal serenity surely waxes and wanes, but it generally correlates with my connection to my program and Higher Power. In a recent meeting, we were joking around, and someone asked, "Wouldn't it be great if a doctor could prescribe a pill to help increase my serenity level?" Thinking about this, later on, it clicked for me that I do have an unlimited supply of spiritual medicine that increases my serenity, but it is not in pill form. The "medicine" that unfailingly provides me with a healthy dose of serenity is CPA!

From CPA members, I have learned some powerful remedies to use when I'm experiencing a serenity deficiency. I have learned to rely on deep breaths, the Serenity Prayer, quiet meditations, or guided imagery. I know the benefits of taking inventories and listening to wise and trusted voices, i.e., Steps Four and Ten. I cry, laugh, and share my truth while witnessing my friends navigate difficult circumstances with fortitude and grace. All these things have also helped me to identify the antagonists of serenity in my life and do my best to limit them.

Even at times of heightened pain and physical symptoms, I am able to use a program tool. My Higher Power gives me this strength or brings me someone who does. I trust that *This Too Shall Pass*. I'm very grateful this prescription for serenity was shared with me.

In this moment, I will take the serenity that CPA offers.

December 30

Chronic pain and chronic illness brought extreme self-loathing to the forefront of my every experience. My diagnoses seemed to prove there was something innately wrong with me. I was sure I would be abandoned, that I had created my health problems, and I had failed at life. Death was the next logical course of action. I cried out to the heavens, and almost immediately, CPA entered my life. I clung to it. I worked the Steps in CPA, and awakening upon awakening occurred.

Through grace and willingness to continue my Twelve Step journey, I am now able to experience freedom. The sinister inner critic has been removed. I now see life as an exciting experiment—no harm, no foul. Self-acceptance, self-care, and self-love—once inconceivable—are now daily experiences. My fear has been replaced by courage and faith. I see the lighter side of situations. I am kind and compassionate with myself and others. My life has a renewed purpose and meaning as I open myself to new beginnings.

I will keep coming back to peel this onion because with every layer, new awakenings are revealed.

In this moment, I will be open to the spiritual awakenings available in Step Twelve.

December 31

"Fear will be replaced by courage, strength, and faith to rise and meet any challenges. We will even see challenges as opportunities for spiritual growth." - The CPA Declaration.

Until I had actually experienced this declaration coming true in CPA, I had absolutely no idea how it would look. My entire journey in CPA has been that way. I cannot predict what the results and gifts of working this program will be. I only strive to work the Step I am on. Usually, I discover that how it works for me is beyond anything my imagination could come up with.

I now have a Higher Power who believes in me and gives me the miracles I need in HP's time. I focus on living with my chronic pain and illness rather than putting my life on hold until I feel better. I pace myself. I slow down. I practice gratitude. I've learned self-compassion and made friends who understand. My pain and illness no longer control my moods. By pacing myself according to what is acceptable for me, not the healthy population, I actually accomplish more.

I actually had a lot of faith before I got sick, but it is the quality of faith that matters when facing fears that come with my chronic pain and illness. Before CPA, my faith and the way I worked the Steps were sufficient for where I was then and helped me recover from addiction. It took a different faith to recover from the debilitating emotional and spiritual effects of chronic illness and chronic pain. My HP provided that faith, and still does, through CPA.

In this moment, I will credit my daily peace, joy, and comfort to CPA and my Higher Power.

Appendix A

The CPA Preamble

CPA is a fellowship of people who share their experience, strength and hope with each other, so that they may solve their common problem and help others to recover from the disabling effects of chronic pain and chronic illness. We believe that changing attitudes can aid recovery. The only requirement for membership is a desire to recover from the emotional and spiritual debilitation of chronic pain or chronic illness. There are no dues or fees for CPA membership. We are self-supporting through our own contributions. CPA is not allied with any sect, denomination, politics, organization or institution; does not wish to engage in any controversy, neither endorses nor opposes any causes. Our primary purpose is to live our lives to the fullest by minimizing the effects of chronic pain and chronic illness in our lives and helping others to do the same. We do this by practicing the Twelve Steps, and welcoming and giving comfort and understanding to each other.

Appendix B

The Twelve Steps of CPA

1. We admitted we were powerless over pain and illness—that our lives had become unmanageable.

2. Came to believe that a Power greater than ourselves could restore us to sanity.

3. Made a decision to turn our will and our lives over to the care of God as we understood Him.

4. Made a searching and fearless moral inventory of ourselves.

5. Admitted to God, to ourselves, and to another human being the exact nature of our wrongs.

6. Were entirely ready to have God remove all these defects of character.

7. Humbly asked Him to remove our shortcomings.

8. Made a list of all persons we had harmed, and became willing to make amends to them all.

9. Made direct amends to such people wherever possible, except when to do so would injure them or others.

10. Continued to take personal inventory and when we were wrong promptly admitted it.

11. Sought through prayer and meditation to improve our conscious contact with God as we understood Him, praying only for knowledge of His will for us and the power to carry that out.

12. Having had a spiritual awakening as the result of these steps, we tried to carry this message to others with chronic pain and chronic illness, and to practice these principles in all our affairs.

Appendix C

The Twelve Traditions of CPA

1. Our common welfare should come first; personal recovery depends upon CPA unity.

2. For our group purpose there is but one ultimate authority—a loving God as He may express Himself in our group conscience. Our leaders are but trusted servants; they do not govern.

3. The only requirement for CPA membership is a desire to recover from the emotional and spiritual debilitation of chronic pain or chronic illness.

4. Each group should be autonomous, except in matters affecting other groups or CPA as a whole.

5. Each group has but one primary purpose – to carry its message to people living with chronic pain and chronic illness.

6. A CPA group ought never endorse, finance, or lend the CPA name to any outside enterprise, lest problems of money, property, and prestige divert us from our primary purpose.

7. Every CPA group ought to be fully self-supporting, declining outside contributions.

8. Chronic Pain Anonymous should remain forever nonprofessional, but our service centers may employ special workers.

9. CPA, as such, ought never be organized; but we may create service boards or committees directly responsible to those they serve.

10. Chronic Pain Anonymous has no opinion on outside issues; hence the CPA name ought never be drawn into public controversy.

11. Our public relations policy is based on attraction rather than promotion; we need always maintain personal anonymity at the level of press, radio, television, film, and the Internet.

12. Anonymity is the spiritual foundation of all our traditions, ever reminding us to place principles before personalities.

Appendix D

Twelve Concepts of Service

1. The final responsibility and the ultimate authority for the CPA World Services should always reside in the collective conscience of our whole Fellowship.

2. The CPA groups delegate complete administrative and operational authority to their World Service Conference and its service arms.

3. As a traditional means of creating and maintaining a clearly defined working relationship among the groups, the World Service Conference, the Service Board of Trustees and its service corporation, staffs, and committees, and of thus ensuring their effective leadership, it is hereby suggested we endow each of these elements of World Service with a traditional "Right of Decision."

4. The "Right of Participation" ensures equality of opportunity for all in the decision-making process. Participation is the key to harmony.

5. Throughout our structure, a traditional "Right of Appeal" ought to prevail, so that minority opinion will be heard and personal grievances will receive careful consideration.

6. The World Service Conference recognizes the chief initiative and active responsibility in most world service matters can be exercised by the trustee members of the Conference acting as the Trustee Board.

7. The Trustees have legal rights while the rights of the Conference are traditional.

8. The Trustees are the principal planners and administrators of overall policy and finance. The Service Board of Trustees delegates full authority for routine management to its executive committees.

9. Good personal leadership at all service levels is a necessity. In the field of world service, the Service Board of Trustees assumes the primary leadership.

10. Every service responsibility should be matched by an equal service authority, with the scope of such authority well defined.

11. The General Service Virtual Office is composed of the Executive Director, selected committees, and staff members.

12. The Conference shall observe the spirit of CPA tradition, taking care that it never becomes the seat of perilous wealth or power; that sufficient operating funds and reserves be its prudent financial principle; that it place none of its members in a position of unqualified authority over others; that it reach all important decisions by discussion, vote, and whenever possible, substantial unanimity; that its actions never be personally punitive nor an incitement to public controversy; that it never perform authoritative acts of government; that, like the Fellowship it serves, it will always remain democratic in thought and action.

General Warranties of the Conferences

- Warranty One: "that it never becomes the seat of perilous wealth or power"
- Warranty Two: "that sufficient operating funds and reserves be its prudent financial principle"
- Warranty Three: "that it place none of its members in a position of unqualified authority over others"
- Warranty Four: "that it reach all important decisions by discussion, vote, and whenever possible, substantial unanimity"

- Warranty Five: "that its actions never be personally punitive nor an incitement to public controversy"

- Warranty Six: "that it never perform authoritative acts of government; that, like the Fellowship it serves, it will always remain democratic in thought and action"

Appendix E

The CPA Declaration

Some of us believe our problems are insurmountable. We have lived with pain and suffering for so long; we have given up hope for happiness. We believe any promises for positive change are only true for others, not for us.

The CPA program of recovery offers new attitudes and ways of thinking. We may start this journey with doubt, yet little by little, through our consistent efforts, we will discover a different way of life in which beneficial habits will begin to replace ones that once brought us misery.

Our spiritual recovery will be accomplished by being open to the experience, strength and hope shared by our friends in the fellowship. We will come to understand if we do what others have done, we will get what others have gotten. As we steadily work the Twelve Steps of CPA and engage in service, our relationship with chronic pain and chronic illness will no longer be adversarial. We will begin our day with gratitude and hope. Possibilities we never dreamed of will be part of our daily existence and we will begin to see that we can have a quality of life despite living with pain and illness.

So, with the little bit of faith and guidance that brought us to CPA, we begin. If we are rigorous in our endeavor, we will be astounded by the results.

CPA Declaration

1. Fellowship, rather than loneliness and isolation, will be present in our life.
2. We will enjoy connecting with other people.
3. We will be compassionate and kind to ourselves as well as consider the needs of others.
4. Fear will be replaced by courage, strength and faith to rise and meet any challenges. We will even see challenges as opportunities for spiritual growth.
5. We will forgive those whom we perceive have harmed us so we can be free from the chains of the past.
6. Remembering progress, not perfection, we will approach each day with a positive attitude. We will choose to focus on gratitude, placing our attention on all that is good.
7. Our pain and illness will no longer be the primary focus of our day. We will feel serenity and peace regardless of what condition our body is in. Our body will not determine the joy we experience in life.
8. We will laugh and see the lighter side of situations.
9. We will value ourselves and believe we have something to give to the world. Self-pity will be replaced by a belief our life has meaning and purpose.
10. We will be open to new beginnings and no longer cling to how things were in the past.
11. We will believe we deserve to love and to be loved.
12. We will have faith in a Higher Power which does for us what we cannot do for ourselves. This Power is the foundation that will support and guide us as we move through each moment. Our life will be far better than we ever imagined possible.

Appendix F

One Day At A Time

One Day At A Time – I will make an effort to participate in the world. I will reach out and connect with another person. I can pick up the phone and call a friend, greet someone on the street, or I can smile at the clerk in the store.

One Day At A Time – I will put my focus on promoting the well-being of someone besides myself. I will take the attention off of me and my issues, and place it on the needs of another being.

One Day At A Time – I will pace myself and trust my body to guide me. I will not push when my body tells me it's time to stop. I will do half of what I think I can accomplish.

One Day At A Time – I will eat well and exercise in moderation. I will take an interest in my appearance and tend to my personal hygiene. I may dress comfortably, but I will try to look my very best.

One Day At A Time – I will ask for help when I need it. I will accept assistance graciously and be thankful. I will appreciate the people in my life who support me.

One Day At A Time – I will live each day to the best of my ability and take responsibility for my own happiness. I will notice the good in life and not dwell on the negative. I will count my blessings and enjoy all that I've been given.

One Day At A Time – I will remember that I am more than my pain or my illness. I will believe that I am perfect exactly as I am. I will accept whatever comes my way with an attitude of gratitude.

One Day At A Time – I will make an extra effort to be patient and gentle with myself and others when I am feeling irritable and frustrated. No blame, no shame. Just because I am in pain doesn't mean I have to be a pain.

One Day At A Time – I will create some quiet moments for myself. I can use them for inner reflection, reviewing my day, or strengthening my spiritual connections. Taking this time each day is a rich and rewarding gift to myself.

One Day At A Time – I will enjoy something that is fun. I will engage my mind in creative activities. I will try something different and be open to new possibilities.

One Day At A Time – I accept the conditions of my life as they are this day. Within any condition I can contribute to myself, my family, and my community. I am a valuable member of society.

One Day At A Time – I will acknowledge feelings of fear and anxiety as they rise up. When they appear, I will remember to put my trust in a Power greater than myself. I will have hope in knowing that this, too, shall pass, and I will have faith that I can thrive through anything when I do it one moment at a time.

Appendix G

One Night At A Time

In CPA we learn to live in the solution and not in the problem. These *One Night At A Time* suggestions can guide us toward serenity. We can't take them all on at once. It helps to take one, study it, and apply it to our lives until we are familiar with it. Over time we will see how changing attitudes and actions can open the door to newfound happiness and a celebration of life.

One night at a time, I will honor my gratitude. Challenges and blessings happened today, and I am grateful for both. I have come to believe that my Higher Power is in charge and is working toward the greatest and highest good for myself and others—regardless of circumstances and appearances. This night, I choose an attitude of gratitude.

One night at a time, I will honor my willingness to surrender. I applaud my willingness to surrender that which no longer serves me or my Higher Power. I surrender my powerlessness and relax. I trust my Higher Power to change my relationship with myself, my body, and all that troubles me. Even in the depths of chronic pain and chronic illness, I am willing to change and be changed. This night, I choose to celebrate my growing faith.

One night at a time, I will honor my courage and my fears. I may have taken risks today, big or small. I may have asked for help and been willing to be of service. I may have felt frightened, may have been reactive, or may have felt hopeless—yet I faced another day with the help of my Higher Power. This night, I choose to acknowledge my courage and bravery when facing my fears.

One night at a time, I will honor myself exactly as I am in this moment. My body, mind and spirit have served me today. Perhaps not in the way I would have liked, but they have served me—and they have served my Higher Power. I remember to pray for Higher Power's will to be done—not my own. I release judgment and criticism. I accept my whole self in its limited functionality as beautiful in the eyes of my Higher Power. This night, I choose self-compassion and self-care.

One night at a time, I will honor self-acceptance. I am a work in progress, a perfectly imperfect human being just like everyone else. I choose to view positive and negative thoughts, sensations, emotions, and behaviors with kindness and gratitude. I release the need to label these experiences as good or bad. Each arrives with wisdom and clarity that Higher Power will reveal to me. This night, I choose self-love.

One night at a time, I will honor others just as they are. I may have felt anger, frustration, or disappointment with others today. I might have had expectations that were not met. These feelings signal my need to practice tolerance, acceptance, and unconditional kindness. In all my relationships, I release my resistance with compassionate self-awareness. This night, I choose to bless everyone in my life and wish them all a serene night.

One night at a time, I will greet all my feelings as valued friends. I may have felt rage, panic, irritability, jealousy, loneliness, or grief today. Although some feelings can be overwhelming and unpleasant, they all have something to teach me. I can acknowledge all my feelings and ask for Higher Power's guidance in processing (not suppressing) them. I do not have to let these feelings dictate the quality of my rest tonight or my actions tomorrow. This night, I will trust Higher Power to show me the wisdom in all of my feelings.

One night at a time, I will remind myself that nothing is required of me in this moment. My day is done, and tomorrow offers a new beginning. I am more open to Higher Power's guidance when I honor my need for rest. I do not need to plan, solve problems, or correct errors. In this present moment, I pray for a quiet mind and a contented heart. This night, I choose to turn over yesterday, today, and tomorrow to the care of my loving Higher Power.

I will rest now, safe in the knowledge of my Higher Power's love for me. I believe the help, guidance, and strength I need for tomorrow will be freely given to me as I continue to pray, "Thy will, not mine, be done." I remember that my Higher Power dreams bigger than I do. I choose to rest in the loving care of my Higher Power.

Appendix H

CPA Suggested Meeting Format

1. Welcome to the _____ meeting of Chronic Pain Anonymous. My name is _____, and I live with chronic pain and chronic illness ("I am a grateful member;" location, etc.). Let's begin the meeting with a moment of silence, followed by the Serenity Prayer.

2. Would someone (or name) please read the Preamble?
   Would someone (or name) please read the Twelve Steps?
   Would someone (or name) please read the Twelve Traditions?

3. Let's introduce ourselves by our first names only. (Optional: People can introduce themselves with their location as well.) If you are new to the group, please let us know so we can welcome you.

4. Group Announcements:
   - Our monthly business meeting is held the _____ of each month. Any group member may call a group conscience at any time.
   - Are there any CPA-related announcements?
   - Is anyone celebrating a CPA milestone?

5. Tradition Seven states, "Every CPA group ought to be fully self-supporting, declining outside contributions." While CPA has no dues or fees, we do have expenses. Our donations pay for services such as literature (professional edits, publishing, printing, and audio recordings), public information, website administration, and bookkeeping. Please give what you can. However, we need you more than we need your money.

   https://chronicpainanonymous.org/contributions/

6. This is a (topic, discussion, speaker, literature, Step study, etc.) group. We will discuss the CPA Twelve Steps and Twelve Traditions, exploring ways to apply the program to living with chronic pain and chronic illness. (We are currently reading _____.)

7. Sharing Guidelines:

In CPA, we concentrate on our feelings and attitudes about our situation rather than on the details of the situation. We reflect on how chronic illness and chronic pain have affected our thinking and our behavior. We look at the part we play in our problems and how the Twelve Steps can guide us toward recovery from the obsession of our chronic illness and chronic pain. When we focus on ways to apply the principles of the program in our daily lives, we discover that our changed attitudes and actions can lead us to a meaningful life of peace and serenity.

Tradition Ten states, "Chronic Pain Anonymous has no opinion on outside issues; hence the CPA name ought never be drawn into public controversy." Therefore, in our meetings we avoid discussions about religion or specific diagnoses, medications, therapies, doctors, insurance providers, and healthcare systems. If referring to our own medical issues, we find it is best to keep to general terms. We do not give medical advice. When we share, we guard against crosstalk. When one person responds directly to another who has shared, this is crosstalk.

8. We come together to share our experience, strength, and hope freely without interruption. We listen to suffering individuals with compassion and understanding, to offer hope and support. We empower each other to be vulnerable by providing a nonjudgmental, safe meeting.

9. This meeting ends at _____ . (Optional: the top of the hour/the bottom of the hour, etc.)

10. Closing:

In closing, I would like to remind everyone that the opinions expressed here were strictly those of the person who spoke. Take what you like and leave the rest. Everything that was shared here was done so in confidence. Please respect the anonymity of this meeting and its members. Discussing who was at a meeting or what they shared is a breach of anonymity. Let what you heard here, stay here. Tradition Twelve states, "Anonymity is the spiritual foundation of all our Traditions, ever reminding us to place principles before personalities."

If you are new to CPA, we encourage you to keep coming back. We have found that while our health challenges may differ, how they affect us is often similar. Although today we may be feeling at our worst, in CPA we see the best in each other. In time, with the love and support we have found here, we begin to see the best in ourselves. We invite you to stay after the meeting and talk with someone who is familiar with CPA and the Twelve Steps. Will all who care to, please join me in the Closing Prayer/Words.

Please see CPA's website under Member Resources > Meeting Materials > for more detailed information.

Index

A

Ability 17, 43, 55, 84, 96, 106, 111, 117, 125, 128, 143, 152, 153, 161, 213, 254, 257, 259, 289, 307, 325, 326, 328, 362, 371, 372, 375, 386, 387, 407

Acceptance 9, 10, 13, 14, 25, 26, 30, 43, 48, 49, 54, 56, 65, 77, 78, 90, 93, 96, 104, 106, 108, 109, 111, 115, 119, 122, 123, 128, 129, 130, 131, 138, 142, 143, 147, 151, 152, 164, 165, 169, 171, 173, 176, 181, 182, 188, 190, 193, 196, 205, 217, 220, 222, 230, 235, 241, 244, 251, 265, 279, 301, 322, 325, 327, 331, 339, 345, 349, 391, 396, 410

Act as if 23, 213, 222, 227, 229

Action 15, 17, 22, 29, 39, 48, 49, 55, 61, 78, 80, 87, 112, 115, 118, 125, 128, 129, 144, 148, 151, 156, 160, 164, 173, 176, 181, 196, 201, 204, 207, 216, 223, 224, 225, 229, 241, 254, 270, 272, 273, 275, 284, 285, 292, 293, 312, 322, 331, 337, 341, 353, 357, 362, 370, 376, 377, 379, 388, 396, 403, 404

Addiction ix, 301, 343, 397

Advice 62, 105, 192, 195, 277, 321, 323, 413

Aging 21

Alone. *See* Loneliness

Amends 13, 57, 89, 94, 103, 123, 124, 129, 141, 148, 149, 171, 242, 248, 254, 257, 271, 277, 290, 305, 315, 316, 379, 399

Anger/Angry ix, 3, 12, 23, 56, 81, 99, 103, 104, 106, 109, 110, 123, 124, 128, 137, 138, 158, 160, 162, 163, 171, 174, 175, 176, 187, 188, 193, 194, 211, 214, 217, 225, 230, 248, 257, 261, 265, 278, 292, 294, 304, 325, 327, 347, 357, 363, 386, 390, 410

Anonymity 3, 107, 121, 186, 194, 256, 367, 391, 401, 414

Anxiety 48, 59, 75, 90, 128, 144, 181, 188, 191, 197, 235, 265, 270, 274, 325, 363, 408

Appointment(s) 47, 81, 108, 116, 117, 139, 225, 230, 306, 313, 328, 385, 389

Art 180, 205, 252

As it is 26, 38, 58, 77, 78, 95, 110, 122, 130, 142, 152, 169, 228, 279

Asking for help 14, 75, 135, 138

Attachment 383

Attitude 7, 16, 18, 19, 31, 42, 47, 49, 52, 60, 61, 69, 78, 80, 106, 156, 195, 198, 202, 207, 221, 225, 229, 236, 241, 242, 252, 253, 254, 257, 265, 271, 283, 290, 297, 301, 305, 309, 349, 360, 363, 367, 373, 383, 385, 388, 406, 407, 409

Authentic 245, 255

Awareness 12, 31, 78, 123, 128, 129, 145, 149, 150, 178, 193, 196, 249, 281, 282, 290, 314, 331, 384, 391, 410

415

B

Bad days xii, 16, 106, 174, 238, 311, 338
Behavior 7, 41, 57, 94, 105, 109, 128, 129, 135, 143, 145, 149, 161, 163, 201, 220, 224, 231, 242, 271, 277, 278, 295, 305, 315, 316, 324, 326, 337, 345, 357, 394, 410, 413
Being still 327
Belief 29, 42, 46, 55, 63, 64, 75, 91, 119, 156, 162, 164, 182, 239, 269, 312, 324, 327, 339, 348, 376, 383, 406
Blame/Blaming 29, 42, 128, 136, 139, 178, 181, 220, 236, 254, 262, 271, 283, 284, 314, 322, 388, 392, 407
Blessings 198, 251, 360, 363, 391, 407, 409
Body's needs 362
Boundaries 9, 79, 137, 220, 237, 246, 251, 276, 281, 282, 283, 302, 358
Breathe 15, 18, 39, 48, 159, 188, 211, 251, 330, 394
Broken 10, 43, 46, 91, 360

C

Calm 51, 70, 90, 251, 275, 303, 345, 379
Care 4, 6, 9, 12, 13, 15, 17, 21, 29, 30, 42, 46, 47, 48, 62, 74, 84, 91, 103, 114, 119, 120, 122, 123, 124, 126, 143, 147, 149, 150, 152, 156, 158, 159, 160, 162, 171, 175, 178, 181, 182, 184, 187, 188, 191, 193, 202, 212, 224, 238, 241, 248, 254, 255, 259, 262, 264, 272, 273, 277, 281, 290, 295, 298, 304, 308, 315, 324, 325, 357, 359, 369, 371, 376, 379, 381, 383, 387, 388, 389, 390, 396, 399, 403, 410, 411, 414
Career 31, 64, 107, 121, 252, 301, 303, 304, 328
Change v, xi, 7, 8, 12, 20, 29, 30, 33, 39, 42, 43, 47, 49, 51, 52, 53, 56, 57, 58, 60, 61, 69, 72, 74, 75, 78, 80, 88, 90, 98, 103, 104, 108, 110, 111, 131, 139, 143, 145, 153, 156, 161, 163, 165, 169, 170, 172, 174, 190, 192, 196, 202, 206, 219, 221, 225, 226, 229, 238, 248, 249, 250, 253, 264, 265, 271, 273, 277, 284, 286, 288, 304, 310, 312, 313, 322, 324, 336, 339, 345, 351, 355, 367, 374, 376, 378, 383, 385, 389, 394, 405, 409, 413
Changed Attitudes 29, 61, 389, 413
Choice 15, 29, 32, 42, 48, 60, 65, 72, 75, 82, 103, 106, 109, 125, 132, 171, 185, 190, 191, 193, 201, 213, 220, 228, 248, 271, 277, 292, 301, 343, 352, 355, 363, 370
Chronic conditions 7, 27, 33, 62, 119, 122, 146, 169, 186, 206, 208, 226, 260, 322, 384, 391
Clarity 15, 44, 96, 105, 125, 141, 144, 149, 204, 228, 285, 325, 371, 410
Comfort ix, xii, 3, 8, 11, 23, 44, 106, 127, 173, 175, 178, 185, 188, 195, 212, 215, 222, 258, 263, 275, 282, 325, 342, 388, 389, 397, 398
Coming to CPA 54, 73, 182, 262, 304

Communication 70, 149, 281, 290, 296, 308, 320, 330, 347, 358
Community 53, 76, 114, 187, 251, 256, 343, 408
Compare 24, 53, 107, 177, 186, 191, 194, 197, 203, 252, 260, 361
Compassion 3, 6, 42, 53, 56, 57, 58, 65, 80, 85, 99, 105, 106, 107, 108, 119, 123, 127, 136, 137, 138, 151, 152, 163, 174, 182, 187, 188, 198, 223, 224, 241, 251, 253, 254, 257, 258, 265, 271, 276, 283, 290, 294, 315, 321, 322, 323, 325, 345, 361, 368, 379, 388, 390, 397, 410, 413
Connection 8, 11, 73, 79, 125, 150, 175, 185, 203, 248, 264, 274, 347, 354, 356, 374, 384, 395
Conscious contact 44, 273, 296, 356, 399
Control 4, 7, 13, 14, 15, 21, 25, 29, 30, 38, 41, 55, 64, 80, 81, 83, 84, 96, 97, 105, 108, 110, 122, 127, 130, 131, 141, 146, 148, 150, 162, 165, 176, 181, 182, 196, 197, 202, 204, 206, 222, 230, 241, 251, 269, 273, 281, 284, 296, 301, 305, 323, 336, 339, 357, 362, 369, 372, 376, 385, 394, 397
Co-travelers 304
Courage v, 7, 49, 55, 60, 61, 78, 90, 96, 120, 126, 138, 147, 180, 185, 225, 255, 293, 297, 301, 308, 312, 313, 315, 328, 329, 350, 369, 379, 386, 396, 397, 406, 409
Creative xi, 10, 32, 47, 55, 123, 143, 180, 247, 252, 278, 294, 313, 373, 408

D

Daily practice 77, 345, 394
Debilitation ix, 4, 164, 182, 185, 186, 189, 244, 376, 398, 400
Declarations xi, 392, 397, 405, 406
Denial 9, 43, 129, 156, 213, 284, 322
Depression ix, 3, 16, 18, 45, 58, 75, 90, 104, 174, 180, 189, 226, 248, 253, 293, 311, 328, 355
Despair 8, 14, 28, 31, 80, 85, 90, 132, 153, 170, 177, 183, 186, 252, 253, 328, 376
Diagnosis 30, 81, 88, 119, 182, 183, 186, 191, 235, 244, 255, 263, 351, 354, 369, 391, 396, 413
Difference v, 6, 7, 9, 18, 48, 52, 58, 60, 63, 70, 89, 93, 105, 112, 117, 121, 135, 139, 143, 144, 148, 152, 155, 169, 177, 178, 190, 197, 203, 208, 212, 222, 223, 225, 229, 236, 246, 253, 265, 269, 271, 273, 274, 279, 280, 284, 296, 297, 298, 317, 319, 324, 331, 339, 349, 359, 367, 370, 375, 376, 377, 387, 397, 405, 408
Diminish 43, 156, 363
Disability 51, 165, 190, 203, 230, 262, 304, 351
Disappointment 5, 25, 52, 119, 145, 252, 292, 376, 410
Dishonesty 23, 125, 147, 262
Distorted thinking 241, 285, 291
Divine 159, 347

Doctors ix, 27, 43, 52, 54, 72, 80, 81, 88, 99, 114, 117, 131, 139, 146, 165, 185, 187, 188, 217, 240, 246, 255, 262, 265, 275, 288, 301, 306, 323, 328, 339, 343, 349, 353, 371, 385, 389, 395, 413
Do/Doing half 112, 241, 287, 407
Don't Quit Five Minutes Before the Miracle 307
Doubt 38, 85, 126, 187, 211, 264, 295, 347, 405

E

Easy Does It 58, 235, 241, 283
Ego 220, 256, 305, 342, 347
Emotions 10, 12, 15, 19, 28, 42, 48, 75, 104, 114, 119, 124, 128, 130, 131, 138, 143, 145, 163, 171, 183, 190, 198, 220, 239, 275, 294, 297, 304, 305, 314, 317, 364, 367, 381, 388, 410
Employer 161, 351
Envy. *See* Jealousy
Exhaustion 19, 33, 58, 114, 128, 226, 291, 381
    Tired 5, 19, 46, 72, 92, 109, 149, 226, 278, 283, 290, 294, 381
Expectations 12, 13, 26, 33, 42, 49, 110, 137, 142, 143, 153, 165, 172, 211, 217, 236, 269, 357, 376, 385, 391, 393, 410
Experience, Strength, and Hope ix, xii, 114, 155, 192, 223, 229, 237, 274, 308, 321, 367, 377, 386, 413

F

Faith 14, 38, 39, 55, 64, 73, 79, 83, 84, 89, 105, 126, 153, 158, 161, 184, 185, 209, 211, 214, 222, 227, 265, 273, 297, 303, 310, 339, 351, 368, 379, 382, 396, 397, 405, 406, 408, 409
Family 17, 56, 76, 81, 99, 106, 120, 161, 174, 175, 185, 195, 203, 204, 256, 269, 271, 278, 281, 288, 302, 316, 331, 349, 374, 375, 381, 408
Fatigue. *See* Exhaustion; *See* Exhaustion
Fear ix, 3, 7, 16, 18, 21, 40, 41, 54, 57, 59, 63, 75, 80, 81, 86, 90, 93, 99, 104, 120, 124, 126, 128, 138, 139, 150, 152, 157, 161, 163, 172, 176, 178, 185, 188, 211, 215, 239, 244, 255, 259, 265, 274, 278, 293, 295, 297, 302, 304, 310, 311, 328, 351, 357, 376, 378, 382, 386, 396, 408
Finances 53, 126, 146, 184, 259, 316, 328, 375
Financial insecurity 259, 351
Forgiveness 57, 143, 150, 173, 182, 187, 193, 258, 271, 280, 345, 406
Freedom/Free x, xi, 12, 52, 61, 78, 83, 98, 105, 111, 121, 126, 143, 144, 148, 150, 151, 157, 205, 206, 209, 236, 256, 262, 277, 302, 312, 321, 322, 349, 355, 363, 367, 375, 396, 406
Friend(s) 5, 6, 11, 13, 31, 42, 59, 81, 85, 91, 99, 106, 110, 113, 114, 115, 118, 130, 137, 138, 146, 147, 149, 154, 158, 162, 175, 177, 183, 185, 190, 192, 195, 203, 210, 211, 213, 227, 229, 238, 241, 242, 249, 253, 254, 255, 256, 261, 262, 269, 271, 273, 275, 276, 277, 281, 282, 284, 293,

294, 304, 315, 318, 321, 330, 337, 342, 347, 352, 354, 357, 363, 373, 374, 375, 379, 386, 389, 390, 395, 397, 405, 407, 410
Frustration 12, 53, 90, 104, 130, 159, 160, 189, 250, 274, 316, 352, 410

G

Gentleness xii, 57, 58, 80, 83, 106, 123, 150, 156, 164, 192, 196, 253, 254, 263, 271, 319, 335, 337, 355, 386, 388, 390, 407
Giving up 25, 65, 77, 82, 90, 118, 136, 159, 252, 301, 303, 328, 337, 339, 349, 364
Goals 23, 107, 165, 284, 318
God's will 49, 71, 96, 125, 130, 228, 261, 296, 351, 352, 364
Going slowly 103, 171
Grace/Graciously 12, 16, 44, 78, 85, 86, 105, 126, 135, 143, 241, 316, 343, 368, 395, 396, 407
Grandiosity 206, 285, 321
Grateful 6, 8, 9, 15, 18, 20, 27, 31, 45, 52, 64, 65, 70, 73, 80, 82, 85, 91, 99, 104, 109, 114, 115, 127, 128, 143, 165, 176, 179, 180, 183, 189, 192, 194, 217, 219, 226, 229, 230, 235, 241, 243, 250, 253, 264, 284, 288, 295, 304, 308, 314, 316, 323, 327, 328, 329, 330, 331, 343, 348, 360, 363, 378, 382, 385, 386, 391, 392, 409, 412
Gratitude 12, 18, 23, 29, 31, 42, 43, 49, 95, 96, 99, 106, 109, 157, 179, 198, 237, 257, 280, 298, 316, 326, 348, 360, 363, 368, 379, 384, 394, 397, 405, 406, 407, 409, 410
Gratitude list 12, 29, 96, 179, 198
Grief 10, 27, 46, 65, 81, 90, 121, 128, 142, 146, 165, 170, 193, 239, 244, 252, 328, 348, 410
Growth xii, 63, 76, 93, 138, 196, 284, 306, 308, 342, 397, 406
Guidance 5, 15, 42, 55, 57, 59, 75, 81, 82, 86, 144, 146, 148, 158, 172, 173, 182, 185, 188, 207, 222, 227, 260, 261, 264, 274, 275, 284, 295, 296, 303, 306, 339, 345, 350, 357, 359, 377, 405, 410

H

Harmony 77, 106, 275, 319, 402
Healthcare system 178, 385
Help ix, xi, xii, 4, 7, 8, 9, 12, 13, 14, 15, 16, 18, 22, 23, 24, 26, 27, 28, 32, 33, 37, 40, 41, 42, 44, 45, 46, 47, 49, 50, 51, 53, 57, 59, 60, 61, 63, 64, 65, 69, 70, 73, 74, 75, 76, 77, 78, 79, 80, 82, 83, 86, 87, 89, 91, 94, 98, 99, 104, 105, 107, 108, 109, 112, 114, 116, 120, 122, 123, 124, 125, 130, 131, 132, 135, 136, 138, 139, 144, 145, 146, 151, 156, 157, 158, 161, 162, 170, 172, 177, 178, 181, 183, 184, 185, 190, 195, 196, 197, 201, 204, 205, 206, 207, 209, 214, 216, 217, 219, 220, 222, 223, 224, 225, 227, 228, 236, 237, 238, 239, 241, 242, 244, 245, 246, 250, 251, 252, 254, 255, 256, 257, 258, 260, 265, 273, 274, 275, 277, 278, 282, 283,

284, 287, 288, 289, 291, 293, 294, 296, 302, 304, 305, 306, 307, 308, 310, 311, 313, 316, 317, 318, 319, 321, 324, 326, 329, 330, 331, 337, 338, 339, 340, 342, 343, 344, 345, 346, 348, 349, 350, 353, 356, 359, 360, 364, 367, 368, 369, 370, 372, 378, 381, 382, 383, 384, 385, 389, 391, 394, 395, 397, 398, 407, 409, 410
HELP (Hungry, Exhausted, Lonely, Pain) 224, 381
Holidays 5, 331, 374, 382, 393
Hope ix, xii, 5, 8, 14, 31, 40, 49, 52, 54, 56, 64, 90, 93, 97, 98, 109, 110, 114, 119, 153, 155, 156, 158, 165, 170, 174, 175, 189, 192, 206, 209, 211, 220, 222, 223, 224, 229, 235, 237, 242, 264, 265, 273, 274, 276, 308, 321, 325, 360, 364, 367, 368, 376, 377, 386, 392, 393, 398, 405, 408, 413
Hopeless 15, 19, 56, 109, 147, 336, 409
HOW (Honesty, Open-Mindedness, and Willingness) 284
Humanness 123, 136, 173, 181, 310
Humility 9, 14, 55, 75, 83, 107, 123, 126, 173, 186, 193, 194, 197, 207, 218, 220, 303, 316, 341
Humor 14, 116, 137, 157, 250, 285, 354

I

Illusion of control 38, 131, 202
Impatience 307
Imperfect 13, 16, 126, 211, 257, 283, 310, 355, 385, 410
In all my affairs 55, 184, 309, 367
Independence 303
Insanity 21, 27, 42, 64, 135, 141, 152, 170, 177, 181, 285
Insecurity 104, 128, 259, 304, 351
Inspiration 175, 195, 252
Intimacy 213, 215, 347, 374, 386
Intuition 312, 377
Inventory 19, 24, 95, 119, 124, 128, 136, 172, 207, 217, 236, 271, 278, 290, 291, 318, 328, 344, 357, 399
Isolation ix, xii, 3, 8, 119, 128, 131, 135, 157, 177, 189, 208, 248, 329, 352, 406

J

Jealousy 3, 128, 410
Joining CPA 59, 295, 362
Journal/Journaling 13, 44, 95, 108, 207, 249, 345, 389
Joy i, 12, 117, 289
Just for now 13, 27, 346
Just for today 21, 77, 108, 110, 205, 286, 346, 382

K

Keep coming back 41, 203, 229, 307, 396, 414
Keep It Simple 270
Kindness 16, 41, 57, 58, 79, 85, 119, 127, 143, 193, 194, 223, 235, 251, 257, 258, 280, 315, 363, 388, 390, 410

L

Laughter 5, 47, 61, 154, 157, 183, 201, 235, 306
Let/Letting go 4, 7, 10, 13, 17, 21, 30, 42, 50, 55, 70, 80, 89, 92, 97, 99, 107, 120, 121, 125, 131, 136, 142, 144, 152, 162, 177, 178, 181, 182, 183, 206, 211, 214, 228, 251, 255, 259, 269, 272, 273, 274, 284, 301, 303, 305, 314, 315, 324, 331, 336, 337, 339, 346, 349, 351, 367, 377, 383, 386, 393
Let/Letting God 55, 89, 144, 214
Lifestyle 165, 190, 247, 328, 352
Limits/Limitations 10, 44, 45, 54, 64, 65, 108, 120, 145, 196, 238, 244, 252, 265, 271, 282, 293, 349, 358, 359, 390, 393
Listening xii, 65, 82, 111, 112, 156, 212, 216, 237, 260, 276, 295, 367, 369, 395
Loneliness 3, 10, 11, 19, 20, 33, 38, 40, 41, 48, 56, 59, 69, 73, 83, 92, 94, 97, 114, 122, 126, 131, 132, 143, 152, 156, 162, 175, 185, 188, 189, 208, 211, 217, 222, 224, 226, 235, 242, 245, 248, 258, 261, 264, 273, 276, 284, 286, 287, 307, 312, 313, 320, 335, 342, 343, 348, 352, 354, 356, 373, 387, 392, 406, 410
Loss. *See* Grief
Loving
  Loving care 15, 48, 184, 369, 379, 411
  Loving Higher Power 7, 33, 48, 91, 181, 184, 295, 410
Lowest 112, 160, 246, 257, 262, 393

M

Marriage 184, 185, 250, 321, 347
Medical 8, 25, 43, 46, 47, 59, 99, 103, 114, 131, 139, 147, 169, 171, 186, 209, 215, 217, 244, 250, 255, 262, 263, 306, 313, 321, 379, 385, 413
Medications 56, 111, 131, 156, 177, 188, 220, 226, 237, 291, 301, 321, 323, 343, 347, 349, 362, 413
Meditation x, xii, 18, 51, 58, 99, 112, 125, 130, 143, 150, 163, 185, 223, 228, 255, 345, 346, 356, 395, 399
Meetings 3, 37, 104, 121
Miracles 114, 227, 249, 389, 397
Mistake(s) xii, 16, 33, 40, 143, 152, 173, 216, 310, 355
Mortality 185

N

Negative attitude 252
Newcomer 3, 137, 192, 235, 237, 241, 321, 378
New normal 17, 55, 169
Next indicated action 15, 80, 87, 112, 125, 164, 181, 207, 225, 229, 292, 322, 357, 362, 370, 377, 379, 388
Not giving up. *See also* Giving up

O

Obsession 4, 5, 15, 19, 24, 28, 29, 46, 52, 55, 62, 88, 130, 141, 148, 156, 176, 181, 191, 241, 265, 296, 298, 339, 376, 389, 413
One day at a time xi, xii, 77, 80, 96, 175, 229, 244, 273, 283, 286, 316, 377, 407, 408
One moment at a time 270
One step at a time 144
Open mind 13, 26, 79, 98
Openness 196
Optimisim 90, 213
Outcomes 4, 55, 80, 81, 83, 84, 128, 142, 159, 171, 181, 211, 217, 230, 259, 318, 349, 385
Overdoing 187, 224
Overwhelmed 15, 19, 81, 125, 141, 144, 187, 191, 208, 242, 276, 278, 292, 338, 346, 359

P

Pacing 45, 55, 240, 261, 272, 387, 397
Painful 47, 93, 123, 139, 248, 275, 294, 317, 322, 342, 354, 389
Panic 70, 80, 126, 176, 248, 362, 410
Partner 10, 91, 111, 123, 145, 151, 184, 190, 223, 259, 260, 343, 344, 386
Patience 123, 127, 216, 241, 283, 327
Pause/Pausing 12, 15, 29, 55, 78, 87, 93, 117, 141, 164, 175, 198, 251, 260, 276, 278, 303, 306, 356, 370
Peace ix, xii, 3, 8, 20, 27, 57, 70, 74, 77, 79, 80, 90, 92, 93, 96, 125, 129, 143, 160, 162, 176, 188, 191, 207, 214, 222, 228, 279, 280, 284, 301, 323, 330, 336, 362, 363, 371, 383, 397, 406, 413
Perception 12, 17, 76, 91, 117, 191, 295
Perfectionism 355
Perseverance 82
Planning 192, 230, 319, 376
Play 4, 47, 89, 125, 137, 145, 180, 188, 204, 217, 246, 314, 373, 413
Power greater than myself, A 64, 98, 303, 371, 392, 408
Powerless 6, 7, 9, 10, 25, 28, 29, 32, 39, 60, 86, 88, 97, 99, 103, 122, 127, 128,

139, 141, 162, 165, 171, 176, 184, 187, 190, 196, 209, 218, 230, 269, 284, 292, 297, 318, 322, 323, 339, 340, 345, 369, 376, 399, 409
Prayer 8, 51, 58, 59, 69, 86, 112, 118, 130, 140, 148, 150, 161, 175, 229, 255, 261, 275, 285, 345, 356, 368, 399
Priorities/Prioritize 22, 64, 87, 141, 204
Progress, Not Perfection 16, 42, 115, 213, 216, 240, 270, 281, 336
Promises 224, 405
Purpose 51, 56, 93, 98, 126, 136, 146, 147, 247, 295, 303, 378, 392, 396, 398, 400, 406
Pushing 70, 141, 160, 182, 224, 293, 364, 372

Q

Quit 9, 151, 203, 227, 307, 381

R

Reach out 5, 15, 37, 40, 42, 44, 59, 73, 79, 82, 94, 99, 130, 142, 178, 224, 235, 251, 255, 263, 287, 297, 308, 358, 377, 378, 388, 407
Reality x, 5, 10, 18, 32, 43, 48, 55, 60, 71, 93, 106, 109, 130, 158, 193, 215, 224, 238, 262, 269, 279, 325, 328, 336, 347, 367, 391
Recipe for Recovery 40, 132, 189, 249, 276, 280
Relationship 4, 11, 30, 33, 46, 54, 56, 57, 58, 64, 87, 91, 98, 131, 141, 142, 149, 172, 173, 196, 241, 245, 249, 250, 261, 263, 265, 281, 290, 306, 318, 335, 356, 364, 368, 383, 402, 405, 409
Relax 11, 12, 15, 18, 39, 44, 48, 108, 125, 126, 136, 159, 171, 176, 195, 264, 271, 330, 368, 409
Release/Releasing 10, 12, 24, 38, 73, 112, 117, 148, 163, 182, 206, 211, 217, 231, 236, 303, 313, 318, 337, 358, 367, 409, 410
Relief 6, 19, 55, 56, 73, 76, 79, 92, 97, 113, 119, 172, 177, 207, 222, 227, 244, 258, 262, 269, 314, 345
Resentful/Resentment 12, 31, 131, 138, 217, 236, 242, 285, 294, 381, 392
Resilience 110, 158, 346
Resistance 77, 90, 119, 142, 410
Resources 414
Responsibility 40, 127, 155, 184, 242, 259, 262, 277, 283, 303, 317, 402, 403, 407
Resting 17, 48, 58, 74, 89, 112, 140, 160, 240, 272, 289, 327, 372, 387
Rest Is an Action 17, 156, 224, 241, 270
Restored to sanity 63, 91, 170, 241, 285, 328, 341
Rewards 78, 195, 198, 202, 249, 255, 349, 408
Risk 7, 123, 135, 152, 358

S

Safety 5, 312, 342, 376, 391
Sanity ix, 15, 37, 63, 64, 72, 91, 92, 132, 141, 170, 194, 222, 229, 241, 253, 257, 285, 303, 312, 328, 341, 382, 399
Saying no 251, 290, 358
Security 211, 259, 323, 351
Self-acceptance 9, 14, 48, 54, 119, 122, 123, 143, 147, 152, 182, 188, 241, 325, 396, 410
Self-care 9, 13, 42, 47, 48, 103, 119, 120, 122, 123, 124, 143, 147, 149, 152, 171, 178, 182, 188, 191, 193, 212, 241, 281, 290, 298, 325, 357, 359, 369, 381, 383, 388, 396, 410
Self-compassion 42, 53, 108, 119, 152, 163, 174, 187, 188, 198, 254, 258, 265, 294, 315, 322, 345, 390, 397, 410
Self-esteem 107, 121, 131, 145, 213, 262, 314
Self-forgiveness 57
Self-love 9, 48, 54, 119, 122, 123, 147, 182, 188, 241, 325, 396, 410
Self-pity 61, 125, 138, 163, 174, 242, 363, 392
Self-sufficiency 303, 309
Serenity Prayer v, vii, 3, 7, 60, 70, 71, 80, 110, 116, 146, 207, 209, 225, 274, 376, 395, 412
Service 11, 16, 31, 45, 70, 79, 99, 107, 187, 263, 285, 291, 322, 327, 340, 352, 375, 400, 402, 403, 405, 409
Set Aside Prayer 241
Setting boundaries 251, 281, 302
Sex 111, 145, 347, 386
Shame 20, 42, 89, 104, 105, 127, 131, 136, 139, 160, 191, 212, 255, 258, 271, 278, 306, 311, 351, 372, 386, 407
Sharing 3, 41, 107, 137, 155, 172, 183, 192, 193, 196, 203, 237, 240, 247, 248, 249, 251, 252, 273, 280, 308, 309, 317, 318, 321, 367, 386, 392, 395, 413
Sleep 13, 19, 32, 54, 87, 108, 140, 144, 156, 162, 224, 258, 291, 361, 383
Solution 5, 27, 33, 52, 87, 93, 98, 107, 108, 114, 138, 156, 162, 176, 197, 213, 244, 259, 263, 264, 305, 306, 310, 329, 330, 342, 357, 358, 409
Spiritual path 132, 301, 303, 342
Sponsorship 37, 127, 155, 249, 308, 329
  Sponsee 23, 37, 155, 249, 277, 285, 321
  Sponsor 13, 16, 19, 23, 27, 37, 40, 44, 57, 63, 64, 65, 70, 72, 81, 84, 91, 97, 98, 103, 104, 108, 115, 119, 120, 122, 128, 129, 131, 142, 151, 154, 155, 161, 163, 171, 172, 177, 180, 193, 205, 207, 209, 212, 216, 217, 218, 223, 237, 238, 242, 249, 251, 256, 257, 262, 263, 265, 269, 271, 276, 277, 280, 284, 292, 294, 297, 304, 306, 308, 312, 314, 317, 318, 320, 324, 328, 329, 337, 341, 350, 353, 355, 357, 358, 370, 377, 378, 379, 382, 384, 385, 386, 393, 394
  Step buddy/Co-sponsor/Co-traveler/Fellow traveler 14, 187, 216, 274, 304

Spouse 104, 120, 149, 161, 165, 174, 184, 191, 213, 242, 259, 282, 343
Stand up (for self) 103, 120, 171
Steps. *See* Twelve Steps, The
STOP (Surrender, Time-out, Observe, Prioritize) 22, 87, 141, 204
Strengths 308, 314, 344, 350
Stress 78, 96, 144, 176, 246, 284, 287, 325, 362, 381
Strong 5, 91, 153, 221, 253, 260, 265, 293, 303, 318, 343
Struggle 5, 20, 39, 130, 131, 135, 138, 142, 150, 159, 174, 181, 273, 317, 325, 331, 349
Successes 286, 308
Support 8, 15, 19, 20, 31, 45, 48, 51, 57, 62, 65, 69, 75, 103, 110, 113, 130, 161, 163, 171, 173, 175, 178, 182, 192, 196, 197, 203, 242, 245, 255, 261, 274, 276, 280, 284, 304, 312, 316, 341, 343, 348, 350, 351, 353, 358, 363, 368, 371, 375, 406, 407, 413, 414
Surrender 6, 13, 27, 29, 32, 39, 41, 46, 60, 61, 71, 93, 103, 118, 120, 130, 135, 146, 158, 159, 171, 176, 181, 190, 193, 214, 222, 230, 259, 278, 305, 318, 322, 325, 339, 349, 370, 409

T

Tenderness 127, 241, 254, 388
Therapy 56, 140, 225, 362, 371
Three A's 129, 196, 331
Three C's 182
Three S's 182
Tired. *See* Exhaustion
To-do list 15, 74, 292
Toolbox 99, 195, 201, 326
Tools 16, 20, 27, 30, 42, 83, 87, 108, 110, 114, 135, 145, 152, 158, 170, 204, 207, 217, 221, 229, 246, 255, 274, 297, 302, 304, 311, 326, 331, 338, 340, 346, 355, 364, 374, 385, 388, 392
Touch 111, 145, 239, 285, 291, 296, 347, 386
Traditions
  Tradition Seven 412
  Tradition Ten 413
  Tradition Twelve 414
Trauma 230, 263, 312
Trigger 159, 265, 285, 359
Trust/Trusting 7, 29, 39, 48, 50, 59, 63, 64, 70, 75, 79, 89, 91, 92, 99, 104, 106, 114, 120, 125, 135, 136, 154, 158, 173, 175, 181, 184, 191, 196, 203, 207, 210, 214, 217, 222, 239, 241, 249, 251, 256, 259, 264, 273, 281, 286, 305, 308, 310, 312, 318, 324, 336, 338, 339, 341, 347, 351, 356, 362, 370, 376, 377, 378, 379, 386, 389, 394, 395, 407, 408, 409, 410
Turning it over 297

Turn it over 94, 209, 336
Twelve Steps, The ix, xi, xii, 4, 7, 20, 28, 61, 64, 69, 73, 75, 76, 86, 88, 91, 98, 104, 106, 107, 122, 127, 151, 155, 172, 189, 203, 208, 209, 221, 235, 241, 245, 265, 275, 284, 290, 295, 306, 308, 309, 312, 313, 314, 321, 329, 335, 339, 342, 350, 360, 367, 391, 396, 398, 399, 405, 412, 413, 414
  Step One 4, 6, 9, 14, 32, 39, 81, 83, 88, 97, 112, 127, 139, 142, 158, 163, 165, 176, 181, 190, 220, 235, 245, 260, 275, 280, 284, 301, 303, 312, 323, 325, 339, 369
  Step Two 37, 39, 63, 64, 76, 91, 98, 158, 170, 176, 222, 264, 270, 275, 285, 303, 341, 371
  Step Three 29, 39, 59, 64, 70, 84, 99, 158, 159, 170, 176, 184, 227, 264, 275, 285, 295, 336, 370, 391
  Step Four 24, 103, 105, 128, 131, 171, 172, 217, 236, 249, 290, 314, 318, 328, 337, 350, 357, 383, 395
  Step Five 95, 122, 136, 151, 172, 249, 337
  Step Six 173, 206, 337, 394
  Step Seven 86, 180, 207, 218, 324, 337, 383
  Step Eight 242
  Step Nine 57, 89, 94, 248, 254, 271, 277, 290
  Step Ten 95, 207, 241, 278, 305, 310, 344, 385, 395
  Step Eleven 95, 96, 180, 296, 345, 356
  Step Twelve 61, 122, 239, 249, 312, 325, 378, 396
  Twelve Traditions, The ix, xi, 400, 412, 413

U

Unity 98, 155, 194, 203, 367, 400
Unmanageable 3, 7, 9, 28, 29, 42, 109, 164, 165, 176, 269, 284, 312, 369, 394, 399
Unrealistic expectations 13, 269, 385
Unsolicited advice 192

V

Vulnerable 6, 119, 154, 196, 318, 381, 391, 413

W

Weaknesses 135, 314, 344, 350
Welcoming 3, 398
Well-being 9, 42, 46, 78, 109, 147, 179, 196, 225, 312, 316, 407
Willingness 15, 32, 83, 84, 111, 122, 125, 152, 190, 218, 228, 235, 249, 257, 277, 281, 295, 309, 318, 324, 328, 329, 396, 409
Wisdom v, 7, 38, 45, 60, 61, 80, 144, 151, 188, 225, 241, 251, 302, 303, 308, 312, 341, 346, 368, 369, 376, 389, 410
Working the Steps 37, 57, 187, 190, 217, 322

Notes

Notes

Notes

Notes

Notes

www.ingramcontent.com/pod-product-compliance
Lightning Source LLC
Chambersburg PA
CBHW071257110426

42743CB00042B/1080